D0948690

Television Aesthetics:

Perceptual, Cognitive, and Compositional Bases

Television Aesthetics:
Perceptual, Cognitive, and Compositional Bases

Nikos Metallinos
Concordia University

 UNIVERSITY OF TOLEDO LIBRARIES

LAWRENCE ERLBAUM ASSOCIATES, PUBLISHERS

1996   Mahwah, NJ

Lawrence Erlbaum Associates, Inc., Publishers
10 Industrial Avenue
Mahwah, NJ 07430

Cover design by Gail Silverman

Library of Congress Cataloging-in-Publication Data

Metallinos, Nikos
Television aesthetics : perceptual, cognitive, and com-
postional bases / Nikos Metallinos.
p. cm.
Includes bibliographical references and index.
ISBN 0-8058-1221-0 (cloth : alk. paper). — ISBN
0-8058-2218-6 (pbk. : alk. paper)
1. Television—Aesthetics. 2. Visual perception. 3.
Auditory perception. 4. Television and the arts. 5. Television—Production and direction. I. Title.
PN1992.55.M46 1996
791.45'01—dc20   95-42621
                                                      CIP

Books published by Lawrence Erlbaum Associates are printed
on acid-free paper, and their bindings are chosen for strength
and durability.

Printed in the United States of America
10 9 8 7 6 5 4 3 2 1

Contents

Preface

Rapid developments, wide application, and people's total dependence on visual communication media define the need for the development of the field of visual literacy. Film, photography, television, and computerized images shape people's images of the world and themselves with astonishing speed, intimacy, and persuasion. The dominance of the 5OO-channel universe offered by direct satellite television and the global, instant, and direct communication offered by the Internet computer network justify the urgency for the establishment of the principles governing the perception, the comprehension, and the synthesis of visual messages. Furthermore, the availability—and easy access—of the visual communication media technologies, along with the power of the visual image and people's fascination with the novelty these technologies provide, dictate the need for teaching visual literacy to both those who create visual images and those who consume them.

This volume offers a response to three ongoing needs: (a) the need to develop the main compositional principles pertinent to the visual communication medium of television, (b) the need to establish the field of television aesthetics as an extension of the broader field of visual literacy, and (c) the need to promote television aesthetics to both students and consumers of television.

The aesthetic principles of television images that I develop are based on effective empirical research on all three axes—perception, cognition, and composition; they are drawn from converging research in academic disciplines such as psychology (perceptual, cognitive, and experimental), neurophysiology, and the fine arts (including painting, photography, film, theater, and music). Although the aesthetics of the fine arts were traditionally built on contextual theories that relied heavily on subjective evaluations, critical analyses, and descriptive research methods, the aesthetics of today's visual communication media consider equally valuable empirical methodologies found in all sciences. In fact, investigations in these different academic disciplines have provided the constructs and have strengthened the foundations of the theory of television aesthetics offered in this book.

In every stage of the production, transmission, and reception of televised images there are hidden agendas, persuasive agents, interferences, deceptions, and noises that often hinder the real purpose of communication, deliberately disturbing the meaning. Visual literacy in general, and television aesthetics in particular, provides knowledge of these dangers by acknowledging the theories pertaining to perception (visual, auditory, and motion), cognition, and composition. The production, transmission, and reception of television pictures are interrelated with these three axes and are interdependent with perception, cognition, and composition, each of which raises these three questions:

- What is the message?
- What does it mean?
- How was it constructed?

Part I of the book deals with the perception of television images and examines the basic theories of perception in the three areas of vision, hearing, and movement in corresponding chapters on visual perception, auditory perception, and vision in motion. Part II is devoted to the review of the main theories of cognition as they relate to television picture comprehension. It also examines the neurophysiologies of the eye, the ear, and the brain, and discusses the process of decodification of visual and auditory messages in respective chapters on the human information systems, the brain and the mind, and the standards for recognizing pictures and sounds. Part III refers to the compositional principles of television pictures with chapters that review and examine the arts, criticism, and applied rules of composition of television pictures, respectively.

The review of the existing theories, the examination of the empirical findings in conventional fields, and the discussions of the principles stemming from research in perception, cognition, and composition constitute the integrated theme and underline the approach of this book. Efforts to develop television aesthetics should increase and the approaches to the study of television aesthetics should be broadened, as the need to enter the information highway is now more demanding than ever.

There are many people who assisted me, directly or indirectly, in writing this book—colleagues, students, and friends. I would like to extend my sincere thanks to all and especially to my three teachers, mentors, colleagues, and now, friends. Dr. Herbert Zettl, from San Francisco State University, inspired me as a teacher and has provided the basic theories of television aesthetics. Dr. Robert K. Tiemens, from the University of Utah, taught me the research methodologies related to visual images and provided valuable guidance in my academic career. Dr. James E. Fletcher provided new, advanced, and accurate research measuring devices for the scientific study of visual images. Dr. Fletcher inspired my research involvement and encouraged and assisted me with this book. Finally, a warm thank you to my wife, Daisy, for her valuable assistance and patience.

—Nikos Metallinos

About the Author

Nikos Metallinos is a Professor of Communication Studies at Concordia University of Montreal. He is a graduate of the Modern School of Theater Arts of Greece (BA) and, before coming to North America, was an actor of the National Theater of Greece where he took part in more than 50 plays—mostly ancient Greek drama. He studied television at the Department of Radio, Television, and Film at San Francisco State University and received his MA from the same department, where he also taught for 2 years. Dr. Metallinos obtained his PhD at the Department of Communication of the University of Utah and later joined the Department of Radio, Television, and Film at Temple University in Philadelphia.

Dr. Metallinos' specialty areas are television production, criticism, aesthetics, and empirical research methods in visual communication media. He has written numerous articles for academic journals in North America and abroad, has provided several chapters in textbooks in the field, and is editor of the book *Verbo–Visual Literacy: Understanding and Applying New Educational Communication Media Technologies* (1994). He has organized and has participated in numerous international symposia and communication conferences, and presented key papers on media research methods, visual literacy, and television aesthetics. Dr. Metallinos has been a consultant on educational broadcasting curricula, television production, and visual communication media aesthetics for various universities around the world, including South Africa's Institute of Communication Research and the Department of Communication and Mass Media of the University of Athens, Greece.

Introduction

A few years ago it was inconceivable to consider television, particularly commercial television, a serious mass communication medium capable of presenting tasteful programs with unique artistic merits and recognized aesthetic qualities. The broadcasting industry that developed the television medium was not truly concerned with people's tastes, artistic expansions, and aesthetic awareness in their television programming. The industry's concern was mass distribution and mass consumption of television programs for huge profits. Knowledgeable electronic engineers, skillful media practitioners, and inspired business entrepreneurs worked hand in hand to develop the broadcasting industry as we know it today. Their backgrounds and motivations were driven mainly by science and technology. Their basic beliefs were practicality, economic gain, marketing, supply, and demand. Business and the desire for success dominated the actions taken by the pioneer developers of the broadcasting industry that Brandford (1987) called the "left brain oriented industry" (p. 36). This phenomenon that is not unique to our times, having occurred repeatedly over the history of media development in the Western world, had profound consequences and caused severe drawbacks in the field known today as *television aesthetics*. It took enormous efforts, perseverance, and persistence of media artists who are predominantly right-brain oriented (Brandford, 1987) to become involved in broadcasting media, particularly in the new medium of television. As McLuhan (1978) observed, it took some time for the atrophic right brain of Western man to develop, to comprehend, and to recognize the media evolution of the 20th century. Gradually, artists already working in other media such as music, theater, and photography transferred their artistry to radio and television. They experimented with the new technology and applied previous, well-established rules of composition to broadcast programs. Inductively, the rules of art composition of the broadcasting media, the grammar of broadcasting, were established and from that, television grammar, the television rules of composition known as television aesthetics was developed.

There was more, however, than the awakening of Western people's holistic right brain that contributed to the development of the grammar of the television medium and the field of television aesthetics. Significant developments that affected the genesis of television aesthetics occurred in various related fields. Herein, I provide: (a) a brief review of the major developments in the evolution of aesthetics, as they relate to media aesthetics; (b) an examination of the roles of perception, cognition, and composition regarding the development of television aesthetics; and (c) a summary of the content of each of the three parts of the book.

AESTHETICS, MEDIA AESTHETICS: MAJOR DEVELOPMENTS

For many centuries the study of the nature of beauty has been a major concern of all people, regardless of the society they lived in and the level of their understanding of it. Although each society and each individual create their own particular ideas and are guided by their own definitions of aesthetics, scholars in the field collectively agree that: "Aesthetics or esthetics [is a] branch of philosophy concerned with the essence and perception of beauty and ugliness, and whether such qualities are objectively present in the things they appear to qualify, or whether they exist in the mind of the individual" (Funk & Wagnalls New Encyclopedia, 1972, pp. 217–218). When aesthetics is considered an academic discipline it is defined as "a branch of philosophy dealing with the nature of the beautiful and with judgment concerning beauty" or as a discipline dealing with "the description and explanation of artistic phenomena and aesthetic experience by means of other sciences (as psychology, sociology, ethnology, or history)" (Webster's Seventh New Collegiate Dictionary, 1971, p. 15).

Among the various other sources and academic disciplines concerned with aesthetics are the arts (e.g., history of the arts, psychology of the arts, and analysis of the arts) and criticism (e.g., literary criticism and art criticism). The close connection of aesthetics, in general, to the fields of philosophy, arts, and criticism was argued quite persuasively by Beardsley (1958), who claimed that "As a field of knowledge, aesthetics consists of those principles that are required for clarifying and confirming critical statements. Aesthetics can be thought of, then, as the philosophy of criticism, or metacriticism" (pp. 3–4).

Beardsley's (1958) theory of aesthetics branches out into two other seemingly related, but for him, distinct fields. The first he called "psychological aesthetics" (p. 7), dealing mostly with questions about causes and effects of works of art; the second he called "philosophical aesthetics" (p. 7), referring primarily to questions about the meaning and truth of critical statements. This is a theory of particular importance because it acknowledges the connection of aesthetics to the disciplines of philosophy, the arts, and criticism and demonstrates how the aesthetics of the arts generally, and media arts particularly, developed through the centuries.

During the Classical Period, the predominant aesthetic theories of any significance were those of Plato and Aristotle, collectively known as the imitation theory of the arts, and that of the Roman philosopher Plotinus (205–270 A.D.), known as the mystical theory. Dickie (1971) described the imitation theory of Plato and Aristotle as the one that "focuses attention on the objective properties of the work of art" (p. 3).

Plato's and Aristotle's imitation theory of the arts, particularly when it refers to dramatic poetry, directly relates to the development of television aesthetics because it (a) outlines and examines the parts that form the art objects or events, (b) points out the manipulative power and the danger of the emotional impact of the art objects or events on the spectators, and (c) refers to the role of the arts toward the cultural development of the society that creates them.

Plotinus, a student of the Neoplatonic theory of aesthetics of the Classical Period, held a more sympathetic and clearer view of the arts than his mentor Plato. His aesthetic view was that "art reveals the form of an object more clearly than ordinary experience does and raises the soul to contemplation of the universe" (Funk & Wagnalls New Encyclopedia, 1972, p. 218).

Plotinus went as far as to advocate a metaphysical and mysterious experience that one lives when contemplating an aesthetically pleasing art object or event. One can see that this aesthetic theory is still supported and practiced by spectators of contemporary media, particularly electronic media.

During the Modern Period that spanned roughly from the Middle Ages to the end of the 19th century, the major protagonists in the development of aesthetics were no longer the Greeks or the Romans, but predominantly Germans who were the most faithful students of the ancient Greek scholars, philosophers, and artists. A brief review of the major philosophical and artistic movements of this long and multifaceted period is necessary as it provides an accurate profile of the development of the field of aesthetics.

The German art critic and philosopher Gotthold Ephraim Lessing (1729–1781) in 1766 argued that art is self-limiting, and reaches its apogee only when these limitations are recognized. Johann Gottlieb Fichte (1762–1814), a German philosopher and metaphysicist, considered the important role played by the artist and the arts in society and stated that "the artist creates a world of his own, in which beauty, as much as truth, is an end and art is individual not social, but it fulfills a great human purpose" (Funk & Wagnalls New Encyclopedia, 1972, p. 218). The great German philosopher Immanuel Kant (1724–1804), the father of transcendental aesthetics, centered his argument on the subject of taste in the arts and claimed that "objects are judged beautiful when they satisfy a disinterested desire. The basis for one's response to beauty exists in one's mind" (Funk & Wagnalls New Encyclopedia, 1972, p. 218). Kant's contemporary adversary, the German philosopher Georg Wilheim Friedrich Hegel (1770–1831) believed that certain things in nature can be made more congenial and pleasing, and it is these natural objects that are recognized by art to satisfy aesthetic demands. For the German philosopher Arthur Schopenhauer (1788–1860) the aesthetic satisfaction that the arts reveal emerges from the individual's own contemplation and experience with the arts.

The prolific German poet and philosopher Friedrich Wilhelm Nietzsche (1844–1900), influenced by his lifelong illness, suggested that life is tragic and considered art as the agent that confronts the terrors of the universe and, therefore, art is good only for those who are strong. For Nietzsche, art can transform any experience into beauty and by so doing transforms its horrors in such a way that man can contemplate them with enjoyment.

The *impressionistic* movement of the arts, represented mostly by the French artists of the last quarter of the 19th century such as André Derain, Paul Cézanne, Paul Gauguin, and Henri Matisse, were more concerned with "symbolizing picture structure, volume, and the artist's own psyche" (Funk & Wagnalls New Encyclopedia, 1972, p. 219). The Swedish playwright August Strindberg (1849–1912) and the German playwright Frank Wedefind were considered responsible for the literary movement known as *expressionism* that influenced the arts in the early 1920s and created the Munich School of the Arts bearing its name. Contrary to impressionism, expressionism subordinates the representation of objects to the expression of emotion. During the late 1890s, the last years of the Modern Period, the artistic movements known as *art for art's sake* and *art as imitation* were predominant; the former advocating that art must criticize and comment on life, the latter suggesting that the artists, unlike the scientists, do not state their meanings but express themselves in a work of art.

The Contemporary Period that started at the end of the 19th century and has reached our times produced four key philosophers and four major movements that substantially influenced contemporary aesthetics in general, and media aesthetics in particular.

The French philosopher Henri-Louis Bergson (1859–1941), the Italian philosopher Benedetto Croce (1866–1952), the American philosopher and poet George Santayana (1863–1952), and the American educator and philosopher John Dewey (1859–1952) had a pervasive influence on contemporary media aesthetics as all four dealt with the relationship of science and art: They sought to discover their differences and similarities; how one influences the other; how both influence aesthetics, pragmatism, idealism, intuition, and reality. Bergson's central belief was that the material universe is subject to the domination of a vital force called *élan vital* and that art is based on intuition, which is a direct apprehension of reality unmediated by thought. Thus art cuts through conventional symbols and beliefs about man, life, and society and confronts one with reality itself.

Croce made a distinction between logic and intuition and suggested that logic is concerned with the apprehension of relationships and deals with universal concepts. On the other hand, intuition has to do with the apprehension of the particular; it deals with concepts of the individual. As far as the arts are concerned, Croce maintained that all works of art are the expression, in general form, of such intuitions. However, beauty and ugliness are qualities not of the works of art but of the spirit expressed intuitively in such works.

In his attempt to unify science and art, Santayana maintained that "reality is actively external to consciousness and is known, therefore, only by inference from the sensory data within consciousness . . . and all beliefs about the external world rest on a so-called animal faith" (Funk & Wagnalls Standard Reference Encyclopedia, 1968, p. 7804). He argued that when one takes pleasure in a thing, he may regard the pleasure as a quality of the thing itself, rather than a subjective response to it.

The American pragmatist and philosopher Dewey insisted on the practical, learning by doing and experimentation, and maintained that the process of thinking is a means of realizing human desire, removing the obstacles between what is given and what is wanted. In the same sense, truth is not absolute but merely an idea or hypothesis that has worked. Although human experience is disconnected, fragmented, and has many beginnings, yet no end, Dewey maintained that aesthetic experience is enjoyment for its own sake; it is complete and self-contained, and it is terminal, not merely instrumental for other purposes.

The four movements that shaped contemporary artists are *Marxism, Freudianism, Existentialism,* and *Semantics.* Founded by Karl Marx (1818–1883) and based on economics and politics, the Marxist theory maintains that art is great only when it is *progressive,* that is when it supports the course of the society that creates it. For the Marxists, art and society are interconnected and one influences the development of the other; the development of the arts depends on the economic structure and perspectives of the society.

Freudianism, developed by the Austrian neurologist and founder of psychoanalysis, Sigmund Freud (1856–1939), had a profound influence not only on the arts and aesthetics, but on other behavioral sciences as well. Drawing from the Aristotelian doctrine of catharsis through art, Freud maintained that: "The value of art lies in its therapeutic use; it is by these means that the artist or the reader can reveal his hidden conflicts and discharge his tensions. Fantasies and daydreams, as they extend into art, are thus transformed from an escape from life into ways of meeting it" (Funk & Wagnalls New Encyclopedia, 1972, p. 220).

The Existentialism movement was formed more recently by Jean-Paul Sartre (1905–1980), a French philosopher, novelist, and dramatist with a profound influence on the arts, aesthetics, and media arts of our times. Existentialists believe, in effect, that art is an expression of the freedom of people to choose, and, as such, demonstrates their responsibilities for their choices. Despair, as reflected in art, is not an end but a beginning, because it eradicates the guilt and excuses from which people ordinarily suffer, thus opening the way to genuine freedom.

The fourth influential movement in the development of aesthetics in the Contemporary era is the Semantic, created primarily by the British literary critic, educator, and semanticist Ivor Armstrong Richards (1893–1972). The movement was created as an attempt to find meaning in the arts. Richards stated, in effect, that language and art are similar and he asserted that there are two types of languages, the symbolic, which conveys ideas and information, and the emotive, which expresses, evokes, and excites feelings and attitudes but contains no symbolic meaning.

The preceding review of the major aesthetics theories of the arts points to the foundations for the development of media aesthetics.

From the significant number of literary sources on media, primarily visual and auditory communication media such as theater, film, radio, and television, a number of contemporary media aesthetics theories are emerging. Although these sources are not concerned specifically with media aesthetics, their subjects and points of view can easily be contained in one of these theories. These are, in my view, four prominent media aesthetics theories that emerged from the literature of contemporary media: (a) the *traditional* (or philosophical), (b) the *formalist*, (c) the *contextualist*, and (d) the *empiricist*. A brief review of each theory is provided herein.

The *traditional media aesthetics theory* stems from the classical studies on the aesthetics of art—as already reviewed—and includes the eternal questions: What is true? What constitutes the beautiful, tasteful, sublime, and picturesque in the arts and literature? The traditional aesthetics theories of arts and literature, according to Dickie (1971), derive from the history of Western civilization, in general, and the history of the arts, in particular. This is also true of the development of the traditional media aesthetics theory that is based on the historical developments of modern media.

According to this theory, the analysis, evaluation, and appreciation of the products of modern media (how beautiful, sublime, and picturesque these products are) must be based on the historical developments of the media that reveal their functions within the societies that have developed them. As such, the traditional media aesthetics theory is not isomorphic because it promotes certain modern media for the products they generate (e.g., theater and film) and devalues others (such as radio and television) for their low-quality products.

Historians of modern mass media, particularly of film and television, such as Barnouw (1956, 1968, 1975), Chester, Garrison, and Willis (1971), Head (1972), Head and Sterling (1990), Marshall (1986), Sterling and Kittross (1990), and Summers and Summers (1966) have provided the foundations of the traditional media aesthetics theory although they have not spoken favorably about the artistic quality and the aesthetic value of radio and television products; neither did the early media critics (as discussed later). Nevertheless, it was these and many other modern media historians who helped to define modern media; they explained the media's functions in contemporary society and provided an account of the products presented. This historic information provides the bases for the traditional media aesthetics theory that helps us to understand the evolution and the drastic changes in media aesthetics during the last 60 years.

The *formalist media aesthetics theory* is constituted by the point of view held by several media observers of the technology of the media, their power to influence each other (as well as numerous other institutions of the society), and the analysis of the forms of the media (e.g., the components that work together to construct the media products).

The proponents of this theory suggest, and support, the following:

1. Every medium is unique in its own right; it is characterized by its unique features, instruments, materials, and techniques, as it is argued, very convincingly, by Antin (1979), Newcomb (1987), Tarroni (1979), Toogood (1978), and Zettl (1978a).
2. There is a logic in the succession and progress of the media in which one form of art helps the development of another, as argued by Arnheim (1969a), D'Agostino (1985), Dondis (1973), Innis (1951), and McLuhan (1962).
3. The holistic analysis and study of both media content and media form contribute to the development of media aesthetics, as strongly suggested and supported by Baggaley, Ferguson, and Brooks (1980), Coldevin (1980), Tiemens and Acker (1981), Williams (1975), and others. This is a widely spread and popular theory supported by a diverse family of media scholars.

The *contextualist theory of media aesthetics* suggests that life and art are interrelated, inseparable, and that different incidents in one's life are interconnected. One's ability to unify them so that they gain prominence and obtain some significance is what contextualism advocates.

The founder and major proponent of the contextualistic theory of aesthetics is Pepper (1938, 1945, 1970), who suggested first, the contextualistic theory of beauty and then developed the four major aesthetics systems that he called world hypotheses. These are the formalistic, organimistic, mechanistic, and contextualistic (Pepper, 1970). The central theme of Pepper's (1938) contextualistic theory of aesthetics refers to the quality of one's life experiences and how one is capable of experiencing an aesthetic event. In his book, *The Basis of Criticism in the Arts* (1945), he elaborated on the theory of contextualistic aesthetics that became the basis of the evaluation of arts events with other aesthetic systems.

On the basis of Pepper's theory of aesthetics, Edman (1939) brought into focus the contextualistic theory of aesthetics of the fine arts and a person's life and stated that: "These three functions, intensification, clarification, and interpretation of experience, the arts fulfill in various degrees" (p. 34). Edman's (1939) concept of contextualistic aesthetics has influenced decisively the development of the media aesthetics theory of Zettl (1990), who related applied media aesthetics and contextualism, stating that:

> Contextualism serves as a convenient frame of reference for the discussion of applied media aesthetics. Despite various interpretations of what this branch of philosophy actually means and includes, its major concepts help establish and describe an operational field within which we can examine the specific elements and processes of applied media aesthetics. The four major concepts are: (1) incidents of life, (2) art and life, (3) art as clarified and intensified experience, and (4) order and experienced complexity. (p. 2)

The most profound statements made by the contextualistic theorists of media aesthetics are that mass media, and particularly television, should not be disconnected from what happens in real life, of which it constitutes an inseparable part, and that contemporary media products can be significant as art forms, expressing the incidents, enormous complexities, and multiple experiences of life.

Interestingly enough, the contextualistic theory of media aesthetics, as advocated by Zettl (1990), has formed the basis for the development of television aesthetics as an acceptable and respected academic discourse in various institutions of higher education in North America, although, only a few years ago, such an undertaking was inconceivable and was considered almost impossible.

The *empiricist theory of media aesthetics* stems from empirical studies on various concepts, constructs, and variables of the developed theories of media composition. It advocates that the development of media aesthetics as an academic discourse should be based on scientific evidence stemming from vigorous empirical studies on media composition- (media production) related issues. It points out the need to correlate (a) the scattered thoughts and rumors circulated about the media, (b) the isolated experiments with video productions, and (c) the numerous content-oriented media studies, into a unified discourse.

A number of media researchers (particularly in television composition) have emerged who have embraced the empiricist theory of media aesthetics and have produced significant findings in the field. For example, Fletcher (1972, 1973, 1979, 1994) and Tiemens (1978, 1994) are among the first empiricist scholars who produced scholarly studies on television composition-related variables developing scientific research designs, advanced measuring devices, and techniques for the analysis of data. Their studies and contributions are both significant and pioneering in the field. Their colleagues Barker (1985, 1988), Coldevin (1980), Herbener, Van Tubergen, and Whitlow (1979), Kipper (1986, 1989), McCain and Rebensky (1972), and Tiemens and Acker (1981), to mention only a few, followed the same trend and helped to form the foundations of the empiricist theory of media aesthetics with their significant findings on media composition-related studies.

This theory of media aesthetics was developed as an answer to the overabundance of existing content-oriented studies in the field, as a solution to the problems created by the lack of scientifically based theories of media composition, and to upgrade the level of studies in media in general, and media aesthetics in particular.

PERCEPTION, COGNITION, AND COMPOSITION: FACTOR ANALYSIS AND SYNTHESIS OF TELEVISION AESTHETICS

The preceding review of the developed aesthetics theories of the arts, and particularly the media, indicates that the study of television aesthetics can be approached from different perspectives and academic disciplines. The traditional, formalist, contextualist, and empiricist media aesthetics theories, in particular, provide a link that bridges the aesthetic concepts of the arts with those of the media products; they cannot provide the decisive foundations on which television aesthetics could be built. These theories, and many other media studies that support them, do not provide solutions to all significant problems raised by the serious attempts to develop the discipline of television aesthetics. The issues regarding the processes of perceiving visual and auditory images in motion, recognizing or interpreting such images, and synthesizing, or composing moving images with sound, are not addressed.

It is my belief that the study of television aesthetics, and its subsequent acceptance as a distinct academic discipline, should be centered on the analysis of three factors: perception, cognition, and composition of television images. These three factors constitute the axes that support television aesthetics (see Fig. A).

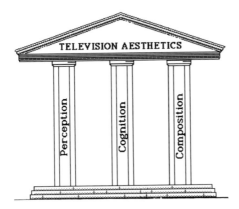

FIG. A. The axes of television aesthetics.

The study of perception in general, and particularly visual, auditory, and motion perceptions, constitutes a fundamental axis for the support of television aesthetics for the following reasons: (a) it provides scientific explanations of the perceptual processes of sight, sound, and motion—the three main elements of television pictures; (b) it explains and underlines the unique functions of each of the organs of visual and auditory perception during the process of watching television; and (c) it distinguishes the role of perception from that of cognition and emphasizes the evolutionary development through the stages of stimulation (receiving sensory data), perception (organizing and coding precepts), and cognition (decoding and creating concepts). Foremost, studies on perception, which are reported in psychological journals (perceptual and experimental) are brought to the attention of communication studies, linking sciences with humanities, and behavioral studies with social studies.

The study of cognition also constitutes a fundamental axis supporting television aesthetics for the following reasons: (a) it provides scientifically based explanations for the complicated process of decodification and recognition of sights, sounds, and motions incorporated in television pictures; (b) it analyzes the organ of cognition, the brain, and underlines the particular functions of the various centers that transform sensoric data into moving images; (c) it distinguishes the role of the brain from the role of the mind in understanding television pictures; and (d) it brings to the field of communication studies neurophysiology and cognitive psychology that broaden the communication field, in general, and enrich the study of television aesthetics, in particular.

Lastly, the study of composition is also a fundamental axis supporting television aesthetics for these reasons: (a) it explains how moving images of television are constructed; (b) it analyzes the basic units of television programs such as lights and colors, cameras, audio, and editing and explains how each works in building the program; (c) it underlines the basic compositional principles and examines the production techniques in the areas of lighting, staging, editing, and audio; and (d) it notes the various empirical studies on television composition—mostly conducted by communication scholars—with studies from the fields of behavioral and neurophysiological studies.

In short, the resulting synthesis of television aesthetics as it is proposed here stems from the detailed analysis and thorough examination of the main factors that constitute the bases of television aesthetics, namely, perception, cognition, and composition.

A BRIEF SUMMARY OF THE THREE PARTS

The first part of this book examines the theories, empirical findings, and established principles of *visual, auditory*, and *motion* perceptions as they relate to television pictures. Chapter 1 is devoted to visual perception principles and defines the visual field of the television screen with sections referring to various stimuli, the description of the visual process of television images, the central and peripheral visions and the television picture, the perception of visual elements with the television picture, and the perceptions of three-dimensional media, including holography. Chapter 2 is devoted to auditory perception principles and contains sections discussing the perception of auditory stimuli, the analysis of the perception of acoustic space, and the distinction between television sounds and noise. Chapter 3 refers to motion. It discusses the principles of vision in motion and explains how we perceive moving images. The first section examines the general theories of motion perception, the second section analyzes real and apparent motion, and the third section is devoted to the organization and the perception of movement in the visual field of the television picture.

The second part of this book explores the empirical findings, examines the theories, and reviews the established principles of cognition, also called comprehension and understanding, relating to television pictures. Chapter 4 discusses the anatomy of the human information system in general, with sections devoted specifically to the neurological factors pertaining to the eye, ear, and the brain; stimuli and the perceptual process; and the process of codification of visual and auditory motion. In chapter 5, the distinction is made between the functions performed by the brain and those performed by the mind, with sections dealing specifically with the divisions of the brain and mind, the special functions of the two hemispheres of the brain, and the continued efforts of the brain and mind in recognizing television pictures. Finally, chapter 6 outlines the recognition standards of visual images with sections devoted to the topics of self-awareness, knowledge, and expertise, understanding society and institutions, and learning the processes and understanding the effects of visual communication.

The third part of this book deals with the development of the compositional principles governing the medium of television and reviews the various areas that have contributed to the development of television composition; one such area referring to the arts is examined in chapter 7. The first section provides a brief review of the history of the arts; the second section is devoted to the philosophy, nature, and characteristics of the arts; and the third section refers to the various functions performed by the arts and provides the various categories of the arts. Chapter 8 provides an introduction to criticism, with sections devoted to the nature, role, and functions of art criticism; approaches to art; visual communication media arts; and television criticism, and it provides an application of television's critical approaches to existing television genres. Finally, chapter 9 introduces the applied rules of composition of television programs. The first section considers television as an art form, the second section discusses the fundamental compositional principles of visual communication media arts, and the third section reviews the production techniques of television and examines the principles on which they have been developed.

I
▼▼▼▼▼▼▼

PERCEPTUAL FACTORS

Knowledge of the processes involved in visual and auditory perception, as well as basic understanding of the mechanisms employed by the human brain in transforming perceptions into cognitions, are prerequisites for the study of television aesthetics. Numerous scientific studies, now found in such diversified fields as perceptual psychology, neurophysiology, experimental psychology, cybernetics, and communication, confirm how fundamentally important perception is to the study of the structure of television images. This, in turn, is of great importance to the study of the field of television aesthetics. This part reviews the most appropriate sources in the literature of visual and auditory perception relating to television aesthetics; examines the dominant visual, auditory, and motion factors involved in the structuring of television images; and discusses the role of perception in the development of television pictures with an artistic merit.

The field of television aesthetics, like the similar fields of aesthetics in painting, photography, and the arts, generally evolved from the field of criticism. The description, interpretation, and evaluation of television programs by various television commentators, observers, and critics generated the need to examine the critical statements more thoroughly and to relate them to the medium of television. For this reason, criticism of the arts has also been named metacriticism (Dickie, 1971), and television metacriticism is synonymous with the term television aesthetics.

The efforts of pioneer television critics of the last 50 years, first to identify and then to describe, interpret, and evaluate the various features of television programs, might have resulted in the development of the field of television criticism. However, because the majority of these critics were from such conventional disciplines as sociology, anthropology, journalism, semiotics, linguistics, and English, the discipline of television criticism as a responsible academic discourse could not be fully developed. It was inevitable that with such limited basic television criticism, television metacriticism or television aesthetics could not progress.

Visual communication media scholars who have observed and noted this phenomenon have suggested that the domain of the field of television criticism, and subsequently the field of television aesthetics, must extend beyond the sociological, semiotic, or linguistic approaches that have been the practice during the last 50 years. The medium is not an isolated sociological or unique linguistic phenomenon to be studied only by these respective fields. It is a complex phenomenon better understood if examined from all aspects and by different disciplines, whether they fall under the arts or under the sciences. Visual communication media scholars of today have observed, studied, and concluded that the development of television criticism, the basis for the establishment of the discipline of television aesthetics, must expand and must consider the findings in the fields of perceptual psychology, neurophysiology, experimental psychology, cybernetics, education, fine arts, and communication studies.

Studies on television criticism and television aesthetics by a great number of pioneer scholars seem to agree with my basic belief that the three axes, the three bases on which the discipline of television aesthetics should be built, are perception, cognition, and composition (Metallinos, 1991).

Television aesthetics is the study of sensory data and images. Consequently, the major fields that contain the bulk of literary sources on the discipline are perceptual psychology, neurophysiology, art criticism, and communication. Because the discipline is still in the making and has not yet fully developed its parameters, scholars of television aesthetics are constantly borrowing from other academic disciplines to support their research. As difficult as this task may be, it has proven to be both necessary and worthwhile.

Among the present-day communication scholars who have borrowed and adopted in their own research primarily from the perceptual psychologists and the neurophysiologists are Fletcher, Tiemens, and Zettl.

Fletcher, a communication scholar at the University of Georgia, has used psychophysiological instruments, mostly the galvanic skin response (GSR), as measuring devices in his television production-related research (Fletcher, 1971, 1976, 1978, 1979, 1985, 1994).

In addition to this particular background in communication research, Fletcher has borrowed heavily from Berlyne (1960), Edelberg (1970), Lykken and Venables (1971), Shapiro and Crider (1969), and Venables and Martin (1967), all renowned researchers in neurophysiology and experimental psychology. Fletcher's empirical studies found in the journals and literature of both fields have contributed decisively to the development of television aesthetics as a distinctive academic study and discipline.

Tiemens, a communication scholar at the University of Utah, has studied and published extensively on such television-production related issues as: "Some Relationships of Camera Angle to Communication Credibility" (Tiemens, 1965), "The Syntax of Visual Messages: An Empirical Investigation of the Asymmetry of the Frame Theory" (Avery & Tiemens, 1975), "A Visual Analysis of the 1976 Presidential Debates" (Tiemens, 1978), "Analyzing the Content of Visual Messages: Methodological Considerations" (Tiemens, 1994), and "Children's Perception of Changes in Size of Televised Images" (Tiemens & Acker, 1981).

In his research, Tiemens borrowed heavily from such known perceptual psychologists as Arnheim (1969a, 1969b), Gazzanika (1967), Gibson (1950, 1979), Goldstein (1975), and Ornstein (1972). Tiemens' research works, articles, and papers can be found in all the major communication journals and have significantly helped the development of television aesthetics as a unique academic discourse.

Zettl, a broadcast communication arts scholar at San Francisco State University, is considered the founder of television aesthetics as a distinct field of study. Zettl is among the most diversified media scholars, having mastered the fields of music, painting, television production, media education, and visual arts. Zettl's two books, *Sight, Sound, Motion: Applied Media Aesthetics* (1990), and *Television Production Handbook* (1992) have been, for the last 30 years, the major textbooks in television production and television aesthetics, respectively, and have been translated into many languages. Among Zettl's other noticeable publications and paper presentations on television aesthetics are: "The Paradox of Education Television and the Educational Process" (1967), "The Study of Media Aesthetics" (1978c), "Languages of Television: The Language of Television Criticism" (1978b), "The Rare Case of Television Aesthetics" (1978c), "Video in Depth: Multiple Monitors Show Subtext" (1985), and "The Graphication and Personification of Television News" (1989). Among the numerous perceptual psychologists, neurophysiologists, Gestalt psychologists, and art psychologists quoted most frequently by Zettl are Arnheim (1953, 1969a, 1969b), Dondis (1973), Goldberg (1951), Goldstein (1975), Kepes (1969), Koffka (1935), and Tarroni (1979). Zettl's basic approach to the study of television is the inductive analysis of the basic picture elements of lights, colors, two- and three-dimensional space, time-motion editing, and sound. He is a contextualist who believes that as life and art are inseparable, so should the television picture and the entire television program be live and artistic, elevating viewers' involvement and appreciation.

From the research works of these and numerous other scholars I have extracted the major perceptual factors—visual, auditory, and motion—that, in my view, constitute the parameters of the first axis of the study of television aesthetics.

1

▼▼▼▼▼▼▼

Visual Perception Principles: Defining the Visual Field of the Television Screen

Any attempt to define the visual field of the television screen is futile unless the main theories, the organs, and the processes involved in visual perception are thoroughly defined and clearly understood. The physiology of the human perceptual organs, mostly the eyes, the ears, and the brain, and their specific functions are discussed in detail in Part II of this book. This chapter briefly examines only the basic anatomy of the eyes to explain how we perceive televised images. Specifically, this chapter introduces the following topics as they relate to the perception of television images: (a) basic approaches of perception, (b) visual stimulation (which includes also the visual sensory processes), (c) the perceptual process of television images, (d) the perception of elements within the visual field (which expands the discussion to include light and color), and (e) the perception of holographic and three-dimensional visual displays.

BASIC APPROACHES TO VISUAL PERCEPTION

Perception, in general, is a process in which objects and events in the environment are received by the sensoric perception organs as stimuli. These organs then organize, codify, and process the stimuli to the brain, where they are turned into structural perceptions, or cognitive units. The normal operation of this process depends on various key factors such as the nature of the stimuli, heredity, memory, and learning. Perception, therefore, is a product of both the physiological and psychological processes.

In visual perception we usually look at the external world (the visual world) to assign meaning to a variety of sensory impulses. We attempt to organize these impulses to identify and understand them. Depending on how familiar we are with the environmental stimuli, we ask, first, what the form of the particular stimulus is. We then try to define its depth and location. Finally, in our effort to determine its nature in relation to the environment, we wonder what the stimulus is doing; whether it is stationary or in motion.

Consequently the perceptual systems, visual perception in particular with its learned and innate characteristics, are committed to organizing impulses, explaining their existence according to the three previous questions and allowing us to understand, adapt to, and better control the external world. As Gleitman (1986) stated: "our perceptual system shapes and organizes the patchwork of different sensations into a coherent whole that has *form*, *depth*, and *motion*. . . . The perceptual system operates to minimize perceptual contradictions and to make all parts mesh in a coherent whole" (p. 191).

Moreover, our perceptions have meanings that illustrate psychological dimensions of visual perception. In an attempt to survive, we draw from experience and search through computed stimuli to define that which is being examined. As a result, although we accept the information garnered through the means of sight, we are dependent on psychological processes for determining what those impulses mean. As stated by Connor and Hawthorn (1985), "Our perceptions do have meaning, they do make sense; and meaning and sense derive from both our experiences and our present purposes. Without the presence of meaning and sense as active organizing agents, perception, as we know it, would not exist" (p. 119).

These physiological and psychological dimensions of visual perception formed the basis for the creation of three prominent analytical paradigms in perception research, which, in turn, formed the constructs on which three basic approaches of perception were built, the *empiricist*, the *nativist*, and the *Gestaltist*.

In simple terms, empiricists maintain that visual perception depends on the following three factors: (a) an object's size on the retina, (b) depth cues that establish an object's whereabouts and distance from the retina, and (c) the necessity of experience and prior learning. For example, we know from experience that small retina objects—when they have been established and measured in relation to the human figure—are farther away (Gleitman, 1986).

An opposite view is held by nativists, who maintain that perception depends on innate factors that provide information about objects. For example, if the size of an object is defined by distance and its related projected image, the variation in size of surrounding elements remains constant. Consequently, it is the texture gradient that produces a higher order pattern of situations that provide information about distance. According to nativists, a person does not measure the differences between the object and its surroundings, but the internal capacity to interpret changes in texture gradients to create a complete picture of distance. They maintain that, "there is a constant ratio between the retinal size cast by an object and the retinal size of its adjacent texture elements—a higher order stimulus relationship that remains invariant over changes of distance" (Gleitman, 1986, p. 181).

This belief that the perceptual process entails an analysis of the entire visual field has been reinterpreted by Gestalt psychologists. Their approach is based on the law of simplicity of parsimony, which states, in effect, that the best scientific explanation is the simplest one that fits the data (Bloomer, 1976). Thus, Gestaltists believe that humans perceive whole shapes as opposed to assessing an object's various elements. Elements, therefore, are grouped into a whole, a shape, to facilitate recognition and simplify the perceptual process. Moreover, a person is only conscious of this activity when confronted with a stimulus that is foreign and requires the creation of meaning. Consequently, the Gestaltists believe humans perform closure, completing forms that are incomplete.

Among these three approaches there are certain similarities worth mentioning. First, the perceiver must be conscious of external stimuli and focus on them. Second, the perceiver must be able to establish distinctions between the object (or stimulus) and its environment, known as *figure–ground relationships* that are further discussed later. Third, the perceiver must be able to attach meaning to a stimulus (after he or she has examined its outline, size, color, and texture) drawn from the stored familiar shapes. This process is called *pattern recognition*, whereby the perceived figure is compared with and defined by its relation to objects previously seen.

These three common grounds of the empiricist, nativist, and the Gestaltist theories of visual perception are of great significance to the perception of television pictures. Viewers' conscious efforts to focus on the visual phenomena depends on the clarity and the attractiveness of visual images. Their ability to differentiate the figures from the grounds depends largely on how visual elements are constructed within the concentrated space of the television screen. Finally, the degree to which television viewers are able to recognize and to give meaning to visual stimuli is determined by the producer's skill in creating readily recognizable television pictures.

VISUAL STIMULATION

Visual perception is an important sensing system. More information reaches the human brain through the eyes than through any other sense organ. Most organisms have two eyes, either both in front or one on each side of their head. For most mammals the gradual change from sideways to frontal-looking eyes occurred as precise judgment of distance became important. The use of two eyes cooperating to give *stereovision* is an important process in visual perception. Sight developed as living organisms needed to react to the electromagnetic energy we call light. Light is essential to life. It is the key ingredient of visual perception and orientation in space and time. The receptors of the eyes are sensitive to only that tiny portion of the vast spectrum of electromagnetic radiation known as light.

Light strikes the eye; it travels through the complex structure of the eyeball to the retina where it is translated into electrical energy and then transmitted to the brain where it is organized, decoded, and perceived.

To understand this entire process we must be aware first of the physiology of the eye. This entails a clear understanding of the various parts of the eye, as illustrated in Fig. 1.1, and their functions (further discussed in Part II).

Because the television camera was developed from the anatomy of the human eye to which it has a great resemblance, knowledge of the physiology of the eye and the nature, role, and specific functions of the lens, iris, pupil, cornea, retina, fovea, rods, cones, and optic nerve are necessary. Second, we must fully comprehend the mechanism of visual perception; what happens in the eye from the moment the light strikes the cornea, transfers to the light-sensitive receptors at the back of the eyeball—the rods and the cones—and then through the optic nerve to the brain. Third, we must learn to distinguish among the potential stimuli (exposed in the visual world), the effective stimuli (picked up by the eye), and the ineffective stimuli (ignored or overlooked by the eye). Herein discussions of these subjects are provided as they relate to television pictures that are moving images accompanied by sounds.

The stimulus of vision is light. Light can be emitted directly by a light source such as the sun or an electric light bulb, or it can be reflected from

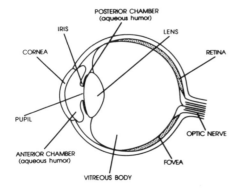

FIG. 1.1. The human eye. Reproduced with permission from Metallinos, N. (1994). Physiological and cognitive factors in the study of visual images. In D. M. Moore & F. M. Dwyer (Eds.), *Visual Literacy: A Spectrum of Visual Learning* (p. 56). Englewood Cliffs, NJ: Educational Technology.

objects. The eye is only sensitive to a relatively small amount of radiation that travels in a wave form, somewhat analogous to the pressure waves that are the stimulus for learning. This radiation can vary in intensity and in wavelength. The range of wavelength to which our visual system can respond is the visual spectrum, extending roughly from 400 (violet) to 750 (red) nm between successive crests.

The eye is the organ that gathers the visual stimulus. As Gleitman (1986) suggested, "Except for the retina, none of its major structures has anything to do with the transduction of the physical stimulus energy into neurological terms. Theirs is a prior function: to fashion a proper stimulus for vision, a sharp retinal image, out of the light that enters the eye from the outside" (p. 153). The particular function of each of the eye structures is examined in detail in Part II.

The resemblance of the eye to the camera, illustrated by Fig. 1.2, has been emphasized by perceptual psychologists and visual communication media researchers such as Hochberg (1978), Zettl (1992), and others. Both the eye and the camera lens bend light rays that pass through and project an image on a light-sensitive surface behind the film in the camera, and the retina in the eye. Both have a focusing mechanism. In the eye, a set of muscles changes the shape of the lens—a process known as *accommodation*. Both have a diaphragm to control the amount of entering light. In the eye, this is the iris, a smooth circular muscle that contracts and dilates by reflex action. The differences, however, are enormous, as explained later.

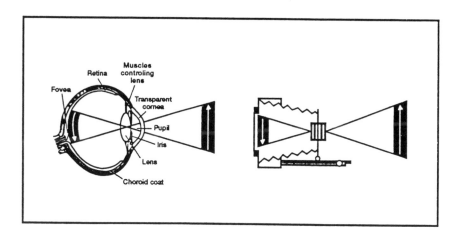

FIG. 1.2. Eye and the camera. Reprinted from PSYCHOLOGY, Second Edition, by Henry Gleitman, with the permission of W. W. Norton & Company, Inc. Copyright © 1986, 1981 by W. W. Norton & Company, Inc.

The receptors do not report to the brain directly, but relay their message upward by way of two intermediate neural links—the bipolar cells and the ganglion cells. The bipolar cells are stimulated by the receptors and they, in turn, excite the ganglion cells. The axons of these ganglion cells are collected from all over the retina, combining into a bundle of fibers that finally leaves the eyeball as the optic nerve. The region where these axons converge contains no receptors and thus cannot give rise to visual sensations; appropriately enough, it is called the blind spot. Visual acuity is greatest in the fovea where the density of the reception is greatest.

According to the *duplicity theory* of vision, rods and cones differ in function. The rods operate at low light intensities and lead to monochromatic sensations. The cones function at a much higher illumination and are responsible for sensations of color. The biological utility of such an arrangement becomes apparent if we consider the enormous range of light intensities that we encounter between day and night.

The first stage in the transformation of light into a neural impulse is a photochemical process that involves the breakdown of various visual pigments that are later resynthesized.

The visual system is not passive as early observers had assumed it to be. It actively shapes and transforms the optic input; its components never function in isolation, they interact. One kind of interaction concerns the relation between what happens now and what happened before. There will be a gradual decline in the reaction to stimulus that persists unchanged. As Bartley (1958) suggested long ago:

> Everyone knows that when we enter an unilluminated or weakly illuminated room, such as a movie theater, from the street on a bright sunny day, we cannot see very well. In a few minutes, this inability diminishes and objects begin to be seen fairly well. This is the experimental aspect of *dark adaptation*. The same initial inability is a well known occurrence when one passes from an unilluminated room to one that is illuminated. The process in this case however, is called *light adaptation*. (p. 109)

Researchers have concluded that in humans, continual involuntary eye movements serve the biologically useful purpose of keeping the visual world intact. As Gleitman (1986) stated:

> Adaptation effects show that sensory systems respond to change over time. If no such change occurs, the sensory response diminishes. What holds for time, holds for space as well, for here too, the key word is change. In vision, the response to a stimulus applied to any one region partially depends on how the neighboring regions are stimulated. The greater the difference in stimulation, the greater the sensory effect. (p. 161)

It is well known that the appearance of a gray patch looks different on a light background than it looks on a black background. This is called *brightness contrast* and its effect increases with intensity differences between the contrasting areas. Such effects serve a vital biological function. They accentuate the edges between different objects in our visual world, and thus allow us to see them more clearly.

The lens and the cones have serious optical aberrations that cause some blur of the retinal image. This blur is further aggravated by light that is dispersed as it passes through the liquid medium of the eye, scattering a diffuse haze over the entire retina. The result is a retinal image in which there are no distinct outlines but only fuzzy fringes. How then do we see the sharp edges of the world around us? The answer is that brightness contrast accentuates intensity differences between adjacent retinal areas, so much so that it sometimes creates perceived boundaries where physically there are none.

Neighboring regions in the retina tend to inhibit each other. The reason for this is a process called *lateral inhibition* (in effect, it is inhibition exerted sideways). When a visual receptor is stimulated, it transmits its excitation upwards to other cells that eventually relay it to the brain. However, this excitation also stimulates some neurons that extend sideways along the retina. These lateral cells make contact with neighboring cells whose activation they inhibit. This process results in increased contrast. The brain gets an exaggerated message. What is dark becomes darker and what is light seems lighter.

The close resemblance of the eye and the camera extends, also, to color, the perceptual properties of which resulted in the development of color photography, film, and television. However, whereas the perception of light depends on its intensity, the perception of color greatly depends on its sensory quality. For example, the sensation of a red color is different than the sensation of a green or a blue color "in a way that it cannot be described as a matter of more or less" (Gleitman, 1986, p. 161).

There are three perceived dimensions of color: hue, brightness, and saturation. *Hue* refers to the chromatic colors but does not include black or white that are known as achromatic or colorless. Hue varies with wavelength. Thus pure blue occurs on the spectrum at about 475 nm, pure green at about 515 nm, and pure yellow at about 580 nm. *Brightness* varies between the chromatic and the achromatic colors and it refers to the amount of light reflected by the color. This can best be understood if we look at the achromatic colors that go from black to white in a succession of steps on the gray scale. *Saturation* is the amount of gray mixed into a specific color hue. It is the purity of the color.

If we consider color patches of maximal saturation and arrange them on the basis of their perceptual similarity, the result is a circular series called the *color wheel*. The red is followed by orange, orange by yellow, yellow-green, green, blue-green, blue, and violet until the circle finally returns to red. To complete our classification of color we need a color solid that incorporates the color wheel with the other two dimensions of perceived color, brightness and saturation.

In the real world, colors are seldom pure. Different objects reflect different combinations of light that strikes them and these reflections strike the same region of the retina simultaneously, causing color mixtures. There are subtractive and additive color mixtures. In *subtractive* mixtures, one set of wavelengths is subtracted from another set. This is demonstrated by color filters that allow some wavelengths to pass through, blocking the others. An example of this is a yellow and blue filter. The blue filter will allow all bright waves between 420 nm and 540 nm to pass through, whereas the yellow filter only passes light waves between 520 nm and 620 nm. If light passes through both filters, the blue filter blocks all light above 540 nm and the yellow blocks all light below 520 nm. As a result, only the light between 520 nm and 540 nm passes through the double barricade and as it happens, this light is seen as green. When the mixture is subtractive, mixing blue and yellow will yield green. The same effect applies to artists' pigments. Any pigment only reflects a certain bond of wavelengths, absorbing the rest. Therefore, mixing yellow and green pigments also yields green.

Additive mixture goes on in the eye itself and occurs when different bonds of wavelengths stimulate the same retinal area simultaneously. Such additive mixtures can be produced by projecting two different colors of light onto the same spot on a wall from two different projectors. The light from each source is reflected back to the same retinal area. One use of additive mixture is color television, in which all colors come from a mixture of red, blue, and green light projected on a phosphorescent screen.

In an additive color mixture, every hue has a complementary one—another hue that, if mixed with the first in appropriate proportions, will produce the color gray. Any hue on the circumference of the color wheel will yield gray if mixed with the hue on the opposite side. Of particular interest are the complementary pairs of red and green and yellow and blue. Hues that are not complementary produce mixtures that preserve the hue of their components: Red and yellow lead to orange, and blue and red yield violet or purple.

Complementary colors are also described as color antagonists because they cancel one another's hues. In general, any region in the visual field tends to induce its color antagonists in adjoining areas. The result is simultaneous color contrasts. For example, a gray patch will tend to look bluish if surrounded by yellow, or yellowish if surrounded by blue. A related phenomenon called *negative afterimage* occurs when a specific color is contrasted with an immediately preceding stimulus. If we look at the green patch for a while and then look at the white wall, we will see a reddish spot. Negative afterimages have the complementary hue and the opposite brightness of the original stimulus. As Gleitman (1986) suggested:

Afterimages are caused by events that occur in the retina and associated visual mechanisms. This is why, when the eye moves, the afterimage moves along with it. One reason for the effect is retinal adaptation. When we fixate a white dish on a black background, the pigments in the retinal region that correspond to the dish will be blended more intensely than those in surrounding areas. (p. 170)

The neurological mechanism that underlines color vision can be explained by asking two questions: How are wavelengths transduced into receptor activity, and how is the receptor output coded into such sensory qualities as hues? Because the raw material of vision is light of different intensities and wavelengths, there are different receptors (types of cones) that are differently attuned to this physical dimension. In fact there are three types of cones that respond to the low, middle, and high bands of wavelengths. The exact color comes from the sensitivity curves of each type and they overlap in their interaction. Each wavelength will produce a different ratio of the outputs of the three receptor types. This factor has, as is shown later, a profound consequence in the composition of color television images.

There are other mechanisms that work on the three receptor outputs and ultimately code them into the sensory qualities that are color. The *opponent process* theory asserts, according to Gleitman (1986):

That there are six psychologically primary color qualities: red, green, blue, yellow, black, and white, each of which has a different neural process that corresponds to it. These six processes are not independent, but instead are organized into three opponent process pairs: red-green, blue-yellow, black-white. The two members of each pair are antagonists. Excitation of one member automatically inhibits the other. (p. 171)

According to the opponent process theory, the experience of hue depends on two of the three opponent process pairs, red–green and blue–yellow. Each pair can be likened to a balance scale. If one arm goes down, the other necessarily comes up.

The brightness or darkness of a visual experience is determined by the activity of a third pair of antagonists—black and white. As Gleitman (1986) suggested: "Every wavelength contributes to the excitation of the white system, in proportion to its intensity and the sensitivity of daylight vision to this point of the spectrum. The black process is produced by inhibition of the antagonistic white process" (p. 172).

So far, we have looked at the way in which the different sensory systems respond to external stimuli, how they transduce the proximal stimulus and convert it to a neural impulse, how they code the message into the various dimensions of our sensory experience, and how activity in any part of a sensory system interacts with the activity of other parts. Next I will examine the three stages in the perception of television images.

THE PERCEPTUAL PROCESS OF TELEVISION
IMAGES

Oversimplified, the perceptual process follows three stages. The potential stimuli of the visual world, the objects, events, and sounds, can all be thought of as *distal* stimuli; they are at a distance and elicit electromagnetic energy in wave form. As long as energy reaches the receptors of our senses and interacts, energy becomes *proximal* stimulus. It arrives at the organs of perception and is ready to be processed. Our sense receptors process the proximal stimulus as a chemical reaction and transmit it to the brain. When the brain receives a stimulus it is perceived as a chain reaction. The responses of the brain are the *perceived* stimuli now known as cognitions (see Fig. 1.3).

Visual perception, as any other sense, depends on incoming stimuli to activate the receptor cells, otherwise we would not sense. Let us see what happens when we watch a television program.

The television set itself and the light coming from the picture on the television screen are the *distal* stimuli. The light that emanates from the screen enters the cornea and the lens of the eyes, travels through the fluid chamber of the eyeball, and strikes the retina. The light impinges on the receptor cells—the rods and cones—and can now be called proximal stimuli. These stimuli are then processed within the light receptors, where they are codified, and then transmitted to the brain for understanding. In the brain, the proxi-

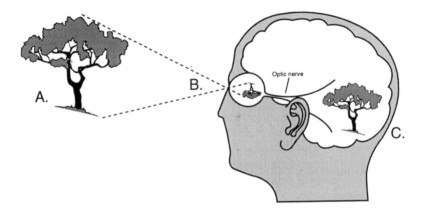

FIG. 1.3. The perceptual process of images: (a) distal, (b) proximal, and (c) perceived stimuli.

mal stimuli become the perceived stimuli. This entire process is further discussed in Part II.

CENTRAL AND PERIPHERAL VISIONS
AND TELEVISION IMAGES

The discussion of the central and peripheral visions as they relate to television images entails an examination of what the domains of these visions are, what the differences between the visual world and the visual field are, and what the differences between the big (film) and small (television) screens are.

Our eyes do not operate independently of each other; one eye cannot move without the other being affected in some way. There is an area in our field of vision where both eyes see the same objects but at slightly different angles. Their overlap measures approximately 120° of *binocular vision*. Binocular vision allows us to see depth. Without it, we would live in a flat world of height and width.

The center of the overlapping field, known as *central vision,* is very precise. At the perimeter of our visual field is our *peripheral vision*. Although it usually remains out of focus, peripheral vision is particularly sensitive to movement and contours.

Our total span of vision is 180° horizontally and 150° vertically. This restriction in our visual field has resulted in the rectangular shape, usually 3:4 aspect ratio, of the television screen, as explained in greater detail later on (see Fig. 1.4).

As we take a look around us, we see objects and experience events as they relate to us. This is our visual world. Streets, people, and objects around us are real and tangible. However, when we see and experience the same objects and events reproduced on the screen, they appear changed, usually smaller, and often less, always relative to their environment. The phenomena of the real world differ when they appear in the visual field in many respects, as explained in the following.

FIG. 1.4. The binocular visual field. The dimensions of the binocular visual field have suggested the 3:4 aspect ratio of the conventional television screen. Reprinted with permission from Ruch, T. C. (1960). Binocular vision and central visual pathways. In T. C. Ruch & J. F. Fulton (Eds.), *Medical Physiology and Biophysics*, 18th ed. (p. 453). Philadelphia: W. B. Saunders.

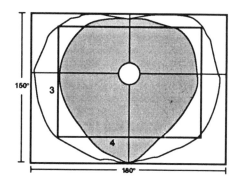

The television camera captures only a small fragment of the visual world. The camera's visual field is transmitted to thousands of television screens around the world. Often we see only a bird's eye view of the world and world events. The images on television are reproductions of the real world that have been edited, manipulated, and squeezed into the small television visual field.

The perception of the television screen is quite unlike that of the film screen. The relatively small size of the traditional television screen means that we usually exercise only our central vision while watching television. The eyes have very little space over which to move. Consequently, most of the information value of objects on the screen is obtained immediately.

At the cinema, we experience both central and peripheral visions because the screen is so much larger. Because we do not see all the screen at once, our eyes move constantly and our brain is more active in its effort to piece all fragments of the screen together; we remain more alert. The size difference of the two screens, film and television, causes the image size of objects and events to look bigger or smaller, more powerful or weaker. Film images are visually louder than images of a small television set. A large image exerts more aesthetic energy than a smaller image, or the same image on a smaller screen. At the theater, people and objects are perceived as being of dramatic proportion not only physically, but psychologically as well. The landscape carries as much energy as the people; both are overwhelmingly strong and in competition for screen space. On the large movie screen, the simple act of a man walking down a country road becomes a gesture; on the small screen this remains a simple act (Metallinos, 1991; Zettl, 1990).

THE PERCEPTION OF ELEMENTS
WITHIN THE VISUAL FIELD

The analysis of the central and peripheral visions that brought into focus the properties of the small (television) and the large (film) screens leads to the examination of the perception of the visual elements of light, color, image size, image pattern, shape, and direction that appear on the small television screen. The analysis of motion of the visual elements is discussed in chapter 3.

The television picture is an interplay of light and colors. It is, therefore, important to understand the properties of light and color to comprehend how this visual medium operates.

As discussed earlier, light is electromagnetic energy. It makes up a small part of the larger electromagnetic spectrum that includes radio waves, infra-red, ultraviolet, X-rays, and gamma rays. What we see as light is the visible part of the spectrum. Color is a property of light; when light is bent by a prism, each wavelength deviates through at a slightly different angle so that the emerging beam comes out of the prism as a fan of light giving all the spectral colors.

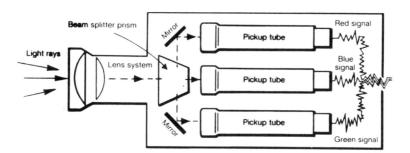

FIG. 1.5. The color television camera. These different pickup tubes (red, blue, and green) create the color television picture. From Thomas D. Burrows and Donald N. Wood, *Television Production: Disciplines and Techniques*, 3rd ed. Copyright © 1986 Wm. C. Brown Communications, Inc. Reprinted by permission of Times Mirror Higher Education Group, Inc., Dubuque, Iowa. All Rights Reserved.

When looking at objects or liquids, we see light as it is reflected from them and when we see color we actually perceive three basic color sensations: the color itself (hue), the color's strength (saturation), and how brilliant a color appears (brightness). Unlike the old black and white television picture, today's color television picture has all these attributes (see Fig. 1.5).

As explained earlier, there are three different types of cones in the retina of the eyes, each of which responds maximally to three different colors: blue, green, and red (Guyton, 1986). The colors we see depend on which of the three cone types are made active and to what degree they are stimulated. Each type of cone is excited most effectively by light of one particular wavelength, but also responds to other wavelengths. According to Vander (1985), "Our sensation of color depends upon the ratios of these three cone outputs and their comparison by higher order cells in the visual system" (pp. 655–656).

Light and color perceptions are also very important as they directly influence the perception of image size, pattern, shape, and duration. The position, direction, and motion of objects and subjects in space are also directly related and can be perceived due to light and color.

THE PERCEPTION OF HOLOGRAPHIC AND THREE-DIMENSIONAL IMAGES

This section briefly examines the perception of holographic images, the perception of three-dimensional images, and the perception of the figure–ground hierarchy in television images.

In the real world, we see and relate to our surroundings in three dimensions. Until recently our artistic expressions in the mass media were confined to two dimensions. Photography, film, and television are two-dimensional or flat media and have no actual depth. The sense of the third dimension is an illusion created by manipulating subjective space. Recent developments in the fields of holography, film, three-dimensional television imaging, and computerized imagery have made three-dimensional images seem almost realistic. Holograms and three-dimensional film and television images appear to extend beyond the screen toward the viewer.

As the words *holo* (total) and *gram* (message) connote, the hologram captures the entire message of the scene in all its visual properties, including the realism of the third dimension. The magic of a hologram can be demystified by an understanding of light and how images are captured on film. In conventional photography, light waves bounce off a subject and pass through a lens. The lens focuses the light waves onto an image and we see a flat two-dimensional photo of the actual object. In holography, however, the lenses precisely guide the light, which must be coherent or monochromatic (known as *laser*, an acronym for light amplification by the simulated emission of radiation), reflecting off all points of the subject. These light rays are recorded in three dimensions. Praising the perceptual property of holograms, Kock (1969) stated, "The hologram plate itself resembles a window with the image scene appearing behind it in full depth. The viewer has available to him many views of the scene to see around the object in the foreground, he simply raises his head or moves it left or right" (p. xi).

The many uses of holography today, including air traffic control, radiative surgery and therapy, topography, computer-aided design, supermarket checkouts, advertising, and education, are additional reasons for the student and the researcher of visual communication media to examine the perceptual properties of holography vis-à-vis their potential covert effects (Metallinos, 1990).

An equally important perception factor is three-dimensional television, which is emerging rapidly thanks to the vigorous research of the Media Lab scholars at the Massachusetts Institute of Technology and Japanese industrial (Sony) and education (NHK) technologists.

Three-dimensional television has not been perfected yet. It is in the experimental stages where either the television cameras, the television sets, or the television viewers must use special converters, apparati that substitute a person's perceptual property of binocular vision. Volumetric three-dimensional imaging methods (Balasubramonian & Rajapan, 1983) and three-dimensional holographic television (Brand, 1987) are among the recent three-dimensional television systems in existence. Their massive application, however, might have negative results. Studies on this issue have shown that there are numerous perceptual and aesthetic drawbacks of the three-dimensional media that should be considered, such as adjusting the depth of field, cardboarding effect, motion parallax, motion perspective, and figure–ground consistency (Metallinos, 1990).

It is very important for television and for any visual art form to maintain a figure–ground segregation; otherwise viewers will not be able to distinguish objects from their background and they will not correctly perceive depth. As Murch (1973) stated, "The exchange [of figure–ground relationship] is marked by a modification of the apparent depth of the figure; the figure portion always appears to be in front of the ground" (p. 147).

We feel compelled to structure what we see in the figure–ground relationship. We constantly see objects relative to a background. Because of this urge, especially startling effects are achieved by rendering the figure–ground relationship purposely ambiguous or by reversing it (Metallinos, 1989). Something like this is common practice in gimmicky advertising. In television, superimposition produces this quite effectively, particularly in dream sequences. Television becomes a blur of moving images, with little comprehension and minimum retention, if the figure–ground relationship is in constant flip flop. Maintaining a consistency in this hierarchy is imperative if we expect viewers to perceive properly and make sense of television images (Metallinos, 1989).

In summary, the study of such visual communication principles in the areas of basic approaches to perception, visual stimulation, perceptual process, central and peripheral visions, perception of visual elements within the visual field, and visual perception of three-dimensional images helps us to define the visual field of the television screen. As is discussed later, the construction of television pictures is guided by and depends on these factors of visual perception.

2
▼▼▼▼▼▼▼

Auditory Perception:
Defining the Sound Dimension
of Television Pictures

Although it is often overlooked and taken for granted, sound is equally important as the sight or vision components of the television medium. Empirical research in television aesthetics on the role of sound in television is very limited (Alten, 1994; Metallinos, 1985).

We live in a society where most means of communication involve the process of sound. Things we see or do often use sounds to be perceived and comprehended. For example, a television picture without its accompanying sound is perceived differently; it assumes a different meaning and at times is meaningless. Sound emphasizes mood and provides meaning in a predominantly visual medium such as television. As Alten (1994) stated: "Sound is a force: emotional, perceptual, physical. It can excite feelings, convey meaning, and, if it is loud enough, resonate the body" (p. 4). As a multilevel force, sound requires thoughtful understanding of its perceptual, cognitive, and compositional properties. This chapter discusses only the perceptual bases of sounds. The cognitive and compositional dimensions of sound are discussed in Parts II and III, respectively.

Specifically, this chapter discusses such basic audio communication-related factors as approaches to auditory perception, auditory stimulation, the process and mechanisms of auditory perception, the perception of acoustic space, and the perception of sound and noise in television images.

APPROACHES TO AUDITORY PERCEPTION

The three approaches to visual perception, *empiricist*, *nativist*, and *Gestaltist*, discussed earlier, also apply to auditory perception. However, the distinct nature of the audio stimuli alters these three approaches to a degree.

The basis for the empiricist approach to sound perception is the necessity of experience and prior knowledge. We receive a great variety of sound stimuli. However, we select, register, and identify readily those sounds of which we have prior knowledge. The faster and more accurately we answer the empirical question "What is it?" the closer we come to identifying the form or the nature of the sound stimulus. For example, by asking what the form of the sound is, empiricists seek to distinguish random noise from purposeful sound. The sound of a church bell is perceived as an organized and purposeful sound exerted by an identifiable source and it has a particular purpose.

For the nativists, whose perception of sound stimuli depends on the innate and intuitive factors, the question "Where is the sound?" satisfies their perceptual curiosity. The location of the sound (along with its depth and its surroundings) automatically comes into focus when the sound is heard by those who have adopted the nativist approach to sound perception. The hierarchy of dependence of all sound stimuli determines all precepts of the nativist listeners. For example, nativists perceive the sound of the church bell, already discussed, as an organized and purposeful sound exerted by the bells that are in a church building. Intuitively, a hierarchy of interdependency is maintained.

The Gestaltist approach to auditory perception (like that of visual perception) maintains that configuration rather than separation provides a better and more accurate perception of the nature (and other characteristics) of the sound.

Incoming sounds are grouped in whole form. They are arranged into known patterns, motives, or schemata to simplify the perceptual process. In their effort to facilitate more accurately the precepts for the perceptual process, Gestaltists ask: "What is the stimulus condition?" For example, the perception of the church bell is influenced by the law of parsimony, which suggests to Gestaltists arranging the sounds into closures of known and readily identifiable patterns.

The preceding analyses of the empiricist, nativist, and Gestaltist approaches to auditory perception lead to the discussion of auditory stimulation and help to clarify the complex process of auditory perception.

AUDITORY STIMULATION

The vibration or mechanical disturbance produced by the physical change of a medium is the stimulus for hearing (Murch, 1973). The sense of hearing, or audition, informs us of the pressure change that occurs at a distance. Its stimulus is a disturbance of the air that is propagated in the form of sound waves (see Fig. 2.1).

Sound waves can vary both in amplitude and in wavelength. *Amplitude* refers to the height of a wavecrest, and *wavelength* is the distance between

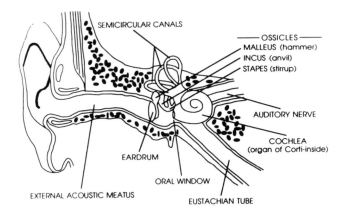

FIG. 2.1. The human ear. Reproduced with permission from Metallinos, N. (1994). Physiological and cognitive factors in the study of visual images. In D. M. Moore & F. M. Dwyer (Eds.), *Visual Literacy: A Spectrum of Visual Learning* (p. 57). Englewood Cliffs, NJ: Educational Technology.

successive crests. Sound waves are generally measured in terms of *frequency*, which is the number of waves per seconds or Hertz (Hz). Our brain translates amplitude and frequency into the psychological dimensions of loudness and pitch.

Humans can respond to a vast range of amplitudes. Researchers have found it convenient to use a scale that compresses this great range into a more convenient form. This scale describes intensities in decibels. Perceived loudness approximately doubles every time the physical intensity goes up 10 decibels.

Young adults can hear tones as low as 16 Hz and as high as 20,000 Hz, with maximal sensitivity in the middle range. As people get older, they lose some sensitivity to sound, especially at the higher frequencies.

There are simple and complex waves. Simple waves, like the sound of a flute, have only one strong frequency, whereas complex waves, like the sound of a violin, have a mixture of several waves or harmonies. The auditory system is able to analyze complex waves into their component parts; we can hear the separate notes that make up a chord. This ability has its limits; if a sound is made up of a great number of unrelated waves, it is perceived as noise that we can no longer analyze.

What the photons are in visual stimulation (which provides information about the objects exposed in the visual world) the acoustic radiations are in auditory perception. They provide information about the environment, but some sounds provide more information about the specific location of the sources. As Bartley (1972) explained, "Vision is a space sense and we are dependent upon it for appreciating the overall pattern and the details of our

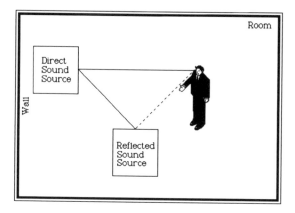

FIG. 2.2. Direct and reflected sound stimulations. The direct source is bounced off the wall and picked up by the reflected sound source by the human ear.

three-dimensional environment, but hearing is a localizing sense. It tells us where *specific* things are in this visual three dimensional space rather than giving us a filled-in area effect such as we obtain in vision" (p. 183).

Sound waves in open space reach the ears straight from the direction of the source. However, in closed environments, acoustic energy splits into two waves: sound waves that arrive directly and sound waves that are echoed, or reach the ear indirectly (see Fig. 2.2). Auditory stimulation of contemporary people is mostly achieved by direct, indirect, and other surface sounds. The surface-reflected auditory stimulation has profound consequences in the perception of sound stimulation of contemporary people. An explanation of the phenomenon and the questions it raises were stated by Bartley (1972) as follows:

> Because you now live in enclosures (buildings) and because artificial acoustic sources have become so potent, a new pattern of acoustic input, which we shall call encompassing, pervades today's living. Through reverberations acoustic waves are reaching the ears from all directions (barring the "sound shadows" made by the head). The question is how does the auditory system handle this kind of an input and does it produce a fuller spatial quality to hearing than an environment in which acoustic waves reach the ear for normally restricted directions? Or does this sort of an environment present an input unfavorable for the listener? (p. 184)

Further insight to this phenomenon and some answers to these questions are provided in the following section regarding the process and mechanism of auditory perception and the perception of acoustic space thereafter.

PROCESS AND MECHANISM OF AUDITORY PERCEPTION

The ear captures sound waves from the surroundings and turns them into bits of information, then processes them to the brain for understanding. Before this entire mechanism of auditory perception is discussed, the fundamentals of the physiology of the ear and the various functions of the auditory stimuli must be explained (see Fig. 2.1).

A number of different organs make up the ear, which divides into three sections: the external ear, the middle ear, and the inner ear. The *external ear* helps to capture and identify the directions of the sound source. It consists of the ear flap, or pinna, and the ear canal, or external auditory meatus, that leads to the eardrum or tympanic membrane. The ear flaps receive the sounds. The ear canal varies both in shape and in size and directs sound vibrations to the eardrum. The outer portion of the canal, about one third of its length, is cartilaginous; the remaining two thirds is bony. The canal takes on a somewhat s-shaped form and has a diameter of about 0.7 centimeters at its entrance; it gets smaller closer to the eardrum.

The middle ear begins with the inside part of the eardrum. In the middle ear cavity there are three tiny bones, the auditory ossicles. These three ossicles, the malleus, the incus, and the stapes, transform sound vibrations to the inner ear. Also found in the middle ear is the Eustachian tube. This tube is responsible for maintaining proper pressure equilibrium in the ear and connects the middle ear with the pharynx. The slitlike ending of the tube in the pharynx is normally closed but during yawning, swallowing, or sneezing, when the muscle movements of the pharynx open the entire passage, the pressure in the middle ear equilibrates with atmospheric pressure or the pressure of the other side of the drum. A difference in pressure is also produced by changes in altitude such as in an elevator or airplane.

The inner ear is the area where sound vibrations convert to electrical impulses, are coded, and propagate through the auditory nerve to the brain for interpretation and understanding. The inner ear structures are contained within a system of spaces and canals—the osseous labyrinth. These spaces and canals generally are divided into three sections: the vestibule, the cochlea, and the semicircular canals.

As stated earlier, the total range of hearing in healthy young adults is between 16 Hz and 20,000 Hz, with few young adults able to hear the entire range. The sounds heard most keenly by human ears are those from sources vibrating at frequencies between 1,000 Hz and 4,000 Hz.

The first step in hearing is the entrance of pressure waves into the ear canal. These pressures, or sound waves, are transmitted to the eardrum, a thin membrane that bows inward under the pressure of the sound waves. The extent to which this membrane moves depends on the force with which the air molecules hit it, and relates to the loudness of the sound.

The second step of hearing is the transmission of sound energy from the tympanic membrane, through the middle ear cavity, and then to the fluid-filled chambers of the inner ear. The total force of the tympanic membrane transfers to the three ossicles in the middle ear. At the end of this bony chain the sound energy transmits to the oral window, a thin membrane that connects the ossicles of the middle ear to the inner ear.

Mechanical vibrations are transformed to electrical signals within the organ of Corti in the inner ear. This organ is a collection of about 23,500 sensitive receptor cells that transduce sound energy into neuronal action. The organ of Corti is located along the top of the basilar membrane. The basilar membrane stands as a thin and stiff organ near the oral window at the beginning of the inner ear. It progressively becomes larger and flabbier as it descends to the wall of the cochlea. Lying like a flap over the organ of Corti is the rectorial membrane. These two membranes are divided from the rest of the cochlea by the Reissner's membrane and are bathed in a fluid called endolymph.

The cells in the organ of Corti are lined with small hairs that stick out through the rectorial membrane. As sound vibrations enter the inner ear, they cause these hairs connecting the two membranes to bend and it is the bending of the hairs that effects the conversion from mechanical sound vibrations to electrical impulses. The bending of the hairs triggers an electrochemical reaction in the cells and the generation of electricity. According to Chedd (1970), "What happens to the sound remains a mystery. All we know is that it is encoded in spikes of electrical activity as each hair cell fires, but the nature of the code is unknown. The unraveling of this code is complicated by the fact that the hair cells continue to fire even in the absence of sound" (p. 29).

Since the 15th century scientists have debated what constitutes sound. If a tree falls in the forest and no one is there to hear it, will there be sound? The answer, of course, depends on whether sound is to be considered a physical vibration transmitted through the ear, or just a sensation inside the mind of the listener. The first statement is the cause and the second is the effect. As a sound receptor, the ear gathers sounds, organizes, manipulates, and processes them to the brain to be decoded just like the eye gathers, organizes, manipulates, and processes sights.

Sound has power. It actually represents a flow of power from one place to another, a flow that can be modified by the medium through which it travels. If the sound elicits a response from the organ of hearing, that sound is an effective stimulus. If the sound goes undetected by the ear the stimulus is then ineffective. Effective sound stimuli travel through the ear, and the brain perceives them and assigns their meanings.

Human efforts to duplicate the mechanism of auditory perception have resulted in the development of various hearing devices, microphones, and sound-generating and sound-control instruments. The television medium in particular, has developed advanced, computerized microphones and sound control equipment that produce, gather, and manipulate, accurately and precisely, the different sounds used by the medium that are thoroughly examined in the third part of this book.

Sound adds new dimensions to the sense of sight. It has the power to alter such emotions as joy, terror, love, and hate. Most importantly, sound forms the basis of speech, our most powerful means of communication. However, the emotional or psychological effects of sound vary depending on the individual's taste and mood and the conditions under which the sound is being heard. Although sounds can produce certain common behavioral effects, tests have shown that individuals provide their own interpretation of sounds. This factor is overlooked by commonly used television measuring devices that insist on homogeneous interpretation of sounds by the television audience.

THE PERCEPTION OF ACOUSTIC SPACE

The perception of acoustic space that examines the issues of sound localization cues, distance, and direction judgments is of great significance to the study of television aesthetics because the television image constructors must work effectively with television audio equipment, microphones, turntables, audio consoles, and so on. Mastering television audio techniques is a slow process that first requires thorough analysis and understanding of the perceptual process of acoustic space.

It is established that because we normally hear with two ears, we can locate sounds in space in a manner "analogous to the visual depth perception and angular acuity that we process within the two eyes" (White, 1975, p. 125). Our two ears permit us to determine the horizontal angle between the line pointing to the two ears and the direction of the incident sound. The perception of the direction of the vertical angle is poor.

Experiments in sound localization have attempted to discover the specific physical sound cues available to the listener and their nature. The ability to localize sound sources is considered to be most important in a person because it helps one to recognize the direction of the objects to look for and to avoid.

According to Moore (1989), "The term 'localization' refers to judgments of the direction and distance of a sound source. Sometimes, when headphones are worn, the sound image is located inside the head" (p. 194). In certain cases not only are we able to figure out the direction of the sound source, but we are able, somehow, to estimate the distance. This ability is most prominent in blind people. Their survival depends on fine acoustical interpretation as they cannot see where they are going; their ears do the seeing for them. Blind people can use information from echoes and sound reflections to determine the position of the objects in the environment.

Among the sound cues that enable us to localize sounds in our environment are the proximity of the sound to our ear, the inequality of the intensity from one ear to the other, and the minute difference in the time arrival of the sound. For example, for low-frequency tones, the difference in phase is the cue for localization, whereas for higher frequencies it is the loudness that allows us to localize the sound. Sound sources located near one side of the head reach the nearest ear before they reach the other. This delay measures a tiny fraction of a second but because the ear is so sensitive it records the discrepancy and interprets it as sound coming from a specific direction.

Sound localization is harder for sounds situated directly in front or behind our heads. There are no cues because both ears receive the same information simultaneously. It is in these instances that the skills and active imagination of the television sound engineer are required the most because in television it is aesthetically important to match the sound levels to the direction and distance of the action.

An important aesthetic principle to consider when trying to make this match is the figure–ground relationship and its perspective. The figure–ground relationship, in the case of sound, concerns itself with the assignment of important sounds such as figures in the foreground and others as background sound. For example, on a set, a couple is sitting in a café whispering thoughts to each other. In a long shot the visual aspects of the waiters and other people talking near the couple are equally prominent; therefore the couple's voices can be mixed with the others. On the other hand, in a close-up of the couple a clearer visual figure–ground relationship is established. The couple will stand out from the other people, therefore the sounds must be matched accordingly.

The perspective of sound parallels that of the signals. It concerns itself with mastering the close-up shots with close (foreground) sounds and the long shots with farther away (background) sounds. When this practice is not considered in television production, the entire aesthetic quality of a program suffers considerably.

SOUND AND NOISE IN TELEVISION IMAGES

It has been established that sound is caused by the motion or vibration of an object. This vibration creates disturbances in the surrounding medium (i.e., the air), causing atmospheric particles (molecules) to be either squeezed closer together than normal (an action known as *condensation*) or to be pulled farther apart from each other (an action known as *rarefaction*).

Noise and sound are both audible vibrations of the air. The distinguishing factors between the two are in the control, the purpose, and the organization. Sounds have purpose and are organized. Noises are random and unwanted.

Sounds can be controlled; they can be regularly switched on or off at will. On the other hand, noise is uncontrollable sound.

In contemporary society, noise pollution has become an environmental problem. Noise is created through technology and there has been little attempt to control it. Some observers believe that "noise as an environmental pollutant has recently become an object of serious social concern" (White, 1975, p. 179). Very intense noise in our society can, over time, cause gradual nervous or mental illness and loss of hearing. This damage occurs mostly to people working in industrial jobs such as construction or metal working, those living near busy airports, and young people listening to today's music.

Bartley (1972) believed that several reasons why young people today listen to very loud music, which older people think of as being unpleasant and even intolerable are:

> (1) Very often the intense acoustic environment involves what is music to them [youngsters]. When enjoyable music is heard, even much older persons can stand or even want it to be intense. (2) The acoustic stimuli that you actively respond to can be far more intense before becoming annoying. (3) Much more of young people's lives are lived in an active fashion and this calls for the intensity we have just been describing. (p. 188)

Visual communication media are also sources of noise when their sounds are abused as explained later. According to Zettl (1990), "Television is definitely not a predominantly visual medium; it is an audio-visual medium. Silent television is inconceivable from an information, as well as aesthetic, point of view" (p. 335).

Consequently, the successful perception of a television picture depends on the proper structure and control of the picture and sound combination. Auditory and visual perceptions must be organized in the same manner; they must be properly and simultaneously combined so they form a synergistic structure. This is not always easy to achieve, and each case has its own requirements. Studies have shown that the matching criteria for pictures and sounds, the ability to simply perceive pictures and sounds together as a unit, can be grouped under such umbrella categories as historical, geographical, tonal, overtonal, and structural (Zettl, 1990). Their application as television sound techniques is discussed in detail in Part III of this book.

Certain efforts to improve the sound quality of commercial television programs by introducing stereo television sound have had negative results, aesthetically speaking. High-quality sound diminishes the presently low definition of the conventional television pictures. When watching a rock concert on television and listening to it through an FM radio channel, the results are disappointing because the high-quality concert sound does not match the low-definition picture of commercial television. However, the arrival of high-definition television will match perfectly the high quality of stereo television sound when the new medium is universally introduced (Metallinos, 1991).

Because it is the sound track that lends authenticity to the picture and not the other way around, television image constructors ought to be aware of the factors of auditory perception specifically covered in the preceding sections.

3
▼▼▼▼▼▼▼

Vision in Motion:
Defining the Dimension of
Movement of Television Pictures

The visual communication media of film and television are called motion picture media because they present pictures—and sounds—in motion. The study of the perception of movement in television images is equally necessary as the study of their visual and auditory perceptions. It provides a significant body of knowledge to the field of television aesthetics and touches all three axes: perception, cognition, and composition.

Although film and television pictures are images in motion enhanced by sound the skillful control of motion and its effective application in structuring visual images is still an occasional practice by film and television program directors. Only sporadically has the role of motion in the study of visual images been theorized by visual communication media scholars (Arnheim, 1969a; Gibson, 1968; Zettl, 1990). Empirical research that verifies the theories is minimal (Metallinos, 1985).

The textbooks of film and television picture composition persistently downplay the importance of perceptual information provided by camera motion (Kipper, 1986); they decisively overlook the significance of object camera motion (Johansson, 1975); their commentary centers, mainly, on the role of motion in film and television editing techniques (Wurtzel, 1983; Zettl, 1992); and occasional articles on the similarities and differences between print (the written word) and electronic media (moving images) consider motion a factor, a construct, that generates a sense of reality (Kaha, 1993; Wober, 1988), bypassing the perceptual, cognitive, and compositional reasons for it.

A review of literary sources regarding the synthesis of moving images indicates that the main reasons that delayed the creation of a universally accepted syntax of moving images are as follows:

1. Most of the influential pioneer scholars of visual communication media claim that there are powerful similarities between still and moving images when we consider their perceptual messages. For example, in *Movement, Film, Communication*, Bass (1966) stated:

> We tend to think of movement and time-span as the unique attributes of film. Yet these qualities are common to both painting and film. If we should examine, let us say, a Rubens painting, we should see that it has a built-in time-motion factor. When a painting surface has objects placed upon it, a sequence in time must be assigned to these objects. We see them sequentially, albeit with infinitesimal time duration between each step. (p. 200)

2. The perception and comprehension of motion, let alone its skillful composition, are considered by most pioneer visual communication media scholars as complex phenomena always interrelated to space and time. As such it was—and still is for many researchers—a compositional factor readily explained with the term adopted by still pictures, including paintings, photographs, frescoes, and so on. Because for some visual media researchers film and television images are still pictures—which these media mechanically turn to moving pictures—they do not need to be examined separately. As Dondis (1973) stated:

> But note, even in this form [motion picture] true movement does not exist as we know it; it lies not in the medium, but in the eyes of the beholder through the physiological phenomenon of "persistence of vision." Movie film is really a string of still pictures containing slight changes, which when reviewed by man in the proper time intervals, are blended together by a holdover factor in seeing so that the movement appears real. (p. 64)

3. The most important reason for the delay in the creation of the syntax of moving images is the lack of communication between academic researchers and the traditional barriers that separate the arts and humanities from the sciences. For example, whereas research findings in the fields of perceptual psychology, physics, neurophysiology, and experimental psychology have studied and have revealed the various motions (real, induced, and apparent) as they relate to visual images, in the field of communication we are either not cognizant of these findings or we are unable to explain them in communication media-related terms (Fletcher, 1985; Metallinos, 1977, 1983).

The information explosion and computer technology have now broken the barriers between disciplines. Consequently, the suggestions of the pioneer scholars of visual communication media to explore the potentials of motion in the kinetic arts media of film and television and to create a unified syntax of motion can now be implemented. We need to point out the differences between still and moving images; to underline their diverse perceptual, cognitive, and compositional properties; and to emphasize the advantages offered by the various forms of motion over the limitations of the still images. As Moholy-Nagy (1969) pointed out:

> While in photography not the camera but the light sensitive emulsion is the key to genuine work, in the motion picture not the emulsion, but the possibility to produce motion is the key to the film production. And yet there is no theory for the use and control of motion. In the majority of films, motion is still so primitively handled that even its basic principles remain to be involved. Practical experience has been confined to a few decades and the eyes apparently are as yet untrained to receive sequences in simultaneous motion. In the majority of cases the multiplicity of movements, even if well controlled, still convey the impression of chaos rather than organic unity. (p. 278)

Advances in new visual communication media, such as three-dimensional film and television, holography, high-definition television, and computerized images, have occurred since Moholy-Nagy (1969) and other pioneers such as Arnheim (1953), Gibson (1968), and Kepes (1966) suggested a closer look at the perceptual, cognitive, and compositional properties and potentials of motion in the structure of moving images. Yet, a unified, confined, and universally accepted syntax of moving images is nonexistent. This chapter provides a theoretical basis for the implementation of the syntax of moving images in an effort to define the various dimensions of the television pictures.

It should be pointed out that there is a substantial body of research dealing with the auditory domain of motion, as well, which is not included in the present discussion, dealing mainly with the perception of motion visually. Studies integrating the two domains of visual and auditory perception of motion provide a valuable holistic approach for the understanding of the perception of motion. For the clarity and direct application of issues pertaining to the television medium, this chapter centers on the visual domain of the perception of motion. Specifically, this chapter examines: the perception of movements in the visual world (the environment); the theories of motion and moving images; the relationships of time, space, and motion; and the origination and the perception of movements in the visual field (the television picture).

THE PERCEPTION OF MOVEMENT IN THE VISUAL WORLD

The perception of motion has traditionally been treated as a troublesome subject among perception researchers. Initially the camera formed a basic analogy with the perception characteristics of our organic eye. To the researchers, the optic stimulation of the retina was essentially similar to a static two-dimensional projection of the interior back wall of the camera. General observations of this phenomenon formed the basis for the initial theories of visual perception. With the arrival of motion pictures, the perception of motion was connected to editing and the sequencing of a series of static images. It was the limitation of this explanation to application of motion, as well as the false belief that motion movie cameras act like the human eyes when recording visuals in motion, that led to the inadequacy of explanations, caused subsequent obstacles to motion perception comprehension, and further delayed the progress of research of this phenomenon.

It was the view of some researchers (e.g., Cutting, 1986) to categorize perception as external presentation (information about objects and events), and as internal representation based on cognitive science research. It is noteworthy that the perception of motion has been of importance not only to contemporary researchers in the domain of psychophysics but throughout the centuries to persons of science as well as philosophy and the arts. Starting with this historical concept of perception and metaphysics we can see why we perceive things as we do. Koffka (1935) and Gibson (1950), for example, were pioneers in this quest. They both understood perception to be based on the process of gathering and absorbing information.

Such information, however, had to be derived from somewhere. It was Gibson (1979) who proposed, only recently, that such information comes from the environment during a given perceptual act. This information is processed according to the laws of optics and perspective geometry. Ullman (1980) also investigated the nature of three-dimensional solutions from two-dimensional projections of objects in motion, in the belief that the eye and the camera are compatible. Recent researchers, however, do not share these views because the eye does not have a shutter or an exposure time and it cannot see or record a moving image the same way the camera does (Berkeley, 1986; Pong, Kenner, & Otis, 1990).

The most common area of investigation relating to the movement of the observer is called *motion parallax*. It refers to the relative displacement of objects due to the observer's change of placement. It was first explored by the Greek geometrician Euclid (around 300 B.C.) and then by the German physiologist and physicist Helmholtz (1821–1894), who observed the effects of the movement of the observer on the perception of distance. What happens to the observers when they are moving is that they continuously fixate on a particular point of reference and that image remains stationary on the retina for a brief period of time. At the same time, images of objects that are further and/or nearer shift in opposite directions over the retina surface. The points that lie farther away than the reference appear to move in the same direction, whereas the objects that are closer seem to move in the opposite direction. This is the basis of motion parallax that has been thoroughly developed by perceptual theorists such as Gregory (1990), Hochberg (1978), and Murch (1973), and is further discussed later on in this chapter.

THEORIES OF MOTION AND MOVING IMAGES

The scientific arguments regarding motion perception and its subsequent movement comprehension, are centuries old, diversified, and still appear inconclusive (Marr, 1982). The study of the perception of motion, on one hand, has always been very complex mostly due to the various extreme and multi-faceted forms by which motion occurs. For example, in addition to the extreme velocities of motion that are present but that we do not perceive (e.g., bullet shots or the gradual process of the growing of plants), in the perception of motion such complex factors as change, time, direction, and distance are involved (Murch, 1973). The study of the comprehension of movement, on the other hand, depends on the observer's own abilities, convictions, beliefs, and memories to transform diverse motion codes into cohesive cognitive movements (Spigel, 1968).

These scientific arguments regarding the study of visually perceived and mentally conceived movements have generated three main theories of motion—real movement, induced movement, and apparent movement—each of which subdivides into various forms (or types of real, induced, or apparent motions).

Real Movement Theory

This theory states that the successions of changes of objects, subjects, or events in the environment are the cues that the observer receives and develops his or her conception of occurrences of motion in the environment. Known also as *absolute*, *threshold*, or *objective movement*, this theory, according to Gibson (1968), incorporates the motions caused by changes of an object in the environment, changes of the position of the observer, changes of objects or subjects as the observer moves and changes of the heads and/or the body of the observers.

Neurophysiologists who have studied the real movement theory suggest that greater visual acuity regarding the perception of motion is found in the periphery rather than the center of the retina, in the rods rather than the cones of the fovea (Bloomer, 1976; Gregory, 1990). The main area of the brain in which the coded motion signals are processed and translated into movements is the visual cortex, also known as the striate cortex (Bloom, Lazerson, & Hofstader, 1985). The degree of comprehension of real movement depends on the degree of homogeneity of the environment, the size of the moving objects, and their brightness. After repeated experiments on these factors, Spigel (1968) concluded that, "the more homogeneous the field the greater the rate of motion required for the emergence of perceived movement. Lower thresholds were also obtained with decreased size and brightness of the moving target" (p. 104).

It is, therefore, easy to understand how significant the real movement theory is for the construction of the syntax of moving images and its subsequent application to film or television programs.

Induced Movement Theory

The induced movement theory states, in effect, that the perception and comprehension of moving objects occur when their hierarchy of interdependence, developed by Duncke (1929), and their relationships as figures and grounds, developed by Hebb (1949), are present during the succession of changes. As Spigel (1968) stated:

> The idea that motion is a quality conferred upon an object by an observer is clearly illustrated by the phenomenon of *induced movement*. With two objects or stimulus elements arranged such that one is the surrounded for the other, regardless of which is set in motion, it is the surrounded target that is inevitably perceived as the element that is moving. (p. 105)

Also known as "figure of reference" (Bloomer, 1976, p. 96), or "relativity of movement" (Gregory, 1990, pp. 121–125), this theory is fundamental to the study of visual images for the following reasons: (a) it provides the foundations on which all objects are perceived in the field, orderly and in accordance with their prominence; (b) it allows the observer to make clear distinctions between objects moving across a particular background and a stationary background that is used as frame of reference, and (c) it identifies and helps to explain motion parallax, an artifact of the visual field that occurs when the observer moves his or her head or body, changing the spatial relationship between the eyes and the environment. These motion syntactic constructs should guide the constructors of moving images, particularly the composition of television images that require constant motion and change.

Apparent Movement Theory

This theory refers to a series of phenomenal displacements that lack physical or real movement; they are illusionary, rather than real; they give the impression of natural movements, when in actuality the displacement of objects in space and their continuity is not physiological; it is indirect, inferred, or apparent (Bloomer, 1976; Gregory, 1990; Murch, 1973; Spigel, 1968).

Visual perception paradoxes created by various apparent movements have been the concern not only of the pioneer neurophysiologists and perceptual psychologists cited earlier, but primarily Gestalt psychologists and visual communication media scholars. Due to the arrival of motion pictures (cinema first, and later television and computer images), advocates of the apparent movement theory have identified and studied more closely the various types or forms of apparent movements known as the phi phenomenon, the persistence of vision, the autokinetic effect, and the movement aftereffect. Each of these forms of the apparent movement theory are discussed in reference to their contribution to the study of the visual communication media of film and television.

The Phi Phenomenon Movement. This movement assumed its name from the pioneer Gestalt psychologists who considered a number of illusionary, somewhat paradoxical, and unreal motion instances and studied them separately as basic types of apparent movements namely alpha (a), beta (b), gamma (g), and delta (d).

The *alpha movement* occurs when a successive presentation of a rotated figure, a trapezoidal window with distinctive lines, appears to expand or contract with the successive presentation of each position of the figure. The basis for the illusion of motion generated by alpha movement relies on the fact that the observer is conditioned to assume that a line is of a constant length and that the illusion is a result of a depth change in which the line moves closer and then retreats. Our firm beliefs and habitual convictions insist that what we see fits our previous experience when in reality, what we think we see is not what it is. These factors are also important. The successful interpretation of visual images depends on the accuracy by which they are constructed in the visual fields of the film and television screens so that they will not be misinterpreted and misunderstood.

Beta movement occurs when two spatially separated stationary targets are presented in succession when the delay intervals and the distance between the targets have been proportionally analyzed to create the illusion—the apparent motion—of a single target moving from the position of the first target to the position of the second (Murch, 1973). For example, if the two targets were two flashing lights, rather than perceiving two lights flashing off and on we see a single light moving back and forth in a lateral direction. The successful beta movement effect can only occur when there is a perfect correlation and an optimal relationship among the temporal intervals, spatial distance, and target illumination. The beta movement effect can be achieved and used successfully in structuring moving images as long as we are aware of their perceptual factors, their relationships with other visual elements, and their interactions.

The *gamma movement* occurs when the illumination level of a target increases or decreases, creating the sense that the size and the depth of the target are increasing or decreasing, thus creating an apparent change or movement. For example, when two targets, separate but equal in size, are independently illuminated in equal temporal intervals, the illuminated target seems to move forward, decreasing the distance from the observer, and vice versa (Murch, 1973). The gamma movement depends on two main factors: the spatial arrangements and temporal intervals of the targets, and their subsequent illumination that maximizes the changes of their size and their depth and creates the apparent motion. These parameters are compositional tools in the hands of constructors of moving images and constitute syntactic rules in the grammar of motion picture composition.

A strange phenomenon known as *delta movement* occurs when the stimulus conditions of the beta and gamma movements are combined. Both the temporal change of flashing lights (beta movement) and the reduction or increase in illumination of the target (gamma movement), when they occur simultaneously, create a change or the illusion of a motion in depth, which was defined by Murch (1973) as "a lateral movement of the target from position 1 to position 2, as well as a movement in the third dimension" (p. 281). Because delta movement when applied to objects in the environment provides a sense of depth it becomes an important syntactic construct of moving images, and is very practical in its adaptation to the construction of moving images.

In his collective examination of these four types of apparent movements, Gregory (1990) emphasized first the importance of the phi phenomenon for the creation and the believability of cinema and television. He commented on the degree of tolerance of our perceptual apparati to provide spatial and temporal connections for the organic operation of these media and concluded that, "The phi phenomenon does tell us something about the image—retina system: namely, that it is reasonably tolerant in its demands—which makes the cinema and television economically possible" (p. 121).

The Persistence of Vision or Cinematic Motion. Closely related to the four types of illusionary motions of the phi phenomenon is yet another type of apparent or illusionary motion that I call *cinematic motion*. It is created by a phenomenon known as *persistence of vision*, which, simply stated, is the inability of the retina to follow the signal stimulation in rapid fluctuations. The process of image stimulation continues beyond the initial stimulation for a fraction of a second, merging separate images with one another, thus creating the illusion of a continuous and organic succession of moving images.

Both media, film and television, rely on the paradoxes of these two distinct visual facts; the phi phenomenon with its various types of movements and the persistence of vision, which is also known as retina lag (Bloomer, 1976). Both media depend on the physical law known as critical fusion frequency, which determines at what point (what speed) the fusion of static pictures into a continuous flow of images occurs. The higher the frequency of flashing lights, the better is the fusion and, therefore, the less the flickering picture effect. The established rates of the 24 pictures per second projection for the cinema and the 30 frames per second for the television frame, although they are both below the critical fusion point, are the standard projection rates with the support of special shutters (in the case of cinema) or faster moving interlaced rasters (in the case of television picture frame generation).

Although film pictures are generated differently than television pictures, both images are subject to the cinematic motion theory. That is, their rapid projections (above the initial fusion frequency point) create persistence of vision, which results in illusionary cinematic motion. In other words, there do not seem to be great differences in perceiving and decoding the cinematic motion of the media of film and television as we were led to believe when television first appeared. There are not grave differences in the aesthetic quality of the images produced by the two media because high-definition television pictures are equal to those of film (Metallinos, 1991). These factors are crucial for the creation of the syntax of moving images and its subsequent application to film and television programs (Mathias & Pattersson, 1985).

The Autokinetic Effect Movement.   A third major category of the apparent movement theory is the so-called *autokinetic effect* (Greek, meaning self-moving, or moving independently), which occurs when a light or a bright object is placed on a homogeneous (mainly black) background and appears to move in all directions and at varying speeds as the observer moves. The illusion of motion is created because the dark background does not provide a clear textured reference for the figure (the light or the bright object). Consequently, the inability of our visual organs to distinguish adequately between the movement or drifting of the eye and the drifting of an object in space are the main reasons for the autokinetic effect (Rock, 1966). The structure of the environment, the background on which objects and events occur, plays a significant role in the perception of figures. Equally significant are the factors of time and the size and intensity of the light, as well as the stored memory of the observer.

Concerning time and place factors involved in the development of autokinetic movement and the factors of size and brightness of the objects, Spigel (1968) suggested that:

> The phenomenon [autokinetic effect] involves movement perception in the absence of displacement of the stimulus in either time, or space. A fixed luminous source in an unarticulated surround—one which reduces to a minimum any frames of reference or stability—is seen as moving in an erratic, unpredictable fashion. . . . Generally, the larger the light the weaker the autokinetic effect obtained. (p. 100)

As far as the role played by memory in decoding and explaining the autokinetic and audiokinetic movements, Murch (1973) suggested that, "The influence of such extrinsic and intrinsic instructions on autokinetic and audio-autokinetic effects suggests that the control processes and long term storage are integrally involved. Faced with an ambiguous stimulus situation the subject produces a perceptual response from his own repertoire of responses" (p. 73). This is true, of course, with the perceptual processes of all phenomena including light, color, and sound. It is for this reason that the construction of easily distinguishable environments, the clear indication of time and location, and the precise identification of size, direction, and shape of objects in the environment are such important motion syntactic factors. To obtain clarity we must consider them thoroughly and we must skillfully apply them in structuring moving images of the film and television media.

The Aftereffect Movement.   The last category of the apparent movement theory is the *aftereffect movement*, also known as the "water-fall effect" (Bloomer, 1976; Gregory, 1990; Spigel, 1968). This effect occurs in several instances such as: (a) when we look steadily and intensely at the center of a moving phonograph record and then we suddenly look away or close our eyes, (b) when we persistently look at the center of a black spiral on a white background and look away or close our eyes, or (c) when we watch flowing water for a while (e.g., a river), and then we turn and look at a fixed subject. In all of these cases, apparent motion is an aftermovement in the opposite direction, which seems to be both paradoxical and inexplicable.

Although the aftereffect movement has been known since ancient Greek civilization, neither physicists, neurophysiologists, nor perceptual psychologists have yet found the exact physiological reasons that cause the aftereffect movement; they have only speculated about it. For example, Gregory (1990), in explaining the aftereffect movement paradoxes, suggested that it must be attributed to the image–retina rather than the eye–head movement system. He proposed that two systems are involved—velocity and positional subserve movement perception. Bloomer (1976), summarizing the scientific speculations, concluded that:

> Just why the waterfall effect occurs is not clear. Some theories suggest that it results from overload firing of the specialized cell circuits in the brain that respond to motion. Other researchers feel that adaptation processes in the retina are at least partly responsible. In any case a stationary reference within the visual field appears essential for the waterfall effect to occur. This illusion, fortunately, does not happen when the moving field covers the entire retina. If it did, we would suffer the waterfall illusion of every sudden automobile stop. (p. 101)

The factors, therefore, that determine the aftereffect movement, such as motion velocity, object position, the cooperative effort of peripheral and central vision, the objective and apparent movement, and the image–retina movement rather than the eye–head movement, are the constructs that comprise the parameters of the syntax of moving images.

An interesting and lengthy dispute has occurred over the years among visual perception researchers regarding the differences between real and apparent visual movement perception processes (Kolers, 1967; Matin & Mackinnon, 1967). The dispute centered precisely on the issue regarding the retina mechanisms for movement perception in real and apparent motion. Gibson (1968, 1979) himself raised the dispute when, in his early experiments with motion, he suggested that the perception of motion should be based on the study of the retina mechanisms. Later on, with new experiments and new findings, he concluded that the perception of all events, real and apparent, depends on "the disturbances of structure on the ambient array" (1979, p. 170). The transformation of the visual array rather than the retina mechanisms can explain the differences between real and apparent movement perception. This argument has prevailed and has been confirmed by all prominent contemporary scholars of visual perception mentioned earlier, and was summarized by Murch (1973) as follows:

> There are meaningful differences between the two [real and apparent movements], particularly in the speed of displacement, since the occlusion and disocclusion of the background are continuous in real movement and discontinuous in apparent movement. Nevertheless, the transformations of the ambient array are very similar in both instances. Therefore, if real motion perception is the result of continuous experience with objects in transformations in the external environment, then the conditions of apparent movement would be those producing highly similar transformations. So similar, in fact, that the observer often cannot discriminate between the two. (p. 287)

Our experience with the various transformations of the ambient array of light that objects in the environment reflect is all we can perceive in either case, for real or apparent motion. Therefore, arguments regarding the relationships between real and apparent motion perception, among other things, reveal to us how significant reflected light is in the perception of still and moving objects as a syntactic factor in the construction of moving images. After all, it is light that we manipulate and control to generate the moving visual images of film and television.

As with most other present-day scientific endeavors, perception of motion research has offered us two different perceptual mechanisms: One is based on shape information and the other on motion between pictures. Thanks to modern-day technological innovations, an immense number of observations, hypotheses, and theories on motion perception have been generated. For the most part, it has been enlightening, providing a clear understanding of the motion phenomena. Yet such studies are not complementary to studies in other fields. For example, film and television viewers' perception and comprehension of moving images is rarely discussed in scientific journals, other than those found in the communication field. The later discussion of the various movements that generate television pictures attempts to bridge this gap. However, we must first examine the relationship of motion to time and space, and explain how each influences the perception of the other.

THE RELATIONSHIP OF TIME, CHANGE, AND MOTION

As it was pointed out previously, motion implies change and change occurs in successive intervals of time. Therefore time is the essence of change sequence or motion. As Marr (1982) pointed out:

More so, perhaps than any other aspect of vision—time is of the essence. This is not only because moving things can be harmful, but also because, like yesterday's weather forecast, old descriptions of the state of a moving body soon become useless. On the other hand, the detail of the analysis that can be performed depends upon the richness of the information on which the analysis is based, and this, in turn is bound to depend upon the length of time that it is available to collect the information. (p. 162)

Arnheim (1969a) also pointed out that motion, change, and time are interrelated and that one is not easily perceived without the other. Furthermore, time as a dimension of change involves the presence of things past (e.g., experiences stored in memory), the presence of things present (e.g., experiences of things happening now), and the presence of things future (e.g., experiences we expect to undergo in the anticipated causality of happenings). Time not only determines the flow of change and motion, it also provides causality and logic to events and happenings, thus providing an orderly, meaningful, and organic sequence of events.

Physicists have provided us with the absolute relationship among these three factors (time, space, motion) with the known formula:

$$V = \frac{D}{T}$$

in which velocity (V; speed of motion) is determined by the time (T; duration) that an object takes to travel a given distance (D; space, or change). Perceptual psychologists and physiologists, however, have discovered that this formula does not apply to visual perceptual motion. Instead, the speed of moving objects can be perceived without the need to involve a time estimate. According to Gregory (1990):

The image running across the retina sequentially fires the receptors and the faster the image travels, up to a limit, the greater the velocity signal this gives. Analogies with other velocity detectors (speedometers and so on) show that velocity could be perceived without the reference to a "clock," but they do not tell us precisely how the visual movement system works. (p. 105)

It is therefore some other perceptual factor, some other time movement, that detects the visual motion, an internal biological measuring device that estimates the perceptors of visual movement.

The various types of time under which the media of film and television operate are, according to Zettl (1990): (a) *objective*, also known as clock time; (b) *subjective*, also known as psychological or emotional time; and (c) *biological* or physiological time.

Physiological time refers to the biological arrangements that determine the organism's changes such as eating time, playing time, seasonal time, and entertainment time. It is not so much the objective time or the emotional experience of time that motivates the actions of an individual but rather his or her own biological clock that dictates change. This factor is an important syntactic component in moving image composition because, biologically, it is known that if the metabolic or physiological time for the perception and enjoyment of moving images is not appropriate, communication breaks down.

Objective time is an equally important compositional factor in structuring moving images because it identifies the real-time event and specifies the exact time it occurs. The media of film and television depend on real time for their operation and every hour, minute, and second of real time means revenues. Time means money to the expensive media of film and television, moreso to commercial television, which operates on the marketing of time.

The emotional, subjective, or psychological time is even more significant as a syntactical factor in the grammar of moving images. In fact, the degree of success of a film or a television program and its aesthetic fulfillment depend on the proper use and manipulation of the emotional time of events involving the presentation and the visual narration of the programs.

The running time of approximately 90 minutes (in objective clock time) is the normal rate of a film, whereas the story time—narrating the fictional events of the movie—varies considerably depending on the script. The running time (actual length) as well as its story time also depend on the nature and the objective of the program and they differ considerably from one program to another.

The control and proper manipulation of these three types of time are the primary tasks of constructors of moving images. The greatest obstacle, however, occurs in the control and the skillful manipulation of the timing of moving events and the temporal order of the succession of images, as it is explained in the next section.

ORIGINATION OF MOVEMENTS IN THE VISUAL FIELD

Now that the perception of movements in the visual world has been discussed and the various theories that generate these movements have been examined, the discussion can turn to the perception of the specific movements generated and used in the concentrated space of the television screen.

As stated earlier, all three major theories—real, induced, and apparent— regarding the perception and comprehension of moving objects are important syntactic constructs for the creation of the grammar of moving images. Some additional types of motions, however, are also in operation when we construct moving images within the visual fields of film and television screens. We call them visual forces operating from within the concentrated space of the film and television screens and they are main direction, magnetism of the frame, attraction of mass, asymmetry of the screen, figure–ground relationship, psychological closure, gestalt, and vectors (Metallinos, 1979; Zettl, 1990). The derived motions from real, induced, and apparent, and the visual forces generated in the visual field are the following three specific motions that we must carefully consider.

The three specific types of motion are known as primary (or movement of objects), secondary (or movement of the camera), and tertiary (or movement created by sequencing images; Arnheim, 1969a; Metallinos, 1992; Zettl, 1990). All three are interrelated; they work cooperatively and they rely on the presence and support of each other.

Movements of Objects or Subjects

The first movement we employ is the movement of the performers or objects themselves in their environmental space in front of the camera. This is the primary motion connoting the event itself and it varies in speed, direction, and duration; that is, it can be a speeding car or a loaded truck driven slowly uphill, an object or a performer moving toward the camera (inward movement) or away from the camera (outward movement), and an accelerated (fast forward) or decelerated (slow motion) movement. Each of these motions constitutes the primary event and their application must be dictated by the script, determined by the producer or director, and justified. However, the aesthetic factor that justifies the application of the primary motion's numerous forms (fast, slow, upward, downward, inward, outward, etc.) must be based on the composer's own experience, knowledge, artistry, and skill. The syntax of motion in the kinetic media will provide such needed guidelines for the constructors of images (Gibson, 1950).

The uses of various forms of primary motion in the construction of moving images are like the various uses of the tenses of a verb (e.g., present, future, past perfect) in grammatically constructing a sentence. The choice in the selection of primary motions must be both logical (or syntactical) and consequential (or grammatical), providing the links that connect the parts of the visual sentence.

Movements of the Camera

The second major type of motion unique to the media of film and television is the motion of the camera that generates a variety of movements and provides various points of view of the recorded event. The average film and television cameras are equipped to dolly-in or dolly-out, to zoom-in or zoom-out, to pan (right or left), to tilt-up or down, to truck or arc in either direction (right or left), to pedestal up or down, and to be craned or boomed in all directions and at varied speeds (Zettl, 1992).

Empirical research on the value and the particular application of each of these camera movements is scarce and has not been considered by visual communication media scholars (Kipper, 1986; Miller, 1969; Monaco, 1981;

Tiemens, 1965), although film and television production practitioners and media theorists have both experimented and theorized with them and about them extensively since the arrival of film and television. Visual communication media producers and/or directors should consider the following:

1. That the value and the subsequent application of each of these camera movements should be based on the logic and the situation demanded by life experience and the story. For example, a slow dolly-in rather than a fast zoom-in should be applied to a scene in which a performer, let us say a teacher in a large classroom, walks slowly from one desk to the next, observing the work of the students.

2. That intuition alone or unintentional experimentation with any such camera movements is often undesirable and unreliable. For example, a sudden and unanticipated camera movement such as a fast pan or tilt is an unrealistic, unnatural, and hence disturbing act that diminishes, rather than enhances, the normal flow of visual communication.

3. That only after careful observation, constant application, and theoretical knowledge of the various effects (perceptual, cognitive, compositional, communicative) of each and every one of these camera movements should the producer of moving images apply them as syntactic factors of such images.

Movements Created by Sequencing Pictures: Editing

A unique form of motion is created within the restricted space of the film and television screens when one visual image is followed by another. The succession or juxtaposition of visual images creates the illusion of motion. The specific direction of such motion is primarily determined by the index and motion vectors of the visual images themselves. The forces in operation that create motion are the psychological principles known as closure (Murch, 1973) and figure–ground interdependence (Bloomer, 1976). Due to psychological closure, when we see two pictures, one following the other, we have the tendency to continue the sequence to complete the action or the event illustrated by the picture. For example, if we see a picture of a man holding a knife succeeded by a picture of a wounded person we immediately conclude that the first person hurt the second person. It is a cause–effect phenomenon that influences our perception of images. The second force in operation in the creation of motion of visual images is the change of the environment and its relation to the figures in front of it. For example, if we see a picture of a car in front of an office building followed by a picture of the same car in front of a house we assume that the two different frames of reference—the two backgrounds—represent the motion of the car from one place to another, the workplace to the home. Both perceptual forces are strong forces that generate otherwise unintentional motion when visual images are juxtaposed.

Yet when the succeeding of visual images is intentional, the resulting motion is called *montage*, or editing. All montage is the result of motion generated by successive visual images appearing on the film and television screens, regardless of the time interval and the duration and speed by which they occur. It is beyond the scope of this chapter to analyze the various forms of editing and to provide their syntactic values in the general grammar of visual communication media composition, which are all discussed in further detail in Part III of this book. Instead, I concentrate on the perceptual and compositional significance of implied, simultaneous, fast, slow, rhythmic, abrupt, and transitional motions that are available and are manipulated at will by the constructors of film and television images.

Implied motion exists in all still art forms such as sculpture, painting, and photographs and it has been known to artists since the dawn of civilization. By manipulating various visual elements within the visual field, the masters of still art have managed to create a sense of motion in otherwise motionless pictures. The graphic forces used to create the illusion of motion vary, but the most commonly used are the directional lines known as vectors (Zettl, 1990). Vectors are not only the strongest indicators of direction, they are the prime generators of implied, inferred, or imaginable motion. The eyes of people of a painting looking toward a direction, fingers pointing, arrows indicating an area, and so on, are either graphic or index vectors that imply motion as they point toward a general or specific direction.

Motion vectors created by moving images within the screens in film and television are, of course, the strongest indicators of direction but they are also indicators of the degree of forcefulness or magnitude of the movement. Continuity and converging vectors are also strong indicators of implied motion that are extensively used in still and motion picture composition (Bloomer, 1976).

Simultaneous motion occurs when both the frame of reference (the background) and the event (the figure) move simultaneously, as for example, in the case of an airplane moving in reference to the sky and the passengers within the plane in reference to the interior of the airplane. Known also as *motion paradox*, this type of motion is very common and is constantly present in recording moving images in which both primary and secondary motion occur simultaneously. Simultaneous motion is a powerful syntactic tool in the hands of moving images directors because it creates this motion paradox in which an object can be interchangeable in motion and at rest at the same time (Zettl, 1990), depending on what frame of reference the viewer chooses to consider in the images he or she observes.

Fast or *accelerated motion* is also a powerful syntactic construct of moving images and has been used extensively and often successfully in films and television programs in such scenes as car chases, car and horse races, and airplane combat. The movements of objects, subjects, and events are sped up, creating a faster than normal flow of action that exaggerates motion and reinforces the meaning, the visual message of the event. Accelerated motion is an excellent indicator of the passage of time when used to speed up a naturally slow process such as the blooming of a flower, the gathering of clouds before a storm, or seasonal changes. The manipulation of accelerated motion by the medium of film has been applied successfully in comic scenes (e.g., the Charlie Chaplin movies) or dramatic scenes (e.g., the famous Eisenstein movies). Accelerated motion is an excellent syntactic factor that constitutes a powerful aesthetic agent when it is not used solely to impress or to attract the attention of viewers (Metallinos, 1989).

Slow motion is also a unique feature of moving images available to film and television directors to be used when the situation demands it. The compositional value of slow motion is very significant when it is used to reinforce the meaning of the visual message, rather than to obscure it. For example, if the communicative purpose of slow motion is to slow down the action so that viewers can see the details of an event that occurred very fast, such as a car crash, the application of slow motion is appropriate. On the other hand, slow motion should never be used to break the normal flow of a scene if the ultimate purpose of the scene is to build up tension.

An extreme form of slow motion is the *freeze frame*, also known as *suspended motion*, or *arrested motion* (Zettl, 1990). The perceptual and emotional effect of the freeze frame is that of suspending an action that wants to continue. It is a useful syntactic factor that provides a sense of suspense, tension, and curiosity to the visual communication circumstance when used sensibly, according to the demands of the script, and tastefully.

Rhythmic motion is the characteristic reoccurrence—in equal temporal intervals—of an event and refers to the flow of the segments of the event. The equal temporal intervals that determine the rhythm and set the pace of the program generate the presence of a motion, physically or emotionally. Music videos are the best examples of the use of rhythmic motion. They are transitions between images, scenes, and sequences that are detectable by the particular rhythm of the musical piece. Once the rhythm of a musical piece is set and the pace is established, it is difficult to break it. Physically and psychologically, we submit to the flow of the event. Rhythmic pace is a strong motion syntactic factor also used extensively and quite successfully in television commercials. However, the establishment of the rhythmic pace, and its subsequent use and control, are not easy tasks and require both "sensibility" and "experience" (Zettl, 1990, p. 281).

Abrupt or *sudden motion* occurs when we suddenly interrupt the normal flow of an action and cut to a new, unexpected environment and event. There is still implied motion, which is created mostly by psychological closure, but the normal expectation of the occurrence of the old event is interrupted by the sudden appearance of a new event (Tiemens, 1994). In the media of film and television, cutting from one picture to the next without the proper warning and anticipation creates the abrupt motion or stopping between shots. Cutting from one visual image to the next is the most common editing technique in television and film. However, if the forthcoming image is not anticipated by the viewer, the sudden motion of cutting creates two serious problems that interfere with the communication process. First, the surprise creates the so-called *jump cut*, in which not only the normal flow of action is interrupted and a new environment appears, but the normal directions of the visual elements within the picture field are scrutinized, resulting in unrelated and unrealistic jumps (Zettl, 1990). Second, the jump cut generates the motion of a missing action between the preceding event and the one that follows. If viewers are unable to fill in the missing link that connects the two events due to the sudden change of the cut, they are disoriented and disturbed. Psychological studies on this issue have shown that abrupt motion generated by cutting should be avoided in programs addressed to preschool children and in programs addressed to those who are visually illiterate or unfamiliar with the media of film and television (Goldberg, 1951; Penn, 1971).

Transitional motions are collectively all other motion effects created by the juxtaposition or sequencing of visual images by way of the unique hardware technologies of the media of film and television such as the dissolve, superimposition, fade, wipe, shrink, stretch, flip, tumble, and glow. Whereas the dissolve, superimposition, and fade are normal transitional modes to both film and television, the rest are special transitional effects found in digital video facilities that vary in technological sophistication and capability. The rapid development of such transitional motion effects does not allow the close study of their syntactic value and their specific application. They are often used because they are available and to impress viewers rather than for particular aesthetic purposes. Consequently, the syntactic value of the dissolve, superimposition, and fade, which have become classic transitional devices in film and television, is briefly examined.

Defined as the gradual transition from one visual image to the next during which the visual elements of the first image temporarily overlap with the visual elements of the second, the *dissolve* is a commonly used, powerful, and effective motion syntactic factor. It indicates the passage of time and the normal transition of events unfolding in front of the viewers' eyes as they occur. The duration of the dissolve (i.e., how fast or slow the transition from one image to the next occurs) is a very significant factor because it alters the reason of its usage. For example, whereas a very slow dissolve temporarily replaces the superimposition and assumes its value, the very fast dissolve almost replaces the cut and assumes its value. The normal flow of the event and the action dictated by the script should be the guidelines for its use.

Superimposition occurs when one visual image is imposed over and blends with another—both visible at the same time and occupying the same visual space. The transition that imposes and blends the two pictures is the factor that creates the motion, which, when completed, becomes a freeze frame of two interwoven images. It is a significant motion component with a serious syntactic value when its use is driven by logic, taste, sensitivity, and knowledge of the medium. It bridges two different events and circumstances that occur simultaneously. Superimposition has been applied successfully in dream scenes, flashback sequences, and other such cases where the past or the future needs to be seen in the present time.

The syntactic value of the motion created by *fade-ins* or *fade-outs* is found in such applications as opening or closing a show, terminating an event and starting a new one, and a plethora of other similar situations. In compositional terms the fade-in assumes the role of the opening of the chapter of a story and the fade-out acts as the closing of it. The gradual transition from black to a visual image opens the visual fields of the film and television screens and gets ready to tell a story, to unfold an event. Conversely, fading gradually to black finishes the story, ending the action and concluding the event. Like the opening and the closing of a store, a theatrical performance, a church mass, or a musical concert, the syntactic value of the motion created by the fade-ins and fade-outs lies in the sensitive, skillful, and tasteful manner by which the fades (opening and closing) are executed.

In summary, all of these specific motions used in the composition of television pictures constitute the syntactic elements that construct the grammar of moving images. Knowledge of their perceptual properties enhances our understanding of them, and this in turn helps us to compose better television images.

In fact, knowledge of the basic principles of all three perceptual factors—vision, hearing, and motion—help us to better understand them and this in turn help us outline the decisive rules of the composition of moving images.

References

Alten, S. R. (1994). *Audio in media* (4th ed.). Belmont, CA: Wadsworth.

Antin, D. (1979). The distinctive features of the medium. In H. Newcomb (Ed.), *Television: The critical view* (2nd ed., pp. 495–516). New York: Oxford University Press.

Arnheim, R. (1953). *Film as art*. Chicago: University of Chicago Press.

Arnheim, R. (1969a). *Art and visual perception: A psychology of the creative eye*. Berkeley: University of California Press.

Arnheim, R. (1969b). *Visual thinking*. Berkeley: University of California Press.

Avery, R. K., & Tiemens, R. K. (1975, December). *The syntax of visual messages: An empirical investigation of the asymmetry of the frame theory*. Paper presented at the annual meeting of the Speech Communication Association, Washington, DC.

Baggaley, J., Ferguson, F. M., & Brooks, P. (1980). *Psychology of the television image*. New York: Praeger.

Balasubramonian, K., & Rajapan, K. P. (1983). Compatible 3-D television: The state of the art. In J. Ebbeni & A. Monfils (Eds.), *Proceedings of SPIE-The International Society of Optical Engineering* (Vol. 3, pp. 100–106). Geneva, Switzerland: Three Dimensional Imaging.

Barker, D. (1985). Television production techniques as communication. *Critical Studies in Mass Communication, 2*, 234–246.

Barker, D. (1988). 'It's been real': Forms of television representation. *Critical Studies in Mass Communication, 5*, 42–56.

Barnouw, E. (1956). *Mass communication: Television, radio, film, press*. New York: Holt, Rinehart, & Winston.

Barnouw, E. (1968). *The golden web: History of broadcasting in the United States*. New York: Oxford University Press.

Barnouw, E. (1975). *Tube of plenty: The evolution of American television*. New York: Oxford University Press.

Bartley, S. H. (1958). *Principles of perception*. New York: Harper & Row.

Bartley, S. H. (1972). *Perception in everyday life*. New York: Harper & Row.

Bass, S. (1966). Movement, film, communication. In G. Kepes (Ed.), *Sign, image, symbol* (pp. 200–205). New York: George Braziller.

Beardsley, M. C. (1958). *Aesthetics: Problems in the philosophy of criticism.* New York: Harcourt, Brace, & World.

Berkeley, G. (1986). An essay towards a new theory of vision. In J. E. Cutting (Ed.), *Perception with an eye for motion* (pp. 213–219). Cambridge, MA: MIT Press.

Berlyne, D. E. (1960). *Conflict, arousal, and curiosity.* New York: McGraw-Hill.

Bloom, F. E., Lazerson, A., & Hofstader, L. (1985). *Brain, mind, and behavior.* New York: Freeman.

Bloomer, C. M. (1976). *Principles of visual perception.* New York: Van Nostrand Reinhold.

Borrows, T. D., & Wood, D. N. (1986). *Television production: Disciplines and techniques* (3rd ed., p. 111). Dubuque, IA: Wm. C. Brown.

Brand, S. (1987). *Media lab: Inventing the future at M.I.T.* New York: Viking Penguin.

Brandford, M. (1987). Technology and creativity [panel discussion]. *Proceedings of the high definition television: Productions of electronic films, strategies, and experiences.* Tokyo, Japan: National Film Board of Canada, Technical R & D Division.

Chedd, G. (1970). *Sound: From communication to noise pollution.* Garden City, NY: Doubleday.

Chester, G., Garrison, G. R., & Willis, E. E. (1971). *Television and radio* (4th ed.). New York: Meredith.

Coldevin, G. (1980). Formative research in television presentation strategies: Guidelines for effective production. *Experimental Research in Television Instruction, 3,* 63–80.

Connor, J., & Hawthorn, J. (Eds.). (1985). *Communication studies: An introductory reader* (2nd ed.). Baltimore, MD: Edward Arnold.

Cutting, J. E. (1986). *Perception with an eye for motion.* Cambridge, MA: MIT Press.

D'Agostino, P. (Ed.). (1985). *Transmission: Theory and practice for a new television aesthetics.* New York: Tanaman Press.

Dickie, G. (1971). *Aesthetics: An introduction.* Indianapolis, IN: Bobbs-Merrill.

Dondis, D. (1973). *A primer of visual literacy.* Cambridge, MA: MIT Press.

Duncke, R. (1929). Uber induzierte bewegung. *Psychologisch e Forschung, 12,* 180–259.

Edelberg, R. (1970). The information content of the recovery limb of the electrodermal response. *Psychophysiology, 6,* 527–539.

Edman, I. (1939). *Arts and the man.* New York: Norton.

Fletcher, J. E. (1971). The orienting response as an index of broadcast communication research. *Psychophysiology, 8,* 699–703.

Fletcher, J. E. (1972). Semantic differential type scales in communications research. *Western Speech, 36,* 269–275.

Fletcher, J. E. (1973). Old time GSR and a new approach to the analysis of public communication. *Quarterly Journal of Speech, 59,* 52–60.

Fletcher, J. E. (1976, December). *Attention, retention, meaning, and popular music.* Paper presented at the annual meeting of the Speech Communication Association, San Francisco, CA.

Fletcher, J. E. (1978, November). *Empirical studies on visual communication: Some methodological considerations.* Paper presented at the annual conference of the Speech Communication Association, Minneapolis, MN.

Fletcher, J. E. (1979). Academic research in retrospect: A final view. *Feedback, 21,* 14–17.

Fletcher, J. E. (1985). Physiological responses to media. In J. R. Dominick & J. E. Fletcher (Eds.), *Broadcast research methods* (pp. 89–106). Boston, MA: Allyn & Bacon.

Fletcher, J. E. (1994). Assessment of the visual image in film, television, and the new visual media research design. In N. Metallinos (Ed.), *Verbo-visual literacy: Understanding and applying new educational communication media technologies* (pp. 21–28). Montreal: 3Dmt Research & Information Center.

Funk & Wagnalls New Encyclopedia, Vol. 1. (1972). New York: Funk & Wagnalls, Inc.

Funk & Wagnalls Standard Reference Encyclopedia. (1968). New York: Standard Reference Works.

Gazzanika, M. (1967). The split brain in man. *Scientific American, 217*, 24–29.

Gibson, J. J. (1950). *The perception of the visual world*. Boston, MA: Houghton-Mifflin.

Gibson, J. J. (1968). What gives rise to the perception of motion? *Psychological Review, 75*, 335–346.

Gibson, J. J. (1979). *The ecological approach to visual perception*. Boston, MA: Houghton-Mifflin.

Gleitman, H. (1986). *Psychology*. New York: Norton.

Goldberg, H. D. (1951). The role of cutting in the perception of the motion picture. *Journal of Applied Psychology, 35*, 70–91.

Goldstein, E. B. (1975). The perception of multiple images. *AV Communication Review, 23*, 34–68.

Gregory, R. L. (1990). *Eye and brain: The psychology of seeing*. New York: McGraw-Hill.

Guyton, A. C. (1986). *Textbooks of medical psychology* (4th ed.). Philadelphia: W. B. Saunders.

Head, S. W. (1972). *Broadcasting in America* (2nd ed.). Boston, MA: Houghton-Mifflin.

Head, S. W., & Sterling, C. H. (1990). *Broadcasting in America* (6th ed.). Boston, MA: Houghton-Mifflin.

Hebb, D. O. (1949). *The organization of behavior*. New York: Wiley.

Herbener, G. F., Van Tubergen, G. N., & Whitlow, S. S. (1979). Dynamics of the frame in visual composition. *Educational Communication and Technology Journal, 27*, 83–88.

Hochberg, E. (1978). *Perception* (2nd ed.). Englewood Cliffs, NJ: Prentice-Hall.

Innis, H. (1951). *The bias of communication*. Toronto: University of Toronto Press.

Johansson, G. (1975). Visual motion perception. *Scientific American, 232*, 76–88.

Kaha, C. W. (1993). Towards a syntax of motion. *Critical Studies in Mass Communication, 10*, 339–348.

Kepes, G. (Ed.). (1966). *Sign, image, symbol*. New York: George Braziller.

Kepes, G. (1969). *Language in vision*. Chicago: Paul Theobald.

Kipper, P. (1986). Television camera movement as a source of perceptual information. *Journal of Broadcasting and Electronic Media, 30*, 295–307.

Kipper, P. (1989, May). *Visual communication, information, and perception*. Paper presented at the annual conference of the International Communication Association, San Francisco, CA.

Kock, W. E. (1969). *Lasers and holography*. Garden City, NY: Doubleday.

Koffka, K. (1935). *Principles of gestalt psychology*. New York: Harcourt.

Kolers, P. A. (1967). Some differences between real and apparent visual movement. In R. N. Haber (Ed.), *Contemporary theory and research in visual perception* (pp. 122–136). New York: Holt, Rinehart, & Winston.

Lykken, D. T., & Venables, P. H. (1971). Direct measurement of skin conductance: A proposal for standardization. *Psychophysiology, 8*, 656–672.

Marr, D. (1982). *Vision*. New York: Freeman.

Marshall, R. (1986). *The history of television*. London: Bison Books.

Mathias, H., & Pattersson, R. (1985). *Electronic cinematography*. Belmont, CA: Wadsworth.

Matin, L., & Mackinnon, G. E. (1967). Autokinetic movement: Selective manipulation of directional components by image stabilization. In R. N. Haber (Ed.), *Contemporary theory and research in visual perception* (pp. 136–139). New York: Holt, Rinehart, & Winston.

McCain, T., & Rebensky, G. (1972, December). *The effect of camera shot on interpersonal attractiveness for comedy performers*. Paper presented at the annual conference of the Speech Communication Association, Chicago, IL.

McLuhan, M. (1962). *The Gutenberg galaxy*. Toronto: University of Toronto Press.

McLuhan, M. (1978). The brain and the media: The "Western" hemisphere. *Journal of Communication, 28*, 54–62.

Metallinos, N. (1977, March). *Biometric research in perception and neurology related to the study of visual communication*. Paper presented at the annual conference of the Broadcast Education Association, Dallas, TX.

Metallinos, N. (1979). Composition of the television picture: Some hypotheses to test the forces operating within the television screen. *Educational Communication and Technology Journal, 27*, 205–214.

Metallinos, N. (1983, January). *Biometric research instruments and measuring techniques.* Paper presented at the Center for Broadcast Studies of Concordia University, Montreal.

Metallinos, N. (1985). Empirical studies on television composition. In J. R. Dominick & J. E. Fletcher (Eds.), *Broadcasting research methods* (pp. 297–311). Boston, MA: Allyn & Bacon.

Metallinos, N. (1989). Figure-ground anomalies in commercial television: A diagnostic study. In R. A. Braden, D. G. Beauchamp, L. W. Miller, & D. M. Moore (Eds.), *About visual research, teaching, and applications. Readings from the 21st annual conference of the International Visual Literacy Association* (pp. 291–303). Blacksburg, VA: International Visual Literacy Association.

Metallinos, N. (1990). Three-dimensional video: Perceptual and aesthetic drawbacks. In H. Thwaites (Ed.), *Three-dimensional media technology: Proceedings from the 1989 International Conference* (pp. 131–144). Montreal: 3Dmt Research & Information Center.

Metallinos, N. (1991). High definition television: New perceptual, cognitive, and aesthetic challenges. *Canadian Journal of Educational Communication, 20*, 121–129.

Metallinos, N. (1992). Perceptual factors in the study of television aesthetics. In J. Clark-Baca, D. G. Beauchamp, & R. A. Braden (Eds.), *Visual communication: Bridging across cultures. Selected readings from the 23rd annual conference of the International Visual Literacy Association* (pp. 359–375). Blacksburg, VA: International Visual Literacy Association.

Metallinos, N. (1994). Physiological and cognitive factors in the study of visual images. In D. M. Moore & F. M. Dwyer (Eds.), *Visual literacy: A spectrum of visual learning* (pp. 53–64). Englewood Cliffs, NJ: Educational Technology.

Miller, W. C. (1969). Film movement and affective response and effect on learning and attitude formation. *AV Communication Review, 17*, 172–181.

Moholy-Nagy, L. (1969). *Vision in motion.* Chicago: Paul Theobald & Co.

Monaco, J. (1981). *How to read a film.* New York: Oxford University Press.

Moore, B. C. (1989). *An introduction to the psychology of hearing.* London: Academic Press.

Murch, G. M. (1973). *Visual and auditory perception.* New York: Bobbs-Merrill.

Newcomb, H. (1987). *Television: The critical view* (4th ed.). New York: Oxford University Press.

Ornstein, R. (1972). *The psychology of consciousness.* San Francisco: Freeman.

Penn, D. G. (1971). The effect of motion and cutting-rate in motion pictures. *AV Communication Review, 19*, 29–51.

Pepper, S. (1938). *Aesthetic quality: A contextualistic theory of beauty.* New York: Scribner's.

Pepper, S. (1945). *The basis of criticism in the arts.* Cambridge, MA: Harvard University Press.

Pepper, S. (1970). *World hypotheses.* Berkeley: University of California Press.

Pong, T. C., Kenner, M. A., & Otis, J. (1990). Stereo and motion cues in preattentive vision processing. *Perception, 19*, 161–170.

Rock, I. (1966). *The nature of perceptual adaptation.* New York: Basic Books.

Ruch, T. C. (1960). Binocular vision and central visual pathways. In T. C. Ruch & J. F. Fulton (Eds.), *Medical physiology and biophysics* (18th ed., p. 453). Philadelphia: W. B. Saunders.

Shapiro, D., & Crider, A. (1969). Psychophysiological approaches to social psychology. In G. Lindsay & E. Aronson (Eds.), *The handbook of social psychology* (Vol. 3, 2nd ed., pp. 6–7). Reading, MA: Addison-Wesley.

Spigel, I. M. (1968). Problems in the study of visually perceived movement: An introduction. In R. N. Haber (Ed.), *Contemporary theory and research in visual perception* (pp. 103–121). New York: Holt, Rinehart, & Winston.

Sterling, C. H., & Kittross, J. M. (1990). *Stay tuned: A concise history of American broadcasting.* Belmont, CA: Wadsworth.

Summers, R. E., & Summers, H. B. (1966). *Broadcasting and the public.* Belmont, CA: Wadsworth.

Tarroni, E. (1979). The aesthetics of television. In H. Newcomb (Ed.), *Television: The critical view* (2nd ed., pp. 437–461). New York: Oxford University Press.

Tiemens, R. K. (1965). Some relationships of camera angle to communication credibility. *Journal of Broadcasting, 14*, 483–490.

Tiemens, R. K. (1978). A visual analysis of the 1976 presidential debates. *Speech Communication Monographs, 45*, 362–370.

Tiemens, R. K. (1994). Analyzing the content of visual messages: Methodological considerations. In N. Metallinos (Ed.), *Verbo-visual literacy: Understanding and applying new educational communication media technologies* (pp. 10–20). Montreal: 3Dmt Research & Information Center.

Tiemens, R. K., & Acker, S. R. (1981). Children's perception of changes in size of televised images. *Human Communication Research, 7*, 340–346.

Ullman, S. (1980). *The interpretation of visual motions*. Cambridge, MA: MIT Press.

Vander, A. J. (1985). *Human psychology: The mechanism of body function* (4th ed.). New York: McGraw-Hill.

Venables, P. H., & Martin, I. (Eds.). (1967). *Manual of psychophysiological methods*. Amsterdam: North-Holland.

Webster's Seventh New Collegiate Dictionary. (1971). Springfield, MA: G. & C. Merriam.

White, F. E. (1975). *Our acoustic environment*. New York: Wiley.

Wober, J. M. (1988). *The uses and abuses of television: A social psychological analysis of changing screens*. Hillsdale, NJ: Lawrence Erlbaum Associates.

Wurtzel, A. (1983). *Television production* (2nd ed.). New York: McGraw-Hill.

Zettl, H. (1967). The paradox of education television and the educational process. *Western Speech, 2*, 224–231.

Zettl, H. (1978a, April). *The study of media aesthetics*. Paper presented at the annual conference of the Broadcast Education Association, Las Vegas, NV.

Zettl, H. (1978b, November). *Languages of television: The language of television criticism*. Paper presented at the annual conference of the National Association of Educational Broadcasters, Washington, DC.

Zettl, H. (1978c). The rare case of television aesthetics. *Journal of the University Film Association, 30*, 3–8.

Zettl, H. (1985, Fall). Video in depth: Multiple monitors show subtext. *Mindport: The Journal of San Francisco State University's School of Creative Arts*, 12–13.

Zettl, H. (1989). The graphication and personification of television news. In G. Burns & R. J. Thompson (Eds.), *Television studies: Textual analysis* (pp. 137–163). New York: Praeger.

Zettl, H. (1990). *Sight, sound motion: Applied media aesthetics* (2nd. ed.). Belmont, CA: Wadsworth.

Zettl, H. (1992). *Television production handbook* (5th ed.). Belmont, CA: Wadsworth.

COGNITIVE FACTORS

Part II concentrates on the cognitive factors by reviewing the empirical data, examining the related theories, and underlining the particular principles of cognition as they relate to moving images. Specifically, this part explores the following three main areas: the anatomy of the human information system, the differences between the brain and the mind, and the standards for recognizing visual images.

Anatomy of the
Human Information System

The organs of visual and auditory perception, the eyes and ears, constitute a complex information system, a network of stations that receive selected signals from the environment either electromagnetically or mechanically (by air vibration), transform them into organized bits of information or codes, and channel them by electrical impulses to the brain. In the brain, these codes are then processed to the appropriate part depending on their nature and particular characteristics where they are decoded, translated, recognized, and assume their meaning. Oversimplified, this is how perception and cognition work.

This chapter describes and exemplifies these processes pertaining to visuals and sounds, both inherent in televised images. Specifically examined are the neurophysiological factors of the information centers (the eyes, ears, and brain), the threefold perceptual process, and the codification of visual and auditory information.

NEUROPHYSIOLOGICAL FACTORS OF THE EYE, EAR, AND BRAIN

To understand how the complex human information networks work, basic preliminary information about the anatomy of these organs is needed. A detailed explanation of the neurophysiology of each part of these three information networks is beyond the scope of this chapter. Instead, the discussion refers to the key stations of each of the three systems involved in the reception, organization, and recognition of visual and auditory signals. The principles of cognition as they relate to visual images in general, and to television images in particular, are underlined. Of particular importance to students of visual literacy are three key factors that relate to the human information organs: duplication, polarization, and interconnection of the eyes, ears, and brain.

Like most other organs of the human body the eyes, ears, and brain are duplicated in the left and right side of a person's head. In our routine activity of receiving and processing images and sounds, the fact that two identical yet separate eyes, ears, and brains are in operation seldom draws our attention. This *duplication* of the information organs, however, benefits us by allowing a larger degree of reception of stimuli, offering a greater flexibility to the delicate processes of perception and recognition, and providing a spare part in case of a loss of or severe damage to one of these organs. In the structuring of visual and auditory images these factors must guide the process; they are fundamental to the study of visual literacy.

The *polarization* of the information organs is also significant. Our two eyes see the phenomena from two different positions. Known as *binocular disparity*, or *stereopsis*, this allows us to see depth. Because of this polarization we perceive the world three-dimensionally. Equally, the perception of stereophonic or three-dimensional sounds is possible because of the polarization of our auditory organs in a left and a right ear separate from each other. Finally, the polarization of the incoming signals (half of which go to the left and half to the right hemisphere of the brain) creates a unique opportunity for the brain to recognize information entering from the left or the right side, known as left or right visual or auditory fields. The polarization of the information organs is a factor of great value to television producers, because (among other things) it indicates where the objects, subjects, or events must be staged in the television studio to be readily perceived and easily recognized when televised (Metallinos & Tiemens, 1977).

The third important factor is that all three systems, the eyes, ears, and brain, are *interconnected*. The process of recognition, translation, or comprehension of visual and auditory information by the brain could not be achieved if all three systems were not interconnected. Such common phrases widely used by people as "Do you see what I mean?" and "Are you listening to me?" are examples of how interconnected, related, and dependent on each other the information organs are.

Misinterpretations and misunderstandings of visuals or sounds are prevented mainly because the organs of perception and recognition are in close contact, supporting and complementing each other. The degree of awareness and understanding of the situation and the circumstances depends on the harmonious coexistence and correlation of the information organs.

Basic Anatomy of the Eye

The most important factor regarding the anatomy of the human eye is that each of its parts are extremely specialized structures, sensibly contrived, and harmonically related to the other organs of the information system.

The basic parts of the human eye principally related to the issues concerning this chapter are the cornea, the aqueous humor, the iris, the pupil, the lens, the retina, the fovea, the vitreous humor, and the optic nerve. Many other smaller auxiliary organs are connected to the human eyes working harmoniously to receive and process visual stimuli to the appropriate hemisphere of the brain (see Fig. 1.1).

The cornea is the foremost external part of the human eye that receives the light that carries information about the shape, texture, and color of an object (Murch, 1973). The aqueous humor is the next external element of the eye that receives the photon beam of the humor that is resecreted and reabsorbed on a cycle of 4 hours' time (Gregory, 1990), regenerating its substance to allow a continuous and uniform reception of light. The internal part of the eye starts with the iris, an annular muscle forming the pupil that regulates the amount of light allowed to pass through to the organ lying immediately behind, the lens. The lens then focuses the light through a semicolorless viscous substance known as the vitreous humor for it to arrive at the sense cells of the retina, which, according to Gregory (1990) "is a thin sheet of interconnected nerve cells, including the light sensitive rod and cone cells which convert light into electrical pulses" (p. 68). These light-sensitive cells of the retina engage in one of the most significant functions of the visual perception process, described by Gregory (1990) as follows: "The cones function in daylight conditions and give color vision. The rods function under low lumination and give vision only to shades of gray. Daylight is referred to as *photopic*, while the gray world given by the rods in dim light is called *scotopic*" (p. 69).

The retina is several layers thick. This thickness allows preprocessing of visual forms. The cones occupy the central region of the retina. Exceedingly close together they form the fovea, the region of the retina that gives the best visual detail and color. The last organ of the eye to receive and process visual information is the optic nerve. Located at the back of the eye, slightly off the center of the eyeball, it receives light impulses from the eye and brings them to the optic chiasma, located in the center of the brain. Here, for all practical purposes, the main task of the eyes to receive and process visual information to the brain ends and the brain takes over.

Basic Anatomy of the Ear

Two important factors regarding the human auditory system are its intricacy and sensitivity. This extremely fragile and delicate auditory system is a complex labyrinth that consists of a great number of chambers and auxiliary organs seemingly different, yet interconnected and related to each other. To compensate for its sensitivity and to prevent deafness should the bloodstream be poisoned by disease, critical auditory parts such as the organ of Corti are isolated from the bloodstream and receive their nutrition from fluids of other organs (see Fig. 2.1).

The most crucial parts of the auditory system directly related to this discussion are (a) the organs of the exterior part such as the pinna, the external auditory meatus, and the eardrum or tympanic membrane; (b) the organs of the middle ear such as the ossicles (malleus, incus, and stapes), the oral window, the tensor tympani, the stapedius, and the Eustachian tube; and (c) the inner ear or central hearing system consisting of three main organs, the semicircular canals that comprise the vestibular systems (unrelated to the acoustic system), the cochlea that furnishes the receptor apparatus of the organ of Corti, and the auditory nerve that transmits sound information to the brain.

Extraneous auditory signals first arrive at the pinna or ear helix for prime selection and are then funneled to the exterior ear, known as the auditory meatus. At the end of the tunnel formed by the auditory meatus, the sound signals resonated impinge on the eardrum or tympanic membrane. This membrane constitutes the gateway that connects the external ear with the middle ear. The resonated vibrations of the tympanic membrane are then picked up by three small bones that form the ossicles called the malleus, incus, and stapes. The main function of the ossicles is to simplify the force exerted by the eardrum, to regulate, and to mechanically transmit the sound vibrations to the oral window, yet another membrane of the middle ear. The regulation of the sound entering the oral window is achieved by two other muscles of the middle ear, the tensor tympani and the stapedius, whose functions are, according to Boddy (1978), "analogous to that of the iris of the eye, as they consequently have the capacity to protect the delicate organs of the inner ear from the damaging effects of very loud sounds, by reflexly dumping their impact at the oral window" (p. 274).

As its name indicates, the function assigned to the oral window is to close the opening end of the tube forming the central organ of the entire auditory system, the cochlea. The successful performance of all key organs of the middle ear, but primarily that of the ossicles, is achieved because they are located in the air-filled cavity formed by the Eustachian tube. This tube forms an opening in the mouth cavity that connects the mouth with the middle ear and maintains an air pressure identical to the exterior one. Adjacent to the cochlea is the vestibular system, an information system formed by the posterior, anterior, and lateral semicircular canals, that "act as transducers for information about orientation with respect to gravity and angular acceleration of the head" (Boddy, 1978, p. 276). In other words, they monitor and report head position. Because of the information provided by this system, we are able to maintain a stable and constant visual world because the vestibular and visual human systems are in perfect correlation and harmony, supporting each other in gathering, classifying, codifying, and processing information to its final destination, the brain. The central most sensitive and complex organ of the auditory system is the cochlea or inner ear, and within this most significant part is the organ of Corti. It is here that the reception of sound signals and their classification into sound information bits is achieved before they are processed to the brain for final reorganization and translation. The acoustic process and functions of the inner ear were described by Murch (1973) as follows:

> The actual process of hearing begins in the cochlea. The vibrations are transmitted through its three fluid-filled canals as a way of movement along the membranes separating the individual canals. On one of the membranes of the cochlea (the basilar membrane) is a cell complex known as the *organ of Corti* which contains rows of hair cells embodied in the membrane. These respond to the physical movement of the traveling wave and translate information concerning its frequency and intensity into impulses into the auditory nerve. (p. 15)

The final organ of the human auditory system connecting the ears with the brain is the cochlear nerve that transmits sound signals to the midbrain's thalamus and the primary auditory area of the cortex of the brain.

Basic Anatomy of the Brain

The brain is divided into three major regions: the forebrain (procencephalon), the midbrain (mesencephalon), and the hindbrain (rhombencephalon). Each of these regions is divided into subregions that perform specific functions that constitute the main purpose of the brain—to perceive, to memorize, and to think.

The forebrain is considered to be the highest intellectual area of the entire brain and consists of the cerebral cortex, the amygdaloid complex or amygdala named for its nutlike shape, the hippocampus named for its seahorse shape, the basal ganglia, and the septum. The two most important regions of the cerebral cortex bearing a direct connection to this chapter are the occipital lobe, where the brain's center for vision is located, and the temporal lobe that includes the brain's center for hearing. The specific structure and particular functions of these two centers are discussed in the following.

The midbrain is considered the relay station of all information coming in and going out of the forebrain and consists of two main regions, the thalamus (from the Greek word meaning large room) and the hypothalamus, a smaller region within the thalamus. Specific structures within these two regions, the thalamic and hypothalamic fields and the nuclei of the midbrain, monitor the incoming information and process it to the forebrain (Bloom, Lazerson, & Hofstader, 1985).

The hindbrain is known as the survival organ and consists of the *pons* or bridges, the medulla oblongata, the brain stem, and the cerebellum. The main functions of these organs are to transform information relating to the body and limb position and to regulate respiration and heart rhythms (Bloom et al., 1985).

According to Boddy (1978), "The hindbrain and midbrain are collectively referred to as the *brain stem* as even in the highest vertebras they form a stemlike structure which merges with the spinal cord at its lower end" (p. 46).

The largest, most complex part of the human brain is the cerebral cortex, which, according to Boddy (1978), "is able to accommodate approximately ten billion neurons, three quarters of the total number in the entire brain, and four times the number found in the brain of the chimpanzee, man's most intelligent cousin" (p. 53; see Fig. 4.1).

The occipital lobe, known also as the striate cortex, occupies the rear parts of the cerebral cortex. When visual signals reach the optic chiasma deep in the thalamus' lateral geniculate body, they divide into two parts. Signals from the left-half portion of the eyes are processed to the left side of the striate cortex, whereas signals derived from the right-half portion of the eyes end up in the right side of the striate cortex. The visual input of the other half of the eyes crosses over and reaches the opposite side of the striate cortex. The two hemispheres of the occipital lobe that form the visual region of the brain, also known as the primary visual area, are connected to the corpus callosum, a massive bundle of fibers also linked to the optic chiasma and the thalamus. Between the optic chiasma and the striate cortex

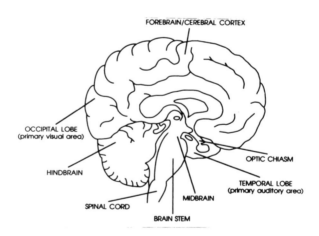

FIG. 4.1. The parts of the human brain. Reproduced with permission from Metallinos, N. (1994). Physiological and cognitive factors in the study of visual images. In D. M. Moore & F. M. Dwyer (Eds.), *Visual Literacy: A Spectrum of Visual Learning* (p. 59). Englewood Cliffs, NJ: Educational Technology.

the signals of vision carried by the optic track pass through a relay station found in both hemispheres of the brain known as the lateral geniculate body (Gregory, 1990). From there the signals "proceed on their way via the optic radiation" (Frisby, 1980, p. 68) and arrive at the striate cortex split in half.

The decodification or signal recognition processes of the visual region are described in the later section on codification of visual and auditory information (see Fig. 4.2).

The temporal lobe of the cerebral cortex occupies the base of the brain and constitutes the primary auditory area. When auditory signals arrive at the cochlea nerve they are processed to the thalamus. The thalamus is "a ·structure composed of two ovoid masses of ganglionic nuclei which are about 4 cc long in humans" (Boddy, 1978, p. 49). The lower thalamic relay nuclei are called the media geniculate body and constitute the final sensory relay of the auditory pathway. When sound signals reach this area, depending on their nature and scope (i.e., sound signals that need to be reproduced or regenerated as visuals or words), they pass through the primary auditory area occupying the temporal lobe of the cerebral cortex, then reach Wernicke's area, which enables comprehension of speech, go through an area called the angular gyrus, and from there pass through an arclike organ called the arcnate fasciculus to arrive at the so-called Broca's area.

Three additional centers within the temporal lobe that are involved in the processing of auditory signals and their final translation as unified auditory messages are the striate cortex already discussed, the motor cortex that is responsible for controlling the motion of the various organs of the body, and the memory engram, the central control system of the memory. The memory engram occupies the entire cerebral cortex and the brain's biochem-

FIG. 4.2. The visual pathways.

istry suggests that "the ultimate basis of information storage in the brain is a modification of synoptic functions" (Boddy, 1978, p. 356).

When we speak either a heard or written word, in addition to the memory engram, the visual cortex and motor cortex are involved, and the pathways of sound signals, passing through the organs of the brain's auditory system, are altered. Excellent descriptions with graphic illustrations of these two auditory processes were given by Geschwind (1979) and Pinchot (1987). Pinchot (1987) specifically stated that:

> When words are heard the sound passes to the auditory area of the cortex flashing from there in neurological codes to the adjacent Wernicke's area, where they are unscrambled into understandable patterns of words. If the words are repeated aloud the patterns must shift forward from Wernicke's area along a handle of linking nerve fibers to Broca's area. Once here they arouse the nearby motor area controlling the movement of speech muscles. (p. 56)

In explaining the involvement of the primary visual area of this process, Pinchot (1987) suggested that:

> This appears to be the task of the third language center, the angular gyrus, a structure lying behind Wernicke's area in the midst of the brain region's sensory signals. The angular gyrus bridges the gap between the speech we hear and the language we read and write. It transforms speech sounds into the visual messages from reading into the sound patterns required to recite poetry from a book. (p. 56)

The decodification process of the auditory area of the brain is described in the later section on codification of visual and auditory information.

In summary, this section provided basic information on the anatomy and broader functions of the three main information systems: the ears, eyes, and brain. The neurophysiological factors that control and dictate the specific functions of the various organs of each of these three major information networks were discussed and the processes that the visual system and the auditory system follow in order to direct the information bits to the particular regions of the brain were underlined. Now that these organs have been discussed and the way they perform their broader functions has been explained, the role of stimulation in the perceptual process is examined.

STIMULI AND THE PERCEPTUAL PROCESSES

This section discusses the role of stimulation in the perceptual process and examines the necessary conditions for the smooth and effective operation of the visual and auditory information processes.

Our interaction with the phenomena exposed in the environment and our mental processes of decoding, recognizing, and interpreting them is a continuous process that starts at birth and increases in complexity and sophistication as we grow older. We all engage in this process, but few of us are aware or even concern ourselves with understanding how it works, how we can improve it, and what the obstacles are that affect the smooth operation of the process. Beyond any doubt, the neurophysiology of the perceptual process is complex. However, students of visual literacy need to be more than aware of its existence.

To simplify matters, perceptual psychologists have adopted the inductive, linear, or mechanical techniques (also known as the stimulus–response process of operation) based on the law of causality, which examines the perceptual process of vision or hearing in terms of cause (stimulus) and effect (response).

Before engaging in the discussion of the various visual and auditory stimuli as causes to the effects of seeing and hearing, the terms *perception* and *sensation* must be distinguished and clarified because both of these crucial psychological constructs include stimulation in their functions. Sensation occurs when a sensoric receptor is stimulated, whereas perception occurs when a stimulus that has reached the sensoric receptor is further processed, codified, and transported to the brain's special center to be translated or decodified. As Murch (1973) stated: "A sensation occurs when neural impulses are transmitted along the afferent [incoming] pathways of the nervous system; perception involves the processing of this input" (p. 5).

Next, the various types of stimuli (visual and auditory), the threefold process of stimulation, and the model of perception and cognition are examined.

Objects and events exposed in the visual world exert electromagnetic energy, making them *potential stimuli*, as all such phenomena are collectively called. The degree of their intensity, strength, and duration determines whether they become *effective stimuli*, capable of reaching the receptors of vision or hearing, or *ineffective stimuli*, unable to stimulate the sensoric organs of vision and hearing.

Scientists have tried to explain at what point potential stimuli become effective or remain ineffective by measuring their intensity, strength, and duration, examining the physical makeup of the organs of vision and hearing, and studying human behavior during the perceptual process. From the observations, hypotheses, and theories developed, scientists have come to the conclusion that the limitations are threefold: (a) insufficient intensity, strength, and duration; (b) physical and/or biological deficiency of the organs of perception; and (c) perceiver's degree of development, receptivity, and awareness. Visual stimuli in regard to their nature, potential, and limitations are discussed next.

Visual Stimulation and Codification

Visual stimuli are electromagnetic energy exerted by objects in the environment that strike the retina of the eye. Light photons transform information about the particular shape, texture, and color of the object and receive stimuli regarding the object's location, size, and whether it is stationary or in motion.

Stimuli that arrive at the retina are not the actual shapes, textures, colors, sizes, locations, and motions of a particular object of the environment but rather a collection of symbols of the object's various parts such as corners, edges, lines, and brightness. When the symbols of a feature are combined and maintain the appropriate relationships in the input image, they form structural descriptions of the particular feature (Frisby, 1980).

Frisby's (1980) theory of structural description of seeing coincides with Murch's (1973) spatial visual fixation, in which a section of the visual field is fixated briefly and followed by another. Sequentially and topographically, bits of information or signals of shapes, borders, straight or curved lines, and edges, are received by the eyes and processed to the brain. In vision, separate inputs are defined primarily by their spatial relationship (Murch, 1973).

Consequently, various visual stimuli are in reality various pieces of an object received individually and sequentially by the visual receptors that, in turn, assemble them into complete structural units and process them to the higher centers of the visual system of the brain. However, only effective visual stimuli reach the brain, where they are stored in either the short- or long-term memories. Furthermore, the effective visual stimulation process offers additional refinement to the reception of the signals.

Auditory Stimulation and Codification

Unlike the stimuli for vision, which are electromagnetic energy that move in an electromagnetic field to reach the retinas of the eyes, the stimulus for hearing "is the physical change of a medium produced by a vibration of mechanical disturbance" (Murch, 1973, p. 12). Sounds produced by a source in the environment become either effective or ineffective stimuli depending on their intensity, strength, and duration. Those effective auditory stimuli that reach the receptors of hearing, unlike the visual ones, are organized by a temporal topographic order. This means that time, frequency, and temporal order rather than spatial order provide the basis for auditory stimulation. Experiments in sound stimulation and sensoric sound perception have shown that the afferent receptors of sensory information in audition are topographic (Erickson, 1968; Murch, 1973) and that each receptor receives only a narrow band of stimulus characteristics.

Effective auditory stimuli arriving mechanically into the hearing receptors are not the actual medium or event of the environment that exerts sounds. They are, rather, bits and pieces of air molecules and tones that stem from the original source. Like visual symbols, sound bits form temporal descriptions of the sound medium that are serially, topographically, and temporally organized and processed. According to Murch (1973), "In audition the nature of an effective stimulus is initially represented mechanically and then translated by topographic receptors into an electrical impulse. This information is then transmitted to the higher centers of auditory reception in the cortex" (p. 107).

Effective stimulation of auditory signals depends on the individual's ability to locate sounds in space. The perception of auditory space, known as sound localization, is an area of immediate concern to the students of verbo-visual literacy. Neuroscientists have suggested several factors that influence the perception of sound localization, such as the restriction or reduction of free head movement, monaural listening, disuse or malfunctioning of the pinna, limited duration of sound vibration, distance of listeners and sound source, and sound frequency (Murch, 1973). These factors must always be recognized and considered in studies that relate to the effects of visual communication media.

Threefold Process of Stimulation and Codification

Now that the visual and auditory stimuli have been defined, their nature discussed, their characteristics underlined, and some of the conditions necessary for their effectiveness pointed out, I turn to the analysis of the threefold process of auditory and visual stimulation: distal, proximal, and perceived (see Fig. 1.3).

Distal Stimuli. All external objects or events are potential stimuli and because they are environmental are called distal stimuli. As stated earlier, in vision all distal stimuli are patterns of ambient light reflected from various objects in the environment. In hearing, all distal stimuli are air molecules disturbed by some medium that travel in waves with a given frequency. The environment provides a continuous flow of countless potential or distal stimuli, most of which go unnoticed and only a fraction of which become effective stimuli.

Proximal Stimuli. Effective stimuli that reach the visual and auditory receptors and cause a sensory reaction that results in the assembling of the individual symbols, or bits of information, of particular objects or events into structural descriptions or representations are called proximal stimuli. The main task of the proximal stimuli is to assemble and codify all input and thus to assist in the building of the precepts that represent, to an extent, the initial distal stimuli (Murch, 1973).

Perceived Stimuli. Proximal stimuli or precepts that reach the appropriate center of the brain and cause the decodification of signals into cognitive structures are called perceived stimuli. The task of the perceived stimuli is to assist the transformation of the proximal sounds to perceived, completed, and recognizable ones.

This threefold process of visual and auditory stimulation is actually an oversimplification, a schematic presentation to explain how the human information system works and improves itself through continuous and systematic elimination and refinement. Furthermore, it helps us to recognize where in this process obstacles occur that need to be overcome and corrected so that the perceptual process will improve. This is precisely the role of the perceptual model provided and discussed next.

Model of Perception and Cognition

Models help to illustrate our thoughts, exemplify a theory, or simplify a complex process. They are graphic explanations or illustrations of complex phenomena, events, or actions. Neuroscientists rely heavily on models to explain the complex process of stimulation, perception, and cognition for various reasons: Models help to clarify these processes, to intensify and focus on specific areas, and to interpret the functions of all parts involved (see Fig. 4.3).

Objects and events that occur in the environment cause stimulation as distal or effective stimuli. This is clarification, the first step of the process. Subsequently, the eyes and ears receive distal effective stimuli in approximate, symbolic, or representative forms constituting the second step, intensification. Finally, the perceptual organs send the intensified and codified signals to the brain. The brain perceives, decodifies, and recognizes. This is the last step of the stimulation process, interpretation.

We must bear in mind the following:

1. This is only a model that helps to explain a process; it is not the process itself.
2. The process itself is much more complex than described here and demands additional advanced models to exemplify it.
3. The steps provided are either unknown or inexplicable and therefore a model that intends to illustrate them is bound to be limited.

Neuroscientists and neurophysiologists originally explained visual and auditory perceptual processes as such, but now suggest that perception starts even before stimulation. Certain neuroscientists and neurophysiologists even equate perception with cognition. Practitioners in the field of visual communication media need to understand and exemplify various perceptual processes because the study of the visual media is in itself a complex undertaking. We analyze, simplify, and model complex phenomena and multilevel communication processes to study them closely and to learn how they affect the visual communication process.

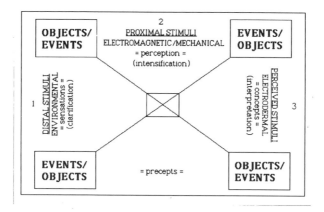

FIG. 4.3. A stimulus/perception/cognition model. Objects and events go through three stages, from (1) environmental (sensations), to (2) electromagnetic (perceptions), to (3) electrodermal (concepts).

CODIFICATION OF VISUAL AND AUDITORY INFORMATION

This section discusses how the organs of perception—the eyes, ears, and brain—receive and codify the complex mixture of visual and auditory stimuli of television pictures. Now that we have a basic understanding of how objects and events of the visual world are received, codified, and processed to the brain for translation and recognition, I move a step further to discuss how moving images within the television screen are received and codified. The first part of this section examines the relationship of the human information organs to the television cameras, microphones, and the control room. The second part discusses the differences between the visual world (the television studio) and the visual field (the television picture), in regard to reception and codification of visual and auditory stimuli. The last part of the section explains how television pictures are perceived and recognized.

The Human Information System and Television ·

Although certain similarities exist between the television medium as an information system and the human information system, there are fundamental differences that are often overlooked. This section discusses the similarities and differences of these two systems.

The key components of the television picture are light and color, sound, and motion, all of which are received from the environment—usually the television studio—by the cameras and microphones and electronically processed and controlled by the switcher and audio console of the television master control room. Cameras receive light reflected from objects on the studio floor as do the eyes from objects in the environment. Objects on the studio floor exposed to the television camera are potential stimuli but the camera, like the human eye, receives only effective stimuli, which are then processed electronically to produce an image. This image appears in the viewfinder located at the back of the camera and is subsequently sent to the television picture switcher in the control room to be integrated into the television program.

This is also the case with microphones, which operate largely on the same principle, receiving the effective sounds from the television studio environment and processing them to the audio console for further manipulation, refinement, and distribution.

Practically all movements performed by a person that looks at a phenomenon can be achieved by professional and technologically advanced television cameras and microphones. Today's television cameras are able to dolly-in and dolly-out, to pan in either direction, to tilt-up or down, to truck or arc left or right, and to zoom-in or zoom-out at the will of the camera operator (see Fig. 4.4).

a. Studio (HK-477)   b. ENG EFP (HC 240A)

c. Convertible (SE-377)   d. Microwave link camera (PITA 2-G)

FIG. 4.4. Samples of various television cameras. Photos courtesy of IKEGAMI Electronics (USA), Inc.

In the same way, television microphones are able to receive sounds arriving with great flexibility, clarity, and accuracy depending on the skill and expertise of the microphone operator.

As the brain receives visual and auditory codes and transforms them into cognitive structures, numerous special image and sound television technologies such as character generators, computerized graphics, television switcher effects, sound or music synthesizers, and sound effects generators, receive images and sounds and further manipulate them to create imaginative and unusual sounds and images that often go beyond the original ones, distorting and exaggerating reality or even creating a new, virtual reality.

Television technology, primarily cameras and microphones, along with their special effects and control systems, will of course never reach the accuracy, sophistication, flexibility, and perfection of the human eyes, ears, and brain. They are mechanical devices that duplicate certain functions of these human information organs. However, they require knowledgeable, skillful, and creative people to operate them effectively. When the instruments of this medium fall into the hands of those who do not have the necessary knowledge, understanding, and creative imagination, the pictures produced are often nothing more than unnatural and tasteless visual and auditory gimmicks. Studies have shown that such tasteless gimmicks often have negative effects on viewers (Metallinos, 1987b). The television camera can zoom in or out at the discretion of the camera operator, whereas the human eye does not possess this flexibility. However, if a fast zoom in or out is performed for the sole purpose of attracting the attention of the viewer, studies have suggested that comprehension and retention of picture content is reduced (Metallinos, 1987a).

The television switcher and audio synthesizer offer a variety of special effects that cannot be performed by the eyes and the ears such as chromakeys, dissolves, flipping and flopping, rolling and expanding pictures, and electronically distorted voices. The technological advantage of the medium in comparison to the human organs, in the hands of the untrained and insensitive, is dangerous and it must be emphasized continuously to visual media communicators that a program's content should determine the use of visuals and sounds, and not the other way around (see Figs. 4.5 and 4.6).

Television Studio (Visual World) and Television Picture (Visual Field)

Events that occur in the studio (visual world) differ considerably from those that appear on the television screen (visual field). Gibson (1950) was the first perceptual psychologist to point out and study these major differences, summarizing them as follows:

> Pictorial seeing, then, differs astonishingly from ordinary objective seeing. The field is bounded whereas the world is not. The field can change in its direc-

FIG. 4.5. Small studio production switcher.

tion-from-here but the world is not. The field is oriented with reference to its margins, the world with reference to gravity. The field is a scene in perspective while the world is Euclidean. Objects in the world have depth-shape and are seen behind one another while the forms in the field approximate being depthless. In the field these shapes are deformed during locomotion, as is the whole field itself, whereas in the world everything remains constant and it is the observer who waves. (p. 42)

(See Fig. 4.7.)
To the student of the anatomy of the human information system these differences provide insightful information often underestimated or over-looked. The camera operator and sound engineer first see objects or hear events in the television studio environment, create retina images and cochlea

FIG. 4.6. An audio control console.

FIG. 4.7. The window of the world. (A) The visual world is boundless and exists beyond the visual field; it is an open world. (B) The visual field is bound, and enclosed with the visual world; it is closed-in and framed.

sound symbols, and operate equipment that re-create them as images and sounds confined in a restricted new environment, mainly representative of the television studio. The camera and microphone operators create pictures from pictures. They re-create observations of the observed phenomena.

First, in the confined space of the television picture produced in the television camera's viewfinder, the camera operator must frame in an event representative of the one that occurs on the studio set. Space restrictions and choice of framing are among the challenges imposed by the bounded field, the television screen. Second, depicted objects and events, when framed, must be assigned a new direction relative to the flow of action of all elements, visuals, and sounds in the new restricted environment. Clear direction of action, ambiguous motion, and constant change are among the key challenges imposed by the transitory visual field. Third, the stable and often horizontal-looking objects and events in the world are framed and photographed and assume their orientation and position in regard to the boundaries that surround them. Maintaining a consistent orientation of the unfolding events within the transitory visual field imposes a serious challenge to the television camera and audio operators. Fourth, the Euclidean theorem that two parallel lines never merge does not seem to be true of pictorial seeing in which the objects and events depicted are seen in perspective, increasingly merging as they approach the vanishing point. Keeping the visuals and sounds of the television picture in perspective and faithful to the Euclidean theorem is also challenging to both the camera operators and the sound engineers. Fifth, the three-dimensional world of the television studio space must be photographed as such so that it reappears in the two-dimen-

FIG. 4.8. The television studio set (visual world). The people in the studio are exposed to the open world. However, when seen by the camera, they are framed into a different, confined unit.

sional visual field, the television picture, as though it has depth. Framing for depth along the z-axis to achieve maximum illusion of three-dimensionality is yet another challenge for television camera and microphone operators (see Fig. 4.8).

Finally, the seemingly constant and stable objects and events of the television studio must be depicted and presented in the picture in a way in which this consistency and stability are similarly maintained. This is a difficult task as the television picture is in constant flux and camera and microphone stabilities, no matter how advanced and sophisticated technologically, require skillful and knowledgeable operators.

Perception and Recognition of Television Pictures

Literature dealing with the perception of still pictures—mainly paintings, photographs, and drawings—is extensive and the theories developed on the perception of each picture category are numerous (Dondis, 1973; Kennedy, 1974). On the other hand, research studies on the perception of moving images—mainly motion pictures and television—are very limited and represented, for the most part, by the pioneering scientific works of Hockberg and Brooks (1974) in motion pictures and Gibson (1979) in television.

In his well-known book titled *The Ecological Approach to Visual Perception*, Gibson (1979) explained how motion pictures in general, and television pictures in particular, are perceived, discussed how they are recognized, and suggested how the study of television picture perception should be approached. In regard to motion picture perception Gibson (1979) stated:

> There is a treated surface, but the treatment has to consist of throwing shadows on the surface by projection instead of depositing traces or pigments on it. An optic array of limited scope is delivered, and it contains information about other things than just the surface itself. The main difference is that the array is not arrested. Its structure undergoes change, disturbance, or transformation. It is not frozen in time. And that is what we need to understand about it. (p. 292)

The television picture is depicted as an optic array of light that contains transformation structures of events. It is interesting to note that (a) the television picture is made of light, and light itself contains information about the things depicted; (b) the television picture is a progressive picture that displays constant transformation and invariant structure; and (c) sound, although not mentioned by Gibson (1979), plays a parallel role in television picture depiction. The first case suggests that the accurate depiction and successful structure of a television picture depend on the lighting operator's knowledge of the technology and artistry in manipulating lighting (Metallinos, 1983). The second case suggests that the camera operator must be aware of the presence and the functions of each of these motions—real, apparent, and implied—connected to television picture perception and always be ready to deal with the additional three motions involving the structuring of television pictures—primary motion (the motion of subjects or events), secondary motion (the motion of the camera itself), and tertiary motion (the motion created by juxtaposition and the succession of the pictures). The third case suggests that in both the perception and in the structure of television pictures, sound is a predominant factor interwoven with visual elements. The perception of the televised picture is either maximized or diminished, depending on the specific use and presence of sound (Metallinos, 1983).

Gibson (1979) also attributed television picture recognition or comprehension to the sequential stimulation of the various parts of the objects and events discussed earlier. However, he considered the television picture as a virtual reality space in which the events are recognized in sequential and hierarchical subordinate happenings. Television pictures are recognized mostly in terms of the continuous flow of events, which implies that recognition of the present moment is greatly dependent on comprehension of the previously depicted moment. Furthermore, recognition of the forthcoming image greatly depends on a clear understanding of the displayed events of the present picture. Describing how the elements of motion and editing contribute to the recognition of motion pictures, Gibson (1979) stated that:

> This awareness [virtual, instead of real] of events is achieved by segmenting the flow of the pictorial optic array so that it specifies the same kinds of

subordinate and superordinate happenings that are specified in a natural optic array. Persons, animals, places, objects, and substances are depicted along with the events. The segments of the optical flow are crucial, that is, the transients between parts as well as the parts themselves. Simply to call them "motion" is not to do justice to them. (p. 301)

Gibson (1979) recognized that the discussion of visual and auditory perception as well as recognition, which he called "awareness" (p. 212) of motion pictures, presuppose an explanation and understanding of such other involved factors as editing (both in film and television), narrative or scriptwriting, and moving images nomenclature. He called film and television images "progressive pictures" as opposed to "arrested pictures" (p. 293), explained how important a role editing plays for the understanding of moving images, and analyzed the cognitive value of panning, dollying, fading, and so on.

Finally, Gibson (1979) suggested that the study of film and television picture perception and recognition requires a holistic rather than a static approach, in which the special features governing the media and the particular ways images are constructed must be studied together because they constitute an inseparable unity. He concluded, "The theory of ecological perception, of perception while moving around and looking around the environment, is better. The various kinds of filming transition—zoom, dolly, pan, cut, fade, wipe, dissolve, and split-screen shot—could usefully be evaluated in the light of ecological optics instead of the snapshot optics that is currently accepted" (p. 303).

This suggestion was also pursued by the pioneering works of numerous other theorists and students of the television medium such as Fletcher (1978), Tarroni (1979), Avery and Tiemens (1975), and Zettl (1990), all of whom studied the aesthetics of television based on its fundamental image elements such as light and color, space manipulation and camera shots, time motion and editing, and sound. The value and function of each of these is described herein.

As the visual elements within the visual field are perceived and recognized, so are the sounds that accompany these visuals. A distinction, however, must be made: The process of perception and recognition of sounds in the visual field differs from that of visuals. As Gibson (1979) pointed out, "But the theory of the invariants under auditory change and their relation to invariants under visual change is another matter entirely. They are not the same for the flow of environmental sounds as they are for the flow of speech sound" (p. 301). In the discussion of television audio, this point is further examined.

Anatomically speaking, the recognition process of television sounds parallels that of the visual recognition process to which sound is subordinate. In summary, the perception and recognition of television pictures presumes the study and understanding of the idiosyncratic nature of a medium that consists of sights, sounds, and motion as the fundamental picture elements.

5
▼▼▼▼▼▼▼

The Brain and the Mind

In visual learning the study of the neurophysiology of the brain is a prerequisite because it provides an explanation of the processes of transforming precepts into concepts. Knowing how the brain works, what tasks are assigned to each part of it, and how they are coordinated enables us to infer how the mind performs its many mental functions relative to the recognition and appreciation of moving images. We observe and study closely the neurochemical reactions of the brain's particular perceptual centers but we can only conclude that the resulting mental functions are caused by specific electrochemical reactions of the nerves of the particular areas of the brain. The workings of the brain, as complex and delicate as they may be to observe and study, are nevertheless tangible; it is possible, with today's advanced neuroscience, to observe them in progress. However, the operations of the mind cannot be seen; they are invisible, and for the most part still mysterious and inexplicable. Although certain scientists suggest that broad localization of various cognitive functions of the brain is possible (Posner, Petersen, Fox, & Reichle, 1988), the observation of such operations is impossible because they are not "performed by any single area of the brain" (p. 1627). Consequently our efforts to distinguish and study the workings of the mind, no matter how complicated, should increase and expand to such other academic disciplines and fields of study as communication and visual literacy.

On the basis of the previous information regarding the anatomy of the human brain, this chapter distinguishes the tasks performed by the various centers of the neurobiological brain from the mental activities of the invisible mind. Specifically, this chapter examines the main functions of the information centers of the brain, discusses the specific functions of the left and right hemispheres of the brain, and identifies both the biological and mental processes involved in recognizing the visual and auditory signals of the television picture.

THE BRAIN DIVIDED: MAIN FUNCTIONS
OF THE BRAIN'S INFORMATION CENTERS

At the outset, three important factors regarding the functions of the various parts of the human brain must be brought into focus. The brain, as a central nervous system responsible for the appropriate functions of all other systems of the human body, is an extremely complex organ. To this day neuroscience has not been able to unveil all the complex functions of every part of the brain, although some areas have been identified and parts of the brain have been given specific names stemming from the functions they seemingly perform (Boddy, 1978). Second, an anatomical description of the human brain vis-à-vis the tasks performed by its parts, regardless of how well thought out and detailed, requires advance knowledge of biological, neurological, chemical, psychological, and behavioral studies, to mention only a few. Artists, scientists, neurologists, and communicators, must work on common ground and in full cooperation to unveil the complex and delicate functions of the various parts of the human brain (Frisby, 1980). Finally, the suggested scientific approach for the study of the brain should be multilevel, combining at least the three methods suggested by Bloom et al. (1985): (a) *Inductive reasoning* in which the scientists and/or artists start with an observation, formulate a hypothesis, and experimentally test this hypothesis; (b) *deductive reasoning* in which the scientists and/or artists start with an overall idea of a phenomenon, a global hypothesis, and formulate experiments to test its truth; and (c) *the analogies* that will help scientists and artists in their investigations of the brain to model brain experiments according to some other ground design already recognized in nature.

Regardless of the method or methods we adopt to investigate the complex functions of the brain, let us not forget that the use of technologically more advanced and scientifically more accurate research instruments and measuring devices is required (Metallinos, 1983) and that the use of computers in correlating both the various methodologies and the data stemming from such studies is strongly suggested by contemporary neurological and computational scholars (Frisby, 1980).

This chapter reviews the key functions of the information centers of the brain, mainly vision and hearing, as they relate to the recognition process of television pictures. Specifically, the basic human activities controlled by the brain as they relate to the recognition of television images are underlined, and the functions of the visual and auditory centers in recognizing television pictures are examined.

Activities Controlled by the Brain

The brain controls all human activity. It not only controls sensation, motion, internal regulation, reproduction, and adaptation to the world that surrounds us (Bloom et al., 1985), but also stimulates the specific centers of each of these categories to cooperate and coordinate their efforts in supporting and complementing each other. As pointed out previously, this is an important factor for the study of perception, recognition, and appreciation of television images. Let us consider some examples.

The category of sensation that constitutes the human information center consists of the specific centers for vision, hearing, taste, smell, touch, and gravity (controlled by the vestibular apparatus located inside the ear). When watching television, besides receiving the sights and sounds of visual and auditory elements exposed within the confines of the television screen, we feel as though we taste, smell, or touch all parts of the picture and particularly those that remind us of the real tastes, smells, and feelings of touch or sense of equilibrium. This is particularly evident with such television programs as cooking shows and instructional programs. In picture recognition, all senses are involved subconsciously although we perceive with our eyes and ears. The degree of picture recognition greatly depends on the picture's ability to reflect the sensations of events in the visual world we have experienced, allowing all senses to participate in the decodification and recognition processes.

Motions, whether voluntary or involuntary, are controlled by the brain and extend to all parts of the body influencing picture recognition—particularly motion pictures such as film and television. Motion makes television pictures seem real, more readily identifiable, and an even closer representation of the objects and events of the visual world, the television studio. Some well-known films and television programs owe their fame to the skillful manipulation and handling of the motions of their visual elements, thereby making them exciting, more readily recognizable, and interesting. How, though, does the brain decodify motion? The actual movements of objects and events in the television studio transform into apparent movement on the television screen. In television pictures, therefore, recognition of motion equals the decodification process of apparent movement, also known as the phi phenomena, of all visual elements within the picture field (Murch, 1973). The brain recognizes visuals in conjunction with their real or apparent motion. However, tertiary motion, inherent in television pictures, is not a biochemical (brain) function but a psychological (mental) function and it is discussed further later.

When our stomachs are empty and gurgle, or when we are in pain, our perceptual as well as cognitive processes are, obviously, affected. Most of our internal regulations go unnoticed when we watch television and this does not seem to influence our thinking. However, the human internal regulatory system is always changing. It exerts its influence on many other activities of the body including viewing, comprehending, and enjoying television, a factor seldom considered by television audience viewing measurement devices and television effects studies.

Reproduction is also a function of our regulatory systems controlled by the brain and it significantly affects the cognitive process of picture comprehension. Pictures that contain sexually related episodes and scenes decisively affect television viewers. Sex, like violence, directly affects television viewers, particularly younger ones, a factor known to television advertisers and commercially oriented television program producers who capitalize on it by producing such images. Reproduction and cognition are interrelated when the performed mental function is picture identification.

Adaptation to the constantly changing world around us is also controlled by the brain and influences our recognition of the visual and auditory environment of television pictures. The result of the adaptation process is a change of behavior that can be either a maladjusted or a well-adjusted one, depending on a person's decision. The mental processes we use to adapt to new situations are carried on in our recognition of television pictures. Usually, we are so drawn into situations created by the inclusive happenings in the picture that we live a new experience, the virtual reality of the television picture. We accept, adopt, and transform the visual field of the television picture into an imaginative world of its own. Here again, imagination, which is not a biological but a mental process, surfaces.

Visual and Auditory Brain Functions in Recognizing Television Pictures

How do the visual and auditory information centers of the brain function in recognizing television pictures? We have seen that the organs of visual and auditory perception bring their respective signals to the visual or acoustic centers of the brain.

As far as the center for visual recognition is concerned, the electrical impulses that bring the signals to the optic chiasma are further split in half and processed electromagnetically to the striate cortex. What arrive in the striate cortex are shades of light and brightness of lines, corners, edges, and the like, all parts of the retina image. The mystery of the brain, the transformation of electrochemical processes into mental functions, occurs at this point. The neurons of the brain start to assemble the parts that constitute the picture on the basis of a stored structural description of the picture existing in the nerves of the entire striate cortex. The assembling of the segmented picture and its final recognition occur at the visual association area, where a two-level analysis of the parts of the picture seems to take place: a low-level analysis involving grouping principles, texture, color, movement, and stereopsis and a high-level contextual analysis of the picture structure that, according to Frisby (1980) "[is] probably achieved by finding a match between a structural description of the segmented feature cluster and a stored structural description of the object" (p. 157).

Memory, therefore, is the basic force that assists the brain in completing its visual recognition functions. But how does the brain store memory? What processes are involved? What types of memories are found? Answers to these questions are provided herein.

As far as the center for sound recognition is concerned, we have seen that sound signals that have been changed to electrical impulses and have left the inner ear's cochlea arrive at the auditory nerve. Nerve fibers of the auditory nerve process sound signals to the auditory centers where they synapse with neurons that carry sound messages to the auditory cortex on either the left or the right side of the brain and to six to eight other sites simultaneously. Like visual signals, sounds originating in each ear travel to both sides of the brain to avoid loss of hearing in case of a dysfunction of the auditory pathway (Sedeen, 1986). There, the recognition of sound signals to complete auditory structures and messages follows—two different processes depending on the auditory task. If sound signals are to be translated into words, Wernicke's area of the brain operates, whereas if the words are to be spoken and repeated as sounds, the signals pass through Broca's area for decodification. When this function is complete, the brain follows the previously described process of transforming sound signals into cognitive auditory structures inherent in television pictures. The auditory cortex performs a low-level analysis of sound codes and a high-level analysis resulting in sound recognition. As with visual recognition, in sound recognition memory is the basic ingredient in the structuring of the auditory message. Memory as a function of the mind is discussed in the next section.

In summary, the brain not only controls all human activities but dictates interconnection and interdependence of such activities in the recognition of the visual and auditory information processes. The final step in the translation by the brain of visual and auditory codes into cognitive images and sounds (television pictures) is a low-level analysis of segmented images and sounds followed by a higher level contextual analysis and matching of pre-existing ones.

LEFT AND RIGHT BRAIN SPECIALIZATIONS

A scientific field of study that helps us to distinguish the functions of the brain from those performed by the mind is hemisphere specialization. Launched in the early 1960s at the California Institute of Technology by psychologist Roger Sparry and his associates (Pinchot, 1987), the field has advanced enormously with vigorous neurophysiological and split brain studies that use computer correlated psychophysiological measuring techniques (Behnke, 1970; Metallinos, 1983). Today, all major research works in visual communication media-related topics acknowledge the findings in the field of hemisphere specialization, particularly those related to the recognition and aesthetic effects of moving images (Fletcher, 1978). In visual learning the discussion of left and right brain recognition of moving images is very important because the composition of visual images is directly related to brain specialization. This section discusses the specific functions performed by each hemisphere of the human brain as they relate to images and sounds. Specifically, this section examines and underlines the decodification of visual signals of the left and right hemispheres, the decodification of auditory signals of left and right hemispheres, and the dichotomy of the logical (rational) and the holistic (irrational) brain's hemispheres.

Left and Right Brain Decodification of Visuals

As previously stated, the brain has two hemispheres connected with fibers in the corpus callosum. If the corpus callosum did not exist, or if it was surgically severed, visual and auditory information input from the left eye and ear would reach only the left hemisphere, and vice versa, as the optic and acoustic chiasma that allows the criss-crossing of the information reaching the brain would no longer exist (see Fig. 5.1).

Extensive correlated studies that started with brain surgeries mostly on epileptic patients and the latest neuroanatomical and neurophysiological

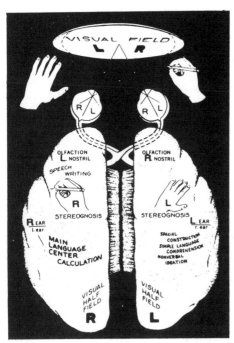

FIG. 5.1. The left and right brains and their specializations. From Eccles, J. C. (1973). *The understanding of the brain* (p. 207). New York: McGraw-Hill. Reproduced with the permission of McGraw-Hill, Inc.

ones that use deoxyglucose to identify which part of the brain is more active (Crick, 1979) have confirmed that recognition of images is a function of the right brain.

Underlining the tasks of the right brain, Ornstein (1972) stated that:

> If the left hemisphere is specialized for analysis, the right hemisphere (again, remember, connected to the left side of the body) seems specialized for holistic mentation. Its language ability is quite limited. This hemisphere is primarily responsible for our orientation in space, artistic endeavor, crafts, body image, recognition of faces. It processes information more diffusely than does the left hemisphere and its responsibilities demand a ready integration of many inputs at once. If the left hemisphere can be termed predominantly analytic and sequential in its operation, then the right hemisphere is more holistic and relational and more simultaneous in its mode of operation. (pp. 52–53)

Image recognition is a function of the right hemisphere of the brain that controls the left side of the body. Pictures are typically images of objects of the real world. Consequently, picture recognition is a function of the right hemisphere of the brain. Recognizing a television picture that combines visuals, sounds, and motion is a holistic process, a task performed by the right brain. Does this imply, therefore, that the success of picture recognition depends on which side of the viewer's body the picture is placed? Is a picture more readily recognizable if its internal structure is such that the visual message is placed on its right or left sides? These are questions that visual communication media researchers have examined over the last few years with considerable success (Avery & Tiemens, 1975; Fletcher, 1978; Metallinos & Tiemens, 1977).

The neurological finding that it is the right hemisphere (which controls the left visual field) that perceives visuals and images more readily was carried a step further. Communication scholars concerned with the comprehension of television images investigated whether left and right brain specialization should be considered in the staging of television programs. The results of these investigations support the theory known among communication scholars as asymmetry of the screen (Zettl, 1990) or asymmetry of the visual field (Metallinos & Tiemens, 1977). It states, in effect, that when viewers watch a television picture they favor one side of it over the other. The sides are not seen evenly; we pay more attention and readily recognize the picture in which the important events occur either on the left or on the right side, asymmetrically dividing the two sides of the visual field. The argument regarding left and right asymmetry of the televised picture grew stronger with publication of empirical research confirming the connection between the neurological findings and the asymmetry of the field theorists. Although communication scholars acknowledge such connections, they are still divided as to which side of the television picture is usually more dominant. For certain communication theorists, it is the right side of the television picture (viewer's left side of the body) that it is visually more predominant (Millerson, 1972; Zettl, 1990), whereas empirical investigations on the asymmetry of the field suggest that it is the left (Metallinos & Tiemens, 1977). The argument continues and more rigorous and scientifically based research is needed instead of speculation and aesthetic intuition. Certainly, studies of the asymmetry of the visual field have concluded that asymmetric placement of visual elements within the concentrated space of the television picture is preferred. Such asymmetry makes the pictures more readily recognizable, dynamic, and artistically pleasing. This important factor should be considered by students of the visual communication media and visual learning.

Left and Right Brain Decodification of Auditory Signals

The auditory cortex of each side of the brain receives information (auditory signals or codes) carried by the fibers that synapse with neurons; it is direct and differs from visual transformation. Auditory signals from the left ear are sent to the brain (half to the right hemisphere and half to the left). In explaining this process Springer and Deutsch (1985) stated, "Unlike the retina which sends projections contralaterally to the brain from one half of its surface, and ipsilaterally from the other half, each ear sends information from all its receptors to both hemispheres. Thus complete information about a stimulus presented to the right ear is presented initially in both hemispheres, and vice versa" (p. 73).

This auditory transformation of information signals might be helpful in preventing hearing loss in case of the dysfunction of an auditory pathway (Sedeen, 1986). It does not, though, indicate hemisphere asymmetry in the decodification of auditory signals because the corpus callosum allows each hemisphere to have equal access to the auditory information input. However, Kimura (1967) and her colleagues at the Montreal Neurological Institute showed that left and right brain specialization and asymmetrical functions in information decodification equally influence the decodification of sounds.

Kimura's (1969) extensive and multilevel studies, which included split-brain tests, sodium amobarbital, and dichotic listening testing in both split-brain and normal subjects have revealed a right ear superiority directly related to left brain function in language-related tests. Neurophysiological and behavioral studies conducted by Kimura (1969) and by several other scholars (Curry, 1967; Dirks, 1964; Rosenzwig, 1951) on the left and right brain decodification process of auditory information confirm that both visual and auditory signal recognition is a function of the right brain. In distinguishing the verbal and nonverbal differences between the left and right hemispheres relating to the studies on left and right brain decodification of auditory information, Springer and Deutsch (1985) suggested that "all language related stimuli are dealt with primarily in the left hemisphere and the right hemisphere is specialized for handling certain types of nonverbal stimuli" (p. 78). However, these authors warn us that although all data gathered so far indicate that decodification of visual and auditory information is mainly a function of the right brain, there are certain inherent drawbacks in interpreting the results of these studies conducted with dichotic (for ear specialization) and tachistoscopic (for eye specialization) measuring devices (Springer & Deutsch, 1985). It is beyond the scope of this discussion to examine these drawbacks, but it is suggested that those interested in visual learning should be familiar with the works of Springer and Deutsch (1985) on this subject.

The right brain superiority in recognizing nonverbal auditory information and vice versa is an important finding directly related to recognizing television pictures. It implies that auditory messages generated in the viewer's left visual field are recognized more readily than if they were to arrive from the right side. This is an important consideration for those who construct television images as well as for those who study them. If the left/right brain recognition of auditory messages of the visual world was carried a step further and applied to the visual field of television pictures, the basis on which the rules for structuring moving images and visual learning could be built.

The Rational Left and the Holistic Right Hemispheres of the Human Brain

The number of scientific studies on the left and right brain specialization is immense, and the range of the fields of study of brain specialization-related investigation is large. An impressive list of such findings illustrating the two modes of operation of the brain was provided by Nevitt (1980–1981). A brief discussion of the application of these findings to the recognition process of television images follows (see Fig. 5.2).

The left brain is occidental, whereas the right brain is oriental. The logical brain recognizes objects and events sequentially and logically. Watching the news delivered by a newscaster without distracting visuals in the background is an occidental function of the left brain that controls the right visual field. However, watching a scene described by a newscaster off camera is an oriental activity of the right brain that controls the left visual field.

The left brain specializes in visual speech and recognizes all activities involving language, logic, and words, whereas the right hemisphere is predominantly musical and acoustic and recognizes more readily melodies and musical tunes (Kimura, 1964). Because of this dichotomy of the brain's functions, speeches on television tend to be monotonous and boring, whereas musical concerts, even when filmed by one camera on a long shot, are interesting to listen to and easier to watch.

Charts, maps, numerical figures, tables, statistics, lists of names, numbered items, and mathematical computations are more readily recognized by the

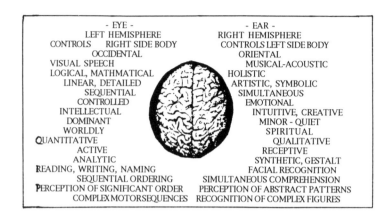

FIG. 5.2. Left and right functions of the human brain. An inclusive list of the specific functions of the two hemispheres of the human brain.

left hemisphere of the brain, found to be specialized in logical, mathematical, intellectual, sequential, and analytic functions.

Complex visual elements and multilevel action scenes placed on the viewer's left side of the screen are recognized by the holistic, simultaneous, intuitive or creative, and synthetic right hemisphere of the brain.

Constructors of television programs that consist primarily of scenes requiring a linear and detailed controlled approach such as instructional or educational programs, cooking shows, and language instruction, should consider placement of such activities on the right side of the screen. However, those producing television programs consisting for the most part of scenes with artistic, symbolic, simultaneous, emotional, and intuitive content (such as experimental television programs, music videos, art shows, and religious programs) should consider placement of the main activities on the left side of the screen for better recognition by the right hemispheres of viewers' brains.

All quantitative activities encompassing the action of a television program such as the recognition of complex motor sequences and significant order, reading, writing, numbering, and analyzing should be placed on the right side of the screen to be more readily recognized by viewers' left hemispheres.

On the other hand, all qualitative activities that characterize the action in a television program such as recognition of complex figures, abstract patterns, or scenes requiring simultaneous comprehension, synthesis, and configurations, have a better chance of being recognized if placed on the viewers' left side of the screen.

In visual learning, knowledge of the special functions of the brain relating to moving images is important because application of these principles in commercial television programming is seldom experienced. It might be true that the left and right specialized functions of the rational and holistic hemispheres of the human brain do not apply when we watch television because, unlike cinema, common television screens are too small to allow such dichotomies in picture recognition (Zettl, 1990). However, acknowledging that scientists in neurophysiology have found and applied such findings to visual communication media-related topics is fundamental for the establishment of the basic rules of composition of visual images. Today commercial television sets are small and the asymmetry of the screen does not have to coincide with the neurological findings regarding right and left functions of the human brain. The arrival of high-definition television and home entertainment center improvements will, however, require a bigger television screen (Metallinos, 1990).

In conclusion, scientific evidence indicating the asymmetries of the human brain and the right brain's dominance in recognizing visuals and sounds should be enhanced with multilevel behavioral studies that use normal subjects and extend their investigation to visual communication media-related issues more widely conducted by communication scholars.

BRAIN AND MIND FUNCTIONS IN TELEVISION PICTURE RECOGNITION

Image recognition involves both the biological brain that contains special regions performing specific tasks, and the invisible mind that controls special mental faculties for specific cognitive processes (Kosslyn, 1988). In this chapter, those special regions of the human brain that receive, reorganize, and decodify the visual and auditory signals, the perceived stimuli, of moving images with sounds such as television pictures have been identified and discussed.

The brain's left or right hemispheres, depending on the nature of the input, receive the codes, organize them, and transform them into precepts. From there on, the mind takes over and turns them into concepts, or cognitive structures. This mental activity depends on a series of other mental activities such as memory, attention, organization, thinking, and imagining, all of which exist in various parts of the brain, yet most, neuroscientists hypothesized, can be localized. According to Posner et al. (1988):

> The hypothesis is that elementary operations forming the basis of cognitive analyses of human tasks are strictly localized. Many such local operations are involved in any cognitive task. A set of distributed brain areas must be orchestrated in the performance of even simple cognitive tasks. The task itself is not performed by any single area of the brain, but the opportunity that underline the performance are strictly localized. (pp. 1627–1631)

To explain how television pictures are perceived and recognized and how biological tasks merge with mental functions in picture recognition, the following topics are discussed: the information storage and retrieval activities, the role of memory in the recognition of moving images, and the contribution of other mental activities such as attention, organization, and thinking, to the final transformation of the biological precepts to the mental concepts in television pictures.

Information Storage and Retrieval

In our discussion of the perceptual process it was stated that when distal effective stimuli are registered by the organs of perception and become proximal stimuli, some are permanently stored in the memory region of the brain (long-term memory) and others are stored for a shorter period (short-term memory). Both categories, however, form the perceived stimulus stage of the perceptual process. Whereas the information storage in both cases seems to be a biological function of the brain, the actual retrieval of the information is definitely a mental function. Memory, or recall of information, is a basic contributor and a fundamental ingredient to picture recognition and must be examined closely.

Neuroscientists have identified and studied two major categories of memories depending on their duration and function. Based on the length of time that memories are stored they are either short term, lasting only a few seconds and vanishing without a trace of their existence, or long term, stored for hours or for a lifetime depending on the needs of the individual. On the basis of the functions that memories perform they seem to be either procedural or declarative. As Pines (1986) explained:

> Scientists believe that humans have at least two memory systems which may reside in different parts of the brain. Procedural memory, a memory for skills, probably developed earlier in life than declarative memory, the ability to recall facts. Fact memory appears to center in the hippocampus, amygdala, and part of the thalamus. Procedural memory, believed more widely dispersed, is therefore less subject to impairment by illness or injury. (p. 359)

These two memory systems, the procedural and the factual, were the basis for the development of the two schools of learning within the field of psychology. The behavioral, which advocates people memorize and learn skills and habits by reinforcement and conditioning, and the cognitive school of thought, advocating that people memorize and acquire information and knowledge intentionally by their own free will without expecting to be rewarded. This type of memory and learning is a function of the higher brain and the conscious mind (Pines, 1986).

Both the procedural and the declarative memories are in operation when one watches a television picture and obtains the ingredient for matching the images by both categories of memory.

The length of the information storage and the behavioral or cognitive manner by which we decide to maintain our memories are connected to numerous other brain and mind operations, the subtotal of which constitutes what is known as the *idiosyncrasy* of an individual. Consequently, recognition and reading of a message in a television picture greatly depend on the nature of the person's stored memory which is strictly idiosyncratic and should not be easily generalized. As Pines (1986) pointed out, "What we choose to store in our long-term memory is closely tied to our emotions" (p. 369). Therefore, an individual's stored experiences are subjective.

The Role of Memory in the Recognition of Television Images

The skillful constructor of images and sounds should meet the consumer or viewer on common ground or recognizable points of reference for the synthesis to be readily and accurately recognized. The conscientious producer or director of television images must understand how information is stored as memory, the duration of its storage, how memory is generated and how it functions, what elements are at work during its successful retrieval. Answers to these questions will provide a basic understanding of the role of memory in the process of recognition of television images. As pointed out previously, the brain controls, coordinates, and interconnects all biological functions of the body. Likewise, the mind interconnects all its operations with mental activities such as the recognition of an image or sound, the result of the cooperation of the organization of thinking, of the emotional state of the individual, and a host of other activities. It is, therefore, difficult to isolate one mental activity without at least acknowledging its interconnection with the others. Let us examine how memory helps in the recognition of television pictures.

As previously stated, we store information in two ways, either procedurally, through repetition and conditioning, or declaratively, through intentionally discovered facts. Television's cultural and social effects studies of the last 60 years suggest that high television viewers are submerged, reinforced, conditioned, and influenced in their judgments and their opinions (Gerbner & Gross, 1979; Gitlin, 1982). Such viewers have chosen to store information procedurally on the basis of images they have persistently been exposed to. It is, therefore, inevitable that the memories they have stored and the experiences they have acquired are totally dominated by images, shapes, sounds, values, habits, and thoughts of television programs they have repeatedly watched. Their understanding and appreciation of television's images and sounds are prejudiced by previously stored information. Such memories are activities of the lower brain region that neuroscientists such as Pines (1986) believe "do not communicate with the conscious mind" (p. 362). Does this mean that the memory of heavy television viewers is of a lower level, therefore their television picture recognition is analogous to the level of the picture's contextual structure? This is an interesting question and an observation that warrants empirical investigation and further verification.

Factual or declarative long-term memory that plays an equally important role in the recognition process of television images is found at the opposite end of the spectrum. Viewers who watch television selectively and sporadically, choosing programs that demand a high level of concentration, constitute the lighter television watching category and are the minority among commercial television audiences. Their selective memory is stored in the cerebral cortex, considered to be the most sophisticated region of the brain, connecting the declarative memory system to the brain's intellectual achievement centers (Pines, 1986). It is common knowledge that television programs that examine important scientific discoveries or those that deal with educational issues are watched by selective (lighter) television viewers. Does this imply that declarative memory systems aid the individual's recognition and appreciation of highly specialized and artistically demanding television pictures? If we choose to memorize and retain objects, events, and situations factually and intentionally, does this mean that we choose to watch those particular television programs that are analogous to the memory system we employ in their final recognition and appreciation? This, also, is an interesting question that requires further investigation and scientific inquiry.

Because we employ both the procedural and declarative memory systems, recognition of television images depends on these two categories of memories. The extent, however, to which television viewers use one more than the other could be determined by both the amount of time spent watching television and the types of television programs they choose to watch (Gerbner, Gross, & Melody, 1973; Hall, 1977).

The Contribution of Selected Mental Activities
Toward the Recognition of Television Images

Memory alone, no matter what the duration of its storage and by which system it is stored in the brain, is not capable of assuming the responsibility of the entire process of television image recognition. Instead, it is aided by a host of other mental activities, all of which are interconnected with memory and with each other. The most critical of these activities such as grouping or psychological closure; texture or contrast and figure–ground distinctions; timing or duration (physical vs. psychological time); and timing, motion or directional vectors; depth or three-dimensionality; and imagination or enlargement of memorable experience are examined briefly and exemplified in the following.

When we look at a picture or hear music, our brain centers of vision or hearing are highly activated to transform the segments or precepts into recognizable pieces of a greater whole. The brain also triggers the memory centers to assist in matching the new pieces to those stored from experience. The mental process involved in grouping the pieces to make completed wholes is called *psychological closure*. The effective recognition of television images is based on the individual viewer's ability to group the segmented process to make completed images, visuals, or sounds. When watching a television program in which visual elements are in constant change and succeed each other, we mentally organize both the images and sounds into *gestalts* or larger configurations stemming from this grouping. We perform a series of mental activities well described by perceptual psychologists as similarity, proximity, common fate, objective set, inclusiveness, good continuation, and closure, all of which relate to grouping elements together to form the real image, the recognized sound (Murch, 1973).

During the process of recognition, while viewing television, we engage in another mental process called *texture recognition*, also known as contrast or figure–ground distinction of the elements exposed to the visual field of the television screen. Pictures and sounds are recognized by identifying their sharply contrasting brightness or darkness, by isolating the figures from their backgrounds, by clearly defining the figures standing in front from those occupying the midground, and finally by the visual and auditory elements that constitute the background of the picture. Assisted by memory, the mind dictates the mental process of texture to aid the cognitive process of television picture recognition and comprehension. We have learned and stored in our memories that all objects have their own specific texture and thus we seek the one that identifies the particular picture image.

Aided by memory or experience, when we watch television we also engage in another mental process known as *timing*. There are three different times: *objective time* measured by the clock; *subjective time*, the duration of the happenings we experience psychologically; and *biological time*, the time kept by our body's regulatory system (Zettl, 1990). Virtually all of these types of time assume a secondary role when we watch a television program because mentally we engage in a totally different type of time and timing; we are subjected to a new environment in which the past, present, and future events are virtually real. They are fictional; they occur on television. The manipulation of television time and timing as structured within the episodes is one of the main tasks of the constructors of television images and one that distinguishes skillful television producers and directors. The mind readily accepts screen time and recognizes the difference between accelerated or slow time and real-life events. However, the representation of life on the television screen relates closely to the way television (or screen time) and timing is manipulated. Generally speaking, the successful recognition and aesthetic appreciation of television images require an evolution of events somewhat faster than real life.

Motion is also a critical mental activity greatly contributing to the recognition process of television images. It, too, is closely related to memory and experience; however, when we watch television, objects and events within the confined space of the screen assume their own types of motion similar to those existing in the real world (real, apparent, and implied), but in the new environment and in the medium's own language. There are three motions. The first is the so-called event motion created by the motion of objects or events in front of the camera. The second is camera motion such as zooms, dollys, pans, tilts, truckings or arcs, pedestals, or booms. The third, called sequence motion, is created by the juxtaposition of the camera shots and the television switcher arranging the sequence of the visual display. This last one is known as editing (Zettl, 1990). The technology of television has enriched the medium with additional motions such as slow or fast-forward motion, simultaneous motion of objects and events, camera movements, and fancy transitions achieved by the television switcher. The mind, assisted by memory and other such mental operations, is capable of recognizing such television images as long as they are kept within the parametric limits of the perceptual organs—mainly the eyes, ears, and brain.

The recognition of *depth* or three-dimensionality of television pictures is a mental activity. The brain receives only relative clues of the images and sounds of the real world and the television screen is a flat two-dimensional surface. It is the mind that suggests and creates the impression that the photographs produced are three-dimensional. The mind sees depth; it places the events of the television picture in accordance to their corresponding places in the environment, their distances, and their sizes. The brain's perceptual processes of segmentation and stereopsis become the mind's high-level contextual activity, transforming the events into cognitive, three-dimensional structures photographically similar to those exposed on the visual field. The contribution of this mental property to television picture recognition is paramount.

The creation of a television program requires extensive *imagination* of the entire television production team. They take aspects of life, certain issues or events that could or could not have occurred in the visual world; manipulate them with the use of the instruments, materials, and techniques of the medium; and present them as episodes and events on television (Metallinos, 1985). Television viewers watching these creations must also use their imagination to recognize and appreciate them. Purely a mental activity, imagination is a fundamental operation for all activities of a person. Imagination is more demanding, however, when we watch television, which is a complicated medium. In television, visuals, sounds, and motions compose a unique mosaic, a metamorphic synthesis, of virtual reality worlds.

In summary, all mental activities mentioned here, which relate to the most fundamental of them all, the memory, are contributory factors for the successful recognition and aesthetic appreciation of television pictures. Those of us concerned with the study of visual composition cannot afford to ignore or underestimate these important mental functions.

6

▼▼▼▼▼▼▼

Recognition Standards of Visual Images

Knowledge of both the neurophysiology of the brain, that underlines the functions of its information centers, and the psychology of the mind, that indicates its mental operations, are important foundations for the study of visual learning. However, they are not enough. To complete the study pertaining to the factors involved in the recognition and appreciation of television images, cultural factors relating to the individual viewer, to society, and the media institutions to which an individual is exposed, and to the idiosyncratic nature of the television medium must also be added and examined. After all, individual viewers control both their biological and psychological activities and make the final cognitive decision as to the meanings they wish to assign to the pictures they watch. However, viewers of the visual communication medium of television do not exist in a vacuum. They belong to a cultural environment that provides them with skills, habits, norms, and learning, all of which shape their behavioral attitudes and form their experiences and memory systems. Standards for the recognition and final appraisal of television images can only be drawn accurately if the cultural factors that relate to individual viewers within society and the media are properly examined. This is precisely the purpose of this chapter.

Specifically, this chapter discusses the following topics: the individual television viewer's general awareness, knowledge, expertise, values, beliefs, and motivations; the individual's understanding of society, institutions, and media; and the individual's knowledge and degree of comprehension of the process, the effects, and the idiosyncratic nature of the visual communication media in general, and television in particular.

SELF-AWARENESS, KNOWLEDGE, AND EXPERTISE

Although all cognitive operations of the human mind including thinking, understanding, interpreting, and recognizing, are, of course, subjective and idiosyncratic to the individual, how the individual will perform such mental operations when given a general task (such as interpreting the message of a common television program) can be predicted. We assume that individual viewers have the necessary knowledge, expertise, skills, and literacy to recognize, interpret, and appreciate the visual images to which they are exposed. From the day we are born to the day we die, our parents, teachers, friends, institutions, and the society we live in all help to provide the guidelines that will help us survive, communicate with each other, and progress. The language, symbols, signs, and arts we learn and to which we are exposed are the common carriers for communication among us. They are the links that tie us together and makes us members of the homogeneous society.

Today's media technologies, predominantly computerized visual communication media, have reached worldwide dimensions and have transformed the citizens of the world into peasants of the global village (McLuhan & Powers, 1989). Inhabitants of the global village are influenced culturally, politically, and socially by media, particularly television—the hegemonies of the global village. Pioneering studies on the process and the effects of mass communication (Jacobs, 1961; McQuail, 1969; Schramm & Roberts, 1971), cultural studies on the influence of the media on the people in mass society (Rissoner & Birch, 1977; Rosenberg & White, 1957), social studies of the influence of the media on the individual's way of living and behaving in the society (Agee, Ault, & Emery, 1988), and critical studies on the artistic merits of programs produced by the media (Burns & Thompson, 1989; Newcomb, 1982) indicate that the visual communication media, particularly television, decisively influence the individual viewer.

Under those circumstances, how then does one obtain the necessary knowledge and experience to recognize accurately, understand clearly, and interpret properly the moving images of the television program one is watching? What should the viewer's standards be for the accurate execution of these cognitive processes? I suggest that self-awareness and knowledge, expertise and confidence, values, beliefs, and motivation are among the most significant standards.

Viewers' Self-Awareness and Knowledge

Although it is increasingly more difficult for the average person to escape the influence of the homogeneous mass society ruled hegemonically by the visual communication media, it is important that parents, family, and peers in the early stages of development, and, at a later stage teachers and learning institutions, assist the individual to develop curiosity, alertness, awareness, and interest in different issues, topics, phenomena, and circumstances. It is important, for example, for parents and teachers to challenge young minds and draw their attention away from the common and the mundane to the diversified, the unusual, and the dynamic.

An individual's escape from the usual will enable him or her to see and to experience different points of view. It will make the individual aware of the different sides of the phenomena and the issues. Exposure to as many points of view as possible is the road that leads to new discoveries and awareness. When challenged and given the chance to experience diversified points of view, individuals form opinions of their own and understand the role they play in the society in which they live. To judge accurately and objectively and to interpret, one must be cognizant of all factors involving the object or event to be evaluated.

Recognition and appreciation of television images require the viewer's general knowledge of academic, social, economic, political, cultural, and media issues. Obviously, to discuss seriously or to communicate responsibly on an issue, one must be aware of it and be knowledgeable about the factors related to it. This is seldom the case in such complex circumstances as viewing a television program. Ignorance in such areas as (a) the message or content of the program; (b) the medium itself, in terms of the visual and auditory choices made by the director to show and tell the story; and (c) the particular types of viewers the program addresses (including their social status and level of intelligence) will result in misinterpretation of the television images. Do all viewers have such knowledge?

The general knowledge required for the proper interpretation of television messages is provided by studies in many different disciplines. However, the specific knowledge one can obtain today to enhance the recognition and appreciation standards of television images can be found in such fields of study as art (art history and appreciation), criticism (particularly mass media criticism), communication (particularly visual communication), semiotics, and media studies (particularly television and films), to mention only a few. Students of visual learning must be aware and fully knowledgeable of these fields. The standards for recognizing and properly interpreting television images are drawn from the findings of all these studies. Television viewers who do not acquire such knowledge do not have solid standards for interpreting televised images. The global village society does not encourage its citizens to acquire both the general and the specific knowledge required to obtain the standards for the recognition and the appreciation of television images. Visual learning that provides such knowledge, it is hoped, will fill this vacuum.

Viewers' Expertise and Confidence

Television viewers' standards for recognition and interpretation of visual and auditory elements that compose the pictures are also based on viewers' expertise in the construction of visual images and their confidence of themselves as individuals. These two factors are combined because a basic and crucial contributor to one's confidence is the acquisition of expertise.

The average television viewer, of course, does not possess expertise in television production techniques. Does high-level exposure to television enhance viewers' understanding of how television works in producing moving images with sounds? It is possible that low-level viewers who watch television sporadically can claim less understanding and knowledge of how the medium works. Viewers who have learned how to think visually, by learning how to draw pictures or by formally studying the media, are considered to be more skillful, experienced, and confident in their cognitive task of recognizing more readily and commenting more intelligently on television images. Today's mass availability of home video cameras has turned the majority of people in technologically developed countries into moving image makers and experts in interpreting visual and auditory messages. Such video camera availability in the homes of a wide variety of individuals has strengthened their confidence not only in handling the image-making tools properly but also in judging how the image maker manipulates the shots to arrive at the intended visual message.

Visual literacy should be a major part of the curriculum at primary and secondary education levels. We must provide students with the experience and confidence needed as viewers of televised messages and with the appropriate standards for such cognitive activity at an early stage.

Viewers' Values, Beliefs, and Motivations

The appropriate recognition of moving images and the final meaning we assign to them are highly influenced by our own values, beliefs, and expectations, which are cognitive operations stemming from our exposure to the values of the society we live in. We form our opinions of how much it is worth our effort to engage in an activity or how important one program is to watch over another. On the basis of these values we judge, comment on, or even act on issues throughout our lives. When such values are wrongly formed due to environmental, cultural, religious, political, and pedagogical reasons, our standards for judging are shattered and misinformed. Forming the appropriate values is not an easy task and we spend our entire lives working toward that goal.

Alongside the values are the beliefs we form on issues and phenomena we assume to be real and truthful. Beliefs seem to be of greater value and individuals seek those figures (political, religious, academic), institutions, or movements that help them form certain beliefs. Human activities are guided by beliefs that consciously or unconsciously constitute the bases that form the standards for our decisions and our cognitive processes. Recognition and appreciation of televised images are based on the beliefs formed by the visual images—the television picture—we watch.

As experience and skills help to build our confidence, so does motivation. It increases our ability to engage in the process of critical viewing, comprehending, and interpreting television images. The accurate recognition and proper interpretation of television pictures are not passive activities as they were once thought to be. Viewers who watch a dramatic program, an interesting information program, or a program of a catastrophic event are totally motivated. For one reason or another, they are totally drawn into the program. The emotional state or mood of viewers determines the degree of their motivation to watch and to appreciate a television program. Consequently, a basic factor (a standard for the accurate recognition and proper appreciation of television images) is motivation or the willingness to engage in such cognitive activities. A television show with a significant subject, an artistically staged play (according to the rules of television image composition), and a clearly defined audience (to which the show addresses itself) will be successful and will most likely motivate viewers to watch it (Metallinos, 1973).

UNDERSTANDING SOCIETY AND INSTITUTIONS

Another prerequisite or standard for the accurate recognition of the message in a given television program is the viewer's knowledge and understanding of how society and institutions are formed, how they function, and how individuals relate to them.

Visual communication media such as film and television are institutions created by people who work under the rules, guidelines, and regulations provided by the society of a particular country. As a creation of a society, media strictly reflect the values and beliefs (political, cultural, economic, religious, etc.) of the people of that society. The institutions and media arts created by a society unavoidably reflect the value system, the philosophies, and the ideologies of the people of the society. They are the modifiers and reflectors of that society (Read, 1970).

As such, media arts of a particular society are created to serve three major purposes: (a) to illustrate the basic values and beliefs of the society, (b) to promote the society's basic philosophies, and (c) to fulfill the needs, aspirations, and desires of the people of the society, which can be multilevel, emotional, psychological, spiritual, ideological, educational, entertaining, and informational. Whereas conventional sociologists theorize that the arts produced by the media of a society are simply institutions like the schools, courts, churches, and so on, contemporary media scholars and sociologists of mass culture suggest that such is the hegemonic power of the mass media in certain contemporary societies (e.g., North America) that they shape the society rather than being a part of it. The powers of the media as conglomerate institutions are such that they dominate, often dictate, impose, and even set the agenda that society is forced to adopt and to follow. It is, therefore, obvious that the understanding of how society and institutions work is a prerequisite for the cognitive process of assigning appropriate meaning and, therefore, of being able to accurately translate televised messages.

This section briefly examines how the mass media, particularly network television, reflect the values and beliefs of American and Canadian societies; how they propagate these beliefs, myths, and philosophies; and how they manage to fulfill the needs, dreams, and expectations of North Americans.

Media and Society in North America

Due to the predominant role of the media, mostly print and electronic media, in the United States and Canada, these countries have been characterized as media, information, and mass societies of the electronic age. They are the perfect paradigm of McLuhan's prophecy of the global village (McLuhan & Powers, 1989). It is imperative that the citizens of these countries realize that the more they depend on the mass media, particularly television, for information, education, and entertainment, the more they become victims of the monopolistic ideology of the producers of these media. Availability of information offered by easily accessible media technology tends to turn individuals into homogeneous, one-track minded, brainwashed, so-called couch potatoes if they are not selective. We must be aware of this danger, and we must realize how some powerful institutions can supersede and surpass the democratic systems governing the people of our societies.

Mass media in North America might work under a democratically free system, but they have the tendency, like totalitarian systems, to impose on their viewers symbols, codes, ideas, messages, signifiers, and ideologies that do not necessarily reflect the society's real concerns and do not have its consensus. Instead, they impose the media institution's own points of view. This has been a serious problem in North America, particularly during the last 50 years since the arrival of network television, and the information explosion with the arrival and the widely explosive application of computers in visual communication media technologies.

The most advanced countries of the world with the most informed people in their societies, the United States and Canada, also have masses of people who are defenseless against the powerful influence and commercially oriented propaganda of mass media. Low-income, ethnic minorities, and even mainstream middle-class heavy television viewers constitute the majority of the viewers in these societies. Decisively influenced by what they watch on and learn from television, they often make such important decisions as voting for government leaders based on media-generated information and propaganda.

In short, the danger in North America is that the monopolistic and manipulative power exerted by the mass media will surpass the governing role of the society. Rather than the media, particularly television, reflecting society and communicating institutional values and beliefs of the society, the media set the agenda and shape the rest of the institutions to such an extent that they become hegemones (leaders) of the society. Students of visual learning must not overlook this factor in the cognitive process of televised picture communication.

Media Myths and Beliefs in North America

As suggested, mass media in North America, and particularly network television, do not simply mirror the culture, political system, values, and beliefs of the society that has created them but rather often suggest and even dictate what these values and beliefs should be. This point must be brought into focus because our cognitive decisions on issues regarding the efforts of the visual communication media are greatly influenced by the media. How this happens and what specific tactics the mass media employ to achieve their influence and control are examined.

The common tactics of persuasion and propaganda are repetition, rhetoric, suggestibility, symbols, and subliminal messages. Some of these tactics used by commercial television in North America, mostly commercials and cultural myths, are briefly examined. The subjects of persuasion, attitude change, and political propaganda are not discussed here. They have been studied in various other fields such as psychology and political science that have shown how successfully the mass media have used them through the centuries (Brown, 1963; O'Keefe, 1990).

Advertising dominates all commercial and business propaganda in North America with persuasion tactics used by the media and employed by businesses. The powerful economies developed in North American societies owe their success to the free market system that encourages competition and is stimulated by sophisticated, aggressive, and vigorous mass media advertising. Television itself, as an institution and a medium of communication in North America, was developed as an advertising medium and this is a fact that should always be remembered. The three most significant factors regarding the persuasive power and decisive influence of network television advertising in North America are as follows: First, commercial advertising in network television is generally slick, better looking, and more interesting than surrounding television programs. Advertising agencies and producers of television advertising realize the importance of persuasion. Having experienced the successful results of commercial network television advertising, agencies spend more money; hire highly competent and knowledgeable writers, producers, directors; and generally apply all the appropriate rules of visual communication media production. Second, commercial advertising in network television in North America is concise, compact, and confined only to the precise persuasive goals set forth by the particular ad. A commercial network television ad of a significant advertising agency often reaches its targeted audience or extends its persuasive visuals and sounds beyond the absolutely necessary. In 10, 20, 30, or 60 seconds (depending on the designated length), the message is clear, the visuals are impressive, and the sounds are selected to match the visual composition, the framing, editing, set, and so on. These elements are all carefully applied and concisely interwoven. Third, television commercials reach a great range of audiences and successfully fulfill their desires, dreams, aspirations, needs, and expectations. Unlike regular television programs, which by necessity appeal only to a certain category of viewers, the average North American network television viewer is exposed to a large number of television ads reaching a vast range of viewers and fulfilling a great variety of the viewers' psychological expectations. Advertising decisively influences viewers' attitudes and cognitive process.

The creation of myths, defined as "a fable or legend of natural upgrowth, embodying the convictions of a people as to their goals or other divine personages, their own origin and early history and the heroes connected with it" (The New Webster's Dictionary, 1965, p. 556), is yet another cultural indicator deeply rooted in the subconscious of regular commercial network television viewers in North American society. Created by either regular, dramatic, or popular television programs, and information-related television shows such as newscasts, magazine programs, talk shows, or television commercials, myths are effective persuasive factors deeply influencing the cognitive process of television viewers. Examples from existing literature on dramatic television series and newscasts confirm the decisive role media myths play in determining the standards for recognizing and assigning meaning to televised images. In his analysis of the former popular dramatic prime time television series *The Waltons*, Roiphe (1979) suggested that by watching the show, the American people created the myth that all was well in American society, just as all was well with the members of the Walton family. Therefore, the mythical world of *The Waltons* offered an escape from the real cultural, political, economic, and other issues of American society's real life. Roiphe (1979) admitted that the creation of myths by television popular programs has some positive aspects to it, particularly in providing a break from the realities of life. However, he warned that, "It could be said that these myths torment us, describing role fulfillments that aren't there, promising marital peace that never arrives and forcing us to stare at the pitiful discrepancy between what is and what we would want" (p. 14).

In his article "Kaptain Kronkite: The Myth of the Eternal Frame," McCray (1979) explained how North American network television viewers who watch various popular television programs for a considerable number of years create mythical heroes of the major characters of these programs who provide entertainment, information, solutions to serious problems, reassurance, and confidence through the television frame. The heroes of the two popular programs *Captain Kangaroo* and *The CBS Evening News with Walter Cronkite* gained mythical proportions from their appearances on the frame. Their behavior and the program's format deeply influenced the cognitive process of viewers. Commenting on this issue, McCray (1979) stated that:

> While I would make no claims for the ultimate artistic greatness of CK or WC, I would argue that formally the shows do tap us somewhere deeply in the recesses of our cultural consciousness. Or, to return to the original question of this essay, I do believe commercial television is engaging man in the growth of his own self-perception—the epic has always done that. (pp. 332–333)

The myths and heroes created by various television programs help North American commercial television viewers to create their values and form their beliefs according to the patterns and examples given by television characters. Our cognitive decisions on matters related to television pictures are highly influenced by such media myths and beliefs.

Media Fulfillments of Viewers' Needs, Dreams, and Desires

Other factors contributing to the establishment of the recognition standards of television images are viewers' needs, dreams, and desires, which various television programs fulfill on different levels. This important factor has a long history and is deeply rooted in the subconscious of people of all cultures. People of a society and a specific culture create their art forms such as music, dance, poetry, and theater to express themselves as artists, reflect their society's values, and fulfill various psychological needs and desires. The psychological functions of the arts in providing the means by which people can rid themselves of inner fears, guilt, sorrow, and so on, and can be inspired, motivated, and fulfilled as well as informed and educated, was first pointed out by the ancient Greeks. Modern psychologists such as Aronoff (1967), Freud (1959, 1960), and Maslow (1954) have given us scientific proof of what was known to Plato and Aristotle some 2,500 years ago. Contemporary media scholars, particularly television program analysts (Adler & Cater, 1975; Novak, 1979; Wood, 1979), have suggested quite accurately the role that various television programs in North American network television play in fulfilling the needs, desires, aspirations, and dreams of a great number of people. Certain examples of these works are provided herein (Hyde, 1970).

Plato and Aristotle were the first to point out the emotional and/or psychological effects of the arts, particularly ancient Greek drama, on spectators. In his dialogues titled *The Laws* and *Ion*, Plato stated that spectators listening to music or watching a drama are often so deeply involved that it can be harmful (Dickie, 1971). Aristotle, a student of Plato, in his work the *Poetics*, not only acknowledged the emotional or psychological effects that drama (in all its forms—tragedy, comedy, and satire) has on spectators, but suggested that the function of a good drama is to stimulate the spectator so deeply that the action on stage will provide emotional catharsis through crying or laughing (Dickie, 1971).

Freud picked up from the works of Plato and Aristotle and used them as the basis for his psychoanalysis, recognizing the emotional impact drama has on spectators.

On the basis of Maslow's (1954) theory of personality, his student Aronoff (1967) developed the theory of psychological needs fulfilled by the cultural activity of a society of which media arts is a part. Maslow's (1954) hierarchy of needs, thoroughly developed in his book *Motivation and Personality*, reached five levels: (a) the *physiological* (air, water, food, shelter, sleep, sex), (b) *safety and security* (fear of death within the family, fear of physical assault), (c) *love and belongingness* (the need to love and to be loved, the need to feel that one belongs to a family), (d) *self-esteem, esteem by others* (the need to acquire strength, dominance, and recognition in a society, thus gaining prestige and self-esteem), and (e) *self-actualization* (the need to explore one's talent, capacity, potential, and skills). To the various levels of the needs expressed by Maslow, Aronoff (1967) added many others stemming from psychology and sociology related to the arts and culture of the people of a society. In short, Aronoff (1967) suggested that all cultural systems and human institutions provide the basis on which the psychological and social issues are explored and therefore concluded that the media arts of the society are created to meet these needs.

Finally, contemporary media analysts such as Novak (1979) and Wood (1979) suggest, quite convincingly, that North American network television programming acts either as a dream for the spectators or fulfills the dreams spectators might have for a better life, luxury homes and cars, prestigious jobs, and so on. Today's great variety of television programs offers notions of living in a dream world while the viewer watches exotic places or people and dreams that take one away from reality for as long as one is engaged in watching television. In either case, television programs fulfill this basic psychological human need, as they do with the entire spectrum of such needs as seeing authority figures either exalted or dishonored, and seeing evil punished and virtue rewarded. The list is as endless and as vast as are the human emotions, psychological desires, and aspirations of every spectator of television programs. Therefore, television programs reach the individual with the dispositions of fulfilling their dreams and satisfying their needs and desires.

STUDY OF THE PROCESS AND THE EFFECTS
OF VISUAL COMMUNICATION MEDIA

In addition to personal awareness, knowledge, and experience, and an individual's knowledge of how society, institutions, and media work, the development of the standards for the recognition and appreciation of television also requires an understanding of the technical aspects of the medium (its hardware) as well as the artistic aspects of the medium (its software). The fulfillment of this prerequisite is extremely crucial because it focuses directly on the medium's two most important areas of study—its processes and its effects—and helps one acquire the value judgments most appropriate for the technical, critical, and aesthetic evaluations of televised images.

This section examines briefly the technical aspects known also as the process of the television medium and the artistic or compositional aspects of the medium, and then provides an inclusive list of criteria for the evaluation of an educational television program.

Technical Aspects of Television Images

In the previous discussion of the similarities and differences between the television camera and the human eye, the microphones and the ear, the television studio and the visual world, and the television master control and the human brain, various technical aspects of television were referred to. Some of the technologies the medium uses are reviewed and the techniques it employs to produce images and sounds are examined.

What characterizes a visual communication medium and distinguishes it from any other are the picture components it uses: television cameras, microphones, switchers, lights, and editors are the specific hardware, the tools the television medium uses to produce its visual messages. Obviously, students of visual literacy must know how these tools work and what their potentials and limitations are. If, for example, a painter does not know how to properly mix colors or how to use a brush, how could that person claim to know about painting? Equally, students of visual learning, particularly of television images, must know how the hardware of the medium work to produce television images. The foremost academic study dealing with this is television production.

In addition to the knowledge of the hardware of visual communication, scholars of the aesthetics of television suggest that the substance or materials of the television medium (which differ decisively from those of other visual communication media such as film or photography), must be studied separately and systematically (Metallinos, 1979b; Tarroni, 1979; Zettl, 1990). The substances from which television images are made of are lights and colors. Consequently, the study of lighting instruments and their subsequent lighting control systems is an important prerequisite for the study of television production and visual learning. The fact that the television picture is made of light not only distinguishes television from other media, but it dictates the particular lighting techniques appropriate only to the television medium. Furthermore, television requires skillful handling of lighting instruments and sensitivity as to what the instruments can or cannot do. This, however, is not always the case with television production lighting engineers.

The third important factor that distinguishes the medium of television (technologically) from other visual communication media is the production techniques used to create television images. The unique way that the lighting engineer handles lighting instruments to create a particular mood of a scene or the way the camera operator frames the picture for a dramatic moment of a scene; the way that the editing was decided by the director, or the different ways that the engineer handles the sounds for the particular scene all constitute the techniques most appropriate for the medium of television. Lighting, framing, editing, or audio techniques for television are not the same as those used by theater, photography, or film. They are different because the medium has developed its own production techniques.

In summary, knowledge and understanding of television hardware and the production techniques used to produce images and sounds are significant factors in building the standards of recognition and appreciation of televised images.

To the knowledge of unique hardware, substance, and production techniques of the medium, one must add the need for a detailed understanding of the four most prominent components (all in the area of the hardware) of the television medium. These are: light and lighting techniques, cameras and framing or staging techniques, time–motion and editing techniques, and audio techniques. In television production the learning of these four components constitutes the bases for the study of the medium. In visual learning the systematic study and knowledge of these components are important, as it is explained herein.

The manipulation of the television lighting instruments to create prominent attached or cast shadows is what television lighting is all about. Learning, therefore, which lighting instruments (directional or diffused) to use, where to place them (e.g., above or below eye level or at what angle), and with what intensity (required number of foot-candles) to create a high key lighting technique or a daytime scene is obviously closely related to picture recognition and appreciation.

The manipulation of television space, both negative (empty) and positive (occupied), is what constitutes the television framing and staging techniques. It is necessary therefore to know where to place the objects or stage the action (positive space) and where to place the cameras in relation to the objects (camera position and angle), the distances allowed for subject (primary) and camera (secondary) movements that depend on the potentially available negative studio space. These factors all determine how the picture is framed by the television camera operator; this, in turn, will enhance television picture recognition and appreciation.

The manipulation of the televised images in regard to their sequential appearance is what television editing is all about. Learning, therefore, which shot was chosen (long, medium, or close-up), by which camera (visual direction), at what time (point of interest and punctuation), are significant factors for the proper flow of information. This is a crucial factor for the recognition and appreciation of televised messages.

Lastly, the manipulation of sounds used to match the visuals that accompany them is what television audio is all about. Learning how each microphone works (omnidirectionally or unidirectionally), where to place the particular microphone for maximum sound pickup, and how to select the appropriate sounds visually compatible to the picture's visual synthesis (matching criteria for pictures and sounds) are all important factors in the construction of televised images and are significant and mandatory knowledge for the proper recognition of television pictures.

In summary, the studies of the technologies used and the techniques employed by the visual communication medium of television provide the basis on which the standards for picture recognition in particular, and visual learning in general, should be built.

Artistic Aspects of Television Images

One of the basic and most crucial prerequisites for proper recognition and appreciation of television images is their analysis as art forms. All art forms, regardless of the category under which they fall, are complicated phenomena and therefore difficult to study. The study of television as an art form is even more difficult for various reasons. There is much confusion in North America as to what network, educational, and video art television are. We call everything television when we must differentiate various categories of it because each one has created several types of programs or production formats that must be analyzed on their own merits. Therefore these three forms of television must be first distinguished. The medium of television, regardless of its category, is a considerably new medium and today there are a limited number of empirical studies dealing with the artistry or the compositional aspects of the medium (Metallinos, 1985; Newcomb, 1982). This lack of vigorous scientific research on the compositional factors of television has considerably delayed the development of those particular compositional principles governing the production of television images. Other factors that made the study of television, as an art form, difficult were its commercial or business origin, its mass communication scope, and the initial belief that television is an advertising device. This business concept dominated the television industry and affected all types of television programming by shaping both the content and its form of presentation.

Serious efforts have been made, however, during the last 10 to 15 years to establish the basis on which television, particularly the educational and video art categories, can be studied as a unique art form with its own merit. Excellent texts on television production (Millerson 1972; Wurtzel, 1983; Zettl,

1992) have been published that provide detailed information on both the hardware and software of the medium. Empirical studies on factors related to various components of the television medium (Fletcher, 1979; Kipper, 1986, 1989; Metallinos, 1979a; Thorburn, 1987; Tiemens, 1965) have been published in the journals of the field, looking at the compositional value of television lighting, staging, editing, and audio and various descriptive, critical studies on the compositional structure of television pictures (Avery & Tiemens, 1975; Newcomb, 1979; Zettl, 1990) have come out as books, articles, or conference papers that look at the medium's production (the television program) as an art form.

This section examines the artistic (or compositional) aspects of television, known also as the medium software, that concentrate primarily on the unique features of television and the primers of television artistry. What makes television unique as an art form? What is the nature and what is the idiosyncrasy of television? Although television categories (e.g., network, cable, educational, or video art) have developed their own unique features and each type of program within each of these categories (e.g., soap operas, detective shows, high drama, experimental video shows) has created its own unique characteristics, some features common to all categories can be generally identified.

Television as an art form produces programs of simultaneous mass audience appeal. Even video art programs, which experiment with both the hardware and software of the medium, are transmitted simultaneously to a great number of viewers. The fact that the transmission of the programs is simultaneous and open to a massive audience dictates the content and outlines the form of program presentation that places it in the broader category of the popular arts. This is a unique feature of television as an art form.

Another unique feature is the threefold synthesis of its pictures that consist of visuals, audio, and movement, all of which work harmoniously to evoke viewers' emotions. Although films also consist of sights, sounds, and motion, television differs from film in that it can present this threefold synthesis of the pictures electromagnetically and live. The television picture, and in fact the entire television program, is composed while in motion, the moment it occurs.

Several observers of the television medium as an art form have suggested that what distinguishes television from other media are its "small size," its "immediacy," its "intimacy" (Millerson, 1972, pp. 198–202), its "viewing intensity," and its "viewing involvement" (Toogood, 1978, p. 16). The programs produced by any category of television are art forms that are given to people who view a small vista screen, are directly in front of it, get deeply drawn into the action, and become totally involved with it (Antin, 1979).

The most emphatically distinct feature of television as an art form is its metamorphic nature, by which images are synthesized to tell the story. The juxtaposition of television images occurs while undergoing a constant metamorphosis. The images, accompanied by appropriate narrative or sounds, are in constant flux changing from long shots to extreme close-ups, sometimes expanding, other times swinging, often flipping over. Only television can achieve this. The art forms produced by television that uses such features are unique. In assessing and evaluating this unique characteristic of the television medium art, Zettl (1978) stated:

> When television is used to *create* it simply grabs from external reality the bits and pieces it needs for this creation. When performing this function television becomes metamorphic. It no longer translates, but transforms, yes, even transcends the raw materials of external reality into an event that cannot exist outside the medium itself. A video synthesized image, is, of course, an extreme case, whereby the image is electronically induced. But even an extensive super, or a key-matte, or a multiple screen events give television its formative metamorphic function. (p. 7)

Let us turn now to the specific new television materials that constitute the primers of the art of television and provide the television literacy in our quest for visual learning. Arnheim (1969) in his book *Art and Visual Perception* and Dondis (1973) in her book *A Primer of Visual Literacy* gave us the basic materials and elements that compose all visual arts. For Arnheim (1969), the basic elements of the visual arts are balance, shape, form, growth, space, light, color, movement, tension, and expression. Paintings, sculptures, architecture, film, photography, music, and theater all have these compositional elements in their synthesis. Their artistic analysis and aesthetic evaluation should be based on the proper syntheses of all these elements. For Dondis (1973), the raw materials in the syntheses of the visual arts, also known as primers of visual communication arts, are the dot, line, shape, direction, tone, color, texture, dimension, scale, and movement. The analysis and aesthetic evaluation of any visual art form should be based on the way these elements are organized to create the art form.

In addition to these materials, most of which are interwoven with the television image, the artistic evaluation of television programs should be based on the way the picture's visual elements are created and composed. They fall into three categories corresponding to the threefold nature of television pictures: visuals, sounds, and movements. In the first category, the lights and colors constitute television's primers and occur either as chiaroscuro lights (characterized by the distinctive darkness or lightness of the cast and the attached shadows that are created by television's directional or diffused lighting instruments) or as flat lights (characterized by the overall unified brightness, and evenly distributed light on the scene). Television colors occur either as primary colors (blue, red, and green) from which all other combinations of colors are achieved or as additive and subtractive colors created by various combinations of primary and secondary colors. The artistic quality of television pictures obviously depends on the proper usage and synthesis of these primers in the entire television program.

Various visuals created by the television camera and manipulated by the television switcher (or special effects video synthesizer) also constitute the primers of television literacy and occur in different forms. They appear as long, medium, or close-up shots depending on the narrative form assigned to them by the director. They are matted, chromakeyed, split-screened, and zoomed in or out, again depending on the audio track and the story they unfold. All visual special effects created by video synthesizers such as fades, dissolves, wipes, and superimpositions constitute the primers of television literacy and are the fundamental elements that compose the television art form.

In the second category of sound, such basic sound elements as literal (e.g., sounds derived from the source that creates them such as waterfalls, airplanes, and traffic), or nonliteral (e.g., music sounds, such as violins imitating the sound of autumn leaves falling) constitute the primers on which the analysis of the television picture and television programs are based. Also, such elements of television sounds as pitch, timbre, duration, loudness, and attack decay, such basic sound structures as melody, harmony, homophonic and polyphonic, or picture sound combinations either homophonically or polyphonically structured; and picture sound matching combinations either thematically, tonally, rhythmically, or historically are the most basic, fundamental elements that compose television art forms (Zettl, 1990).

The real, apparent, and implied perceptual motions discussed earlier, as well as particular movements that occur when a television program is videotaped (such as the movements of subjects, camera, and that created by the flow of the action within the visual fields) are the motion primers of television programs as art forms. They constitute television literacy. To these various types of movement in television pictures, the roles of slow and accelerated motion are significant and unique only to television. The ability to accelerate, slow down, and replay moments of the past are not only unique primers of television but help to form the unique structures of television programs.

In summary, the study of the primers of television found in either images, sounds, or movements of visual elements provides the necessary criteria for the evaluation of television programs as art forms. The study of the artistic aspects of television based on the knowledge of the software of the medium is a prerequisite for the establishment of the appropriate criteria for the accurate recognition and evaluation of televised images.

Established Criteria for the Evaluation of Educational Television Programs

Based on existing literature on television criticism (including several well-written books, research articles, and conference papers) extracted from critical studies on related fields such as theater, visual arts, and film criticism, and from our own studies on television production-related topics, a list of value judgments or applied criteria for the evaluation of educational television programs has been constructed. A thorough discussion on television criticism is contained in Part III of this book. Before referring to the inclusive list of criteria, the three major compositional principles that apply unilaterally to all art forms must first be underlined and a definition and explanation of what an educational television program is must be provided to make the criteria list more explicit.

The compositional principles underlining all art forms, regardless of their nature or form of presentation are direction, proportions, and balance. Critics of the performing, visual, and media arts evaluate art forms on the basis of these three inherent elements.

Direction refers to the way the flow of action moves. It could be from left to right in the case of a moving image, or from morning to night in a play. The established direction determines the flow and continuity and the sequence of events and actions followed within the narrative of the art form. The events of a theatrical play, like those on a television screen, follow, or should follow, an established direction that establishes continuity, which is the foundation of the art form. Disorientation resulting from lack of direction causes confusion and breaks down the communication process of the art form. It is a fundamental compositional principle of all true art forms.

Proportions refer to the way artists adjust various parts of the art form to make them symmetrically or asymmetrically harmonious. Artists proportionally divide the art forms in their effort to make the forms attractive. A dramatist divides the dramatic form, the play, into acts with portions of plain dialogue or high conflict; a painter divides the canvas into areas depicting intensive action and areas of background visual information; a television camera operator, at the will of the director, divides the television picture into areas of prominence (foreground figures) and others with secondary importance (background) elements. A good work of art is aesthetically pleasing when proportionally divided to harmonize its various parts. This is a fundamental compositional principle for all art forms.

Balance, the third basic principle found in all art forms, refers to the degree of stability produced by the distribution and interaction of various parts of the art form and results in an aesthetically pleasing composition. According to Arnheim (1969), "An unbalanced composition looks accidental, transitory, and therefore invalid" (p. 12). Balance, as a compositional principle, can occur either as unstable, stable, or neutral, depending on the particular art form. In television picture composition, all three forms of balance can be found interchangeably as television pictures are, as stated earlier, transitory and metamorphic and create an even greater challenge to the producer or artist of televised images.

Educational television programs do not necessarily refer exclusively to those programs produced by such educational television networks as the Public Broadcasting System (PBS) in the United States, the Canadian Broadcasting Corporation (CBC) in Canada, or the British Broadcasting Corporation (BBC) in Great Britain. The term refers to television programs whose central theme is to present topics strictly referring to education and to others produced by individual educational stations, networks, or organizations such as the National Geographic Society. Such recently televised programs as *The Civil War* or *Nova* are the most representative of the educational television programs referred to in this section. Although these programs place a strong emphasis on their central theme of learning and encyclopedic information, they are written for, produced by, and presented through television. Consequently, the criteria for their evaluation are both specific, referring exclusively to their educational genres, and general, referring to television programs as an art form.

The list of criteria provided here is divided into three major areas according to the three most important functions or purposes television programs serve: to explore the issue, present it, and reach a targeted audience (Metallinos, 1973).

Criteria Concerning the Content or Message. Although not exclusive, the basic criteria for discussing, analyzing, and evaluating the issues explored by an educational television program are as follows:

- Content and message significance and importance.
- Accuracy of ideas and documentation, research.
- Writing style and format (or genre).
- Composition and dramaturgy of story.
- Order and balance of segments.
- Simplicity and complexity of treatment of the story.
- Pedagogical impact and importance of the message.

Criteria Concerning the Medium or Form. The medium shapes the form and creates the art as a communicative agent. The criteria for the evaluation of an educational television program should be based on the two factors, production and performing, as follows:

Production Factors

- Lighting technique usage and effects, colors, and visual clarity.
- Cameras, lenses, effects, framing, staging, space utilization, and background/middle-ground/foreground interrelationships, screen composition, setting, and so on.
- Pace, motion, rhythm, editing techniques, special effects, graphics, image continuity.

- Audio sound clarity, sound consistency, and coherence. Audio perspective, matching visuals with sounds, audiovisual reinforcement, audiovisual balance, and so on.

Performing Factors

- Performer's appearance, clothing, colors, and so on.
- Age, sex, and character choices.
- Body movements, stage (or camera) presence.
- Eye contact, lens acting, naturalness.
- Character interpretation and fitness within the context of the program.
- Delivery and believability of characters, and so on.

Criteria Concerning the Program's Impact and Effects on Viewers. The third important purpose of the educational television program, as is the case with all television program formats, is to stimulate the audience and to cause reactions, to have an effect on them that is closely related to the message. Such criteria are as follows:

- Audience identification. Who are the viewers?
- Does the program fulfill its intended scope?
- Audience reactions. Do they like it? If so, why? If not, why not?
- Overall importance/significance/usefulness of the program to the target audience and to society at large?
- Is the program tasteful? Does it contain violence, conflicts, models, or concepts that should not be aired?
- What specific public needs does the program fulfill (i.e., sociological, aesthetic, psychological, physiological, etc.)?
- Innovation—to what degree is the program different? etc.

In summary, the criteria for the evaluation of educational television programs should be drawn from the three main purposes of the program: the message, the medium, and the viewer.

References

Adler, R., & Cater, D. (Eds.). (1975). *Television as a cultural force.* New York: Praeger.

Agee, W. K., Ault, P. H., & Emery, E. (1988). *Introduction to mass communication* (9th ed.). New York: Harper & Row.

Antin, D. (1979). The distinctive features of the medium. In H. Newcomb (Ed.), *Television: The critical view* (2nd ed., pp. 495–516). New York: Oxford University Press.

Arnheim, R. (1969). *Art and visual perception: A psychology of the creative eye.* Berkeley: University of California Press.

Aronoff, J. (1967). *Psychological needs and cultural systems: A case study.* Toronto: Van Nostrand.

Avery, R. K., & Tiemens, R. K. (1975, December). *The syntax of visual messages: An empirical investigation of the asymmetry of the frame theory.* Paper presented at the annual conference of the Speech Communication Association, Washington, DC.

Behnke, R. R. (1970). Psychological technologies. In P. Emmert & W. D. Brooks (Eds.), *Methods of research in communication* (pp. 429–452). Boston, MA: Houghton Mifflin.

Bloom, F. E., Lazerson, A., & Hofstader, L. (1985). *Brain, mind, and behavior.* New York: Freeman.

Boddy, J. (1978). *Brain systems and psychological concepts.* New York: Wiley.

Brown, J. A. C. (1963). *Techniques of persuasion: From propaganda to brainwashing.* Baltimore, MD: Penguin.

Burns, G., & Thompson, R. J. (Eds.). (1989). *Television studies: Textual analysis.* New York: Praeger.

Crick, F. H. C. (1979). Thinking about the brain. In Scientific American (Eds.), *The brain* (pp. 132–137). New York: Freeman.

Curry, F. W. K. (1967). A comparison of left-handed and right-handed subjects on verbal and non verbal dichotic listening tasks. *Cortex, 3,* 343–352.

Dickie, G. (1971). *Aesthetics: An introduction.* Indianapolis, IN: Bobbs-Merrill.

Dirks, D. (1964). Perception of dichotic and monaural verbal material and cerebral dominance in speech. *Acta Otolaryngologica, 58,* 73–80.

Dondis, D. A. (1973). *A primer of visual literacy.* Cambridge, MA: MIT Press.

Eccles, J. C. (1973). *The understanding of the brain* (p. 207). New York: McGraw-Hill.

Erickson, R. P. (1968). Stimulus coding in topographic and nontopographic afferent modalities. *Psychological Review, 75*, 447–465.

Fletcher, J. E. (1978, November). *Empirical studies of visual communication: Some methodological considerations.* Paper presented at the annual conference of the Speech Communication Association, Minneapolis, MN.

Fletcher, J. E. (1979). Academic research in retrospect: A final view. *Feedback, 21*, 14–17.

Freud, S. (1959). *Collected papers of Sigmund Freud* (E. Jones, J. Prince, J. Strachey, & A. Strachey, Eds. and Trans.). New York: Basic Books.

Freud, S. (1960). *The complete introductory lectures in psychoanalysis* (J. Strachey, Ed. and Trans.). New York: Norton.

Frisby, J. P. (1980). *Seeing: Illusion, brain, and mind.* Oxford, England: Oxford University Press.

Gerbner, G., & Gross, L. (1979). Living with television: The violence profile. In H. Newcomb (Ed.), *Television: The critical view* (2nd ed.). New York: Oxford University Press.

Gerbner, G., Gross, L., & Melody, W. H. (1973). *Communication technology and social policy.* New York: Wiley.

Geschwind, N. (1979). Specialization of the human brain. In Scientific American (Eds.), *The brain* (pp. 107–117). New York: Freeman.

Gibson, J. J. (1950). *The perception of the visual world.* Boston, MA: Houghton-Mifflin.

Gibson, J. J. (1979). *The ecological approach to visual perception.* Boston, MA: Houghton-Mifflin.

Gitlin, T. (1982). Prime time ideology: The hegemonic process in television entertainment. In H. Newcomb (Ed.), *Television: The critical view* (3rd ed., pp. 426–453). New York: Oxford University Press.

Gregory, R. L. (1990). *Eye and brain: The psychology of seeing.* New York: McGraw-Hill.

Hall, S. (1977). Culture, the media, and the ideological effect. In J. Curran, M. Gurevitch, & J. Woolbicott (Eds.), *Mass communication and society* (pp. 315–348). Beverly Hills, CA: Sage.

Hockberg, J., & Brooks, V. (1974). The integration of successive cinematic views of simple scenes. *Bulletin of the Psychonomic Society, 4*, 263–281.

Hyde, S. (1970). *The history and the analysis of the public arts.* Unpublished course syllabus, Department of Broadcast Communication Arts, San Francisco State University, San Francisco, CA.

Ikegami Electronics Inc. (1995). *Products pocket guide: NAB 1995.* Maywood, NJ: 07607.

Jacobs, N. (Ed.). (1961). *Culture for the millions.* Boston, MA: Beacon.

Kennedy, J. M. (1974). *A psychology of picture perception.* San Francisco: Jossey-Bass.

Kimura, D. (1964). Left and right differences in the perception of melodies. *Quarterly Journal of Experimental Psychology, 16*, 355–358.

Kimura, D. (1967). Functional asymmetry of the brain in dichotic listening. *Cortex, 3*, 163–178.

Kimura, D. (1969). Spatial localization in left and right visual fields. *Canadian Journal of Psychology, 23*, 445–458.

Kipper, P. (1986). Television camera movement as a source of perceptual information. *Journal of Broadcasting and Electronic Media, 30*, 295–307.

Kipper, P. (1989, May). *Visual communication, information, and perception.* Paper presented at the annual conference of the International Communication Association, San Francisco, CA.

Kosslyn, S. M. (1988). Aspects of cognitive neuroscience of mental imagery. *Science, 240*, 1621–1626.

Maslow, A. H. (1954). *Motivation and personality.* New York: Harper & Brothers.

McCray, C. L. (1979). Kaptain Kronkite: The myth of the eternal frame. In H. Newcomb (Ed.), *Television: The critical view* (2nd ed., pp. 319–333). New York: Oxford University Press.

McLuhan, M., & Powers, B. R. (1989). *The global village: Transformations in world life and media in the 21st century.* New York: Oxford University Press.

McQuail, D. (1969). *Towards a sociology of mass communication.* London: Collier-MacMillan.

Metallinos, N. (1973). Criteria for evaluating the performing arts. *Interchange, 3,* 11–17.

Metallinos, N. (1979a). The composition of the television picture: Some hypothesis to test the forces operating within the television screen. *Educational Communication and Technology Journal, 27*(8), 204–214.

Metallinos, N. (1979b). Visual communication: Its process and its effects. In O. J. Constandelos & C. J. Efthymiou (Eds.), *Greece today and tomorrow* (pp. 221–233). New York: Krikos.

Metallinos, N. (1983). Biometric research instruments and measuring techniques. In R. A. Braden & A. D. Walker (Eds.), *Seeing ourselves: Visualization in a social context. Readings of the 14th annual conference of the International Visual Literacy Association* (pp. 171–175). Blacksburg: Virginia Polytechnic Institute and State University.

Metallinos, N. (1985). Empirical studies of television composition. In J. R. Dominick & J. E. Fletcher (Eds.), *Broadcasting Research Methods* (pp. 297–311). Newton, MA: Allyn & Bacon.

Metallinos, N. (1987a). Computerized television. *Journal of Visual-Verbal Languaging, 7,* 25–32.

Metallinos, N. (1987b). Comprehension and recall of television's computerized images: An exploratory study. In M. R. Simonson & S. M. Zvacek (Eds.), *Proceedings of selected research paper presentations of the 1987 annual convention of the Association for Educational Communication and Technology* (pp. 481–512). Ames: Iowa State University.

Metallinos, N. (1990). Information design in educational media: Structure, evaluation, and study. *The Visual Literacy Review, 19,* 1–3.

Metallinos, N., & Tiemens, R. K. (1977). Asymmetry of the screen: The effects of left versus right placement of television images. *Journal of Broadcasting, 21*(1), 21–23.

Millerson, G. (1972). *The technique of television production* (9th ed.). New York: Hastings House.

Murch, G. M. (1973). *Visual and auditory perception.* New York: Bobbs-Merrill.

Nevitt, B. (1980–1981). Visible and invisible bias via media. *Canadian Journal of Communication, 7,* 9–42.

New Webster's Dictionary of the English Language. (1965). New York: Grolier.

Newcomb, H. (Ed.). (1979). *Television: The critical view* (2nd ed.). New York: Oxford University Press.

Newcomb, H. (1982). Towards a television aesthetic. In H. Newcomb (Ed.), *Television: The critical view* (3rd ed., pp. 478–494). New York: Oxford University Press.

Novak, M. (1979). Television shapes the soul. In H. Newcomb (Ed.), *Television: The critical view* (2nd ed., pp. 303–318). New York: Oxford University Press.

O'Keefe, D. J. (1990). *Persuasion: Theory and research.* Newbury Park, CA: Sage.

Ornstein, R. E. (1972). *The psychology of consciousness.* San Francisco: Freeman.

Pinchot, R. B. (1987). *The brain: Mystery of matter and mind.* Washington, DC: U.S. News Books.

Pines, M. (1986). Landscapes of the mind. In R. M. Poole (Ed.), *The incredible machine* (pp. 325–377). Washington, DC: National Geographic Society.

Posner, M. I., Petersen, S. E., Fox, P. T., & Reichle, M. E. (1988). Localization of cognitive operations in the human brain. *Science, 240,* 1627–1631.

Read, H. (1970). *Art and society.* New York: Schocken Books.

Rissoner, F., & Birch, D. (1977). *Mass media and the popular arts.* New York: McGraw-Hill.

Roiphe, A. (1979). Ma and Pa and John-Boy in mythical America: The Waltons. In H. Newcomb (Ed.), *Television: The critical view* (2nd ed., pp. 8–15). New York: Oxford University Press.

Rosenberg, B., & White, D. M. (Eds.). (1957). *Mass culture: The popular arts in America.* New York: Collier-MacMillan.

Rosenzwig, M. R. (1951). Representation of the two ears of the auditory cortex. *American Journal of Psychology, 166,* 147–158.

Schramm, W., & Roberts, D. F. (Eds.). (1971). *The process and effects of mass communications.* Chicago: University of Illinois Press.

Sedeen, M. (1986). In touch with the world. In R. M. Poole (Ed.), *The incredible machine* (pp. 261–324). Washington, DC: National Geographic Society.

Springer, S. P., & Deutsch, G. (1985). *Left brain, right brain* (Rev. ed.). San Francisco: Freeman.

Tarroni, E. (1979). The aesthetics of television. In H. Newcomb (Ed.), *Television: The Critical View* (2nd ed., pp. 437–461). New York: Oxford University Press.

Thorburn, D. (1987). Television as an aesthetic medium. *Critical Studies in Mass Communication, 4,* 161–173.

Tiemens, R. K. (1965). Some relationships of camera angle to communication credibility. *Journal of Broadcasting, 14,* 483–490.

Toogood, A. (1978). A framework for the exploration of video as a unique art form. *Journal of the University of Film Association, 30,* 15–19.

Wood, P. H. (1979). Television as a dream. In H. Newcomb (Ed.), *Television: The critical view* (2nd ed., pp. 517–535). New York: Oxford University Press.

Wurtzel, A. (1983). *Television production* (2nd ed.). New York: McGraw-Hill.

Zettl, H. (1978, November). *Languages of television: The language of television criticism.* Paper presented at the annual conference of the National Association of Educational Broadcasters, Washington, DC.

Zettl, H. (1990). *Sight, sound, motion: Applied media aesthetics* (2nd ed.). Belmont, CA: Wadsworth.

Zettl, H. (1992). *Television production handbook* (5th ed.). Belmont, CA: Wadsworth.

III

COMPOSITIONAL FACTORS

The third axis on which the study of visual communication media aesthetics is built is composition. For any attempt to understand clearly, let alone to analyze and to discuss the products generated by the visual communication media such as the various television genres, in addition to the basic knowledge of perception and cognition discussed in Parts I and II, a basic understanding of art composition in general, and composition of the visual communication media products in particular, is needed. The understanding of the complex web of the visual communication art products, through the study of composition, will also improve the ability to analyze and to appreciate such art products, thus completing the threefold linear process of perceiving, understanding, and appreciating visual communication media arts that encompasses the field of visual communication media aesthetics in general, and television aesthetics in particular.

This part examines the axis of composition in the three distinct, yet interrelated areas of arts, criticism, and applied rules of composition of visual communication media products, particularly television programs. The analysis and examination of an art form leads to the establishment of the appropriate value judgments or criteria that evaluate the art form—criticism. However, when art critics question the value judgments pertaining to an art form and engage in discussions regarding taste, harmony, unity, and balance, they further progress beyond criticism, to a higher level of scholarly activity that Beardsley (1958) called "philosophy of criticism, or metacriticism" (p. 4). This hierarchy of composition that starts with the study of the arts, engages the study of criticism, and results in the establishment of the field of aesthetics, has a strong link that ties all three together. As Beardsley (1958) stated: "We shall think of aesthetics as a distinctive philosophical inquiry: it is concerned with the nature and basis of criticism—in the broad sense of the term—just as criticism itself is concerned with works of art" (p. 6). Let us examine, first, the history, philosophy, nature, character, functions, and the various categories of the arts to obtain a broader spectrum of the evolution of visual communication media arts, and specifically television.

7
▼▼▼▼▼▼▼

Introduction to the Arts

The development of the arts of all Western societies coincides with the development of their religious, socioeconomic, cultural, and political beliefs and practices. It is, therefore, natural that to gain a clear understanding of their philosophical base, the evolution of the arts of a society should be examined historically. It is also necessary to look at the specific needs that generated the creation of the various art forms, as this will reveal the various functions of the arts and will underline their nature and character. Today's visual communication media arts, such as entertaining television programs, should be examined on the basis of their historical evolution, nature, character, philosophies they embody, and functions they perform.

The beginning of the civilization of the Western world started with the arts created by prehistoric people. An examination of prehistoric art is a critical starting point because it assists us in understanding not only where and how humankind evolved, but what humans believed in and what they understood. In fact, that is the strength of all works of art, ancient and contemporary. When tracing the evolution of art one traces the evolution of people's aspirations, fears, and basic beliefs; in short, one traces people's philosophies.

From the ancient worlds of Egypt and Mesopotamia evolved civilization and the historic revolution of the written word. To admire the perfection, harmony, and beauty of ancient Greek sculpture or Roman architecture is to react to the clarity of thought that was a unique characteristic of those historical periods.

The Middle Ages brought the beginning of the reign of Christianity; the Church dominated all aspects of life and its importance is reflected in the arts of that period. As the European Renaissance came to be in the 15th century, art took another turn by adopting the new and more scientific reading of the world to its techniques. By contrast, the Romantic Era responded to the logical and intellectual constraints of the Renaissance by appealing to the emotive side of humans. With contemporary artistic movements, artists leaped away from conformity and created their own interpretations of the many different movements that developed simultaneously during the last century.

A closer look at these periods suggests that the various art products reflect the societies that created them. The arts provide the philosophical basis on which society is built. However, it is impossible to properly understand the philosophy reflected in the arts without having a clear understanding of their nature. Once that nature is reviewed, the characteristics of what one can label as art, and more specifically, visual communication media arts, is defined. When drawing these limits and defining the meaning of art, the examination of the functions of the arts becomes simpler and more meaningful.

This chapter first introduces the history of the arts in the Western world from prehistoric times through the Greek and Roman periods, the Middle Ages, the Renaissance, the Romantic Era, and the contemporary art movements. The second section deals with the philosophy of art from ancient to modern thinkers along with the nature and the characteristics of major works of art. The third section of this chapter pertains to the various categories of the arts as they are illustrated through their major psychological, social, and communicative functions.

A BRIEF HISTORY OF THE ARTS OF THE WESTERN WORLD

Whether consciously or totally unaware of their presence, all artists are influenced by the arts of the past, although some artists may have never studied them. However, among all artistic creators, those who know the historical evolution of the arts they nourish not only reflect such knowledge in their art products, but foremost provide a sense of continuity and a logical progression in the evolution of the society they live in. The developers of television entertaining programs—the producers, directors, and writers—should follow and practice this principle faithfully, which will result in the desirable development of television aesthetics.

The brief historical review of the evolution of the arts of the Western world that follows emphasizes how important it is for the study of visual communication media aesthetics to link the past with the present and to have the roots of their compositional principles governing media aesthetics.

The evolution of the most significant works of art of the Prehistoric, Egyptian, Greek, and Roman eras is traced, the artistic movements of the Western Middle Ages and the evolution of the arts in the Renaissance and Romantic

Eras are outlined, and, finally, the contemporary movements in various forms of art that generally reflect the modern Western notion that art is created for art's sake are discussed.

The Prehistoric, Ancient Greek, and Roman Eras

Although our early ancestors began to walk on the earth with two feet more than 1 million years ago, it was not until approximately 600,000 years later that civilization, with the earliest traces of humans as tool makers, hence art makers, began. On the shores of the Nile River in Egypt, and the Tigris and Euphrates rivers in Mesopotamia (Assyria and Babylon), the prehistoric era began with the formation of societies. Defined as the phase of the human evolution that occurred before the arrival of writing, prehistory is not without significance. The development of the written word that began about 5,000 years ago distinguishes prehistoric from historic societies. Yet human beings of both eras felt the need to express themselves in artistic form by dancing around fires, exorcising the inexplicable natural phenomena, drawing pictures on the walls of their caves, and so on.

As a response to the impending threat of physical extinction, the first human inhabitants of the earth created the primitive arts. The major works of this period are classified into three groups: Paleolithic (Old Stone Age), Mesolithic (Middle Stone Age), and Neolithic (New Stone Age). Before social organization that evolved for the sake of the group, humans struggled against the forces of nature rather than fighting against the forces of humans. Examples of artistic forms of the late stages of the Old Stone Age, some 30,000 years ago, such as the drawings of bison, deer, horses, and cattle are found in caves in the regions of Chauvet and Lascaux in France. Located in the deepest hidden places of the caves, the pictures served a practical rather than a decorative or aesthetic purpose in the life of the hunters who could not yet distinguish reality from image. Drawing a picture of an animal served to bring the animal itself within one's grasp. Thus, primitive artists were magicians whose drawings served as an incantation through which they asserted mastery over their world. The Paleolithic Era ended when the Ice Age ended and people left the caves. Then the Mesolithic Period began, characterized by rock paintings and drawings of human figures that are seldom found in the cave art of the Paleolithic Era. During this period, people began to control the world by creating living settlements, domesticating animals, and cultivating plants; humans sought to control the physical environment through developing technologies. The most representative example of the architecture of this era is Stonehenge, located in the Salisbury Plane in Wiltshire, England.

As stated earlier, history began with the invention of writing, an achievement of the historic civilization of Egypt and Mesopotamia. The roots of this development are not known. However, it is suspected that writing was invented several centuries after the first stages of the new societies. History was underway by the time writing could be used to record historic events. Generally, the Egyptian civilization is considered as one of the most rigid and conservative. The basic patterns of Egyptian institutions, beliefs, and artistic expressions were formed between 300 and 2500 B.C. and reasserted themselves for the next 2,000 years so that all Egyptian art appears to have a certain similarity. It is said that it alternates between conservation and innovation but is never static. Some of its great achievements had a profound influence on Greek civilization in general, and the development of Greek theater in particular (e.g., the birth, death, and resurrection of Osiris of ancient Egypt), transforming the cult of Dionysian festivities in Greece that generated the Dythyrambus, the song and dance in honor of Dionysus, from which ancient Greek drama was developed.

During this period the most significant paintings were profiles of human figures, the most prominent being the figures of Egyptian pharaohs. Common belief was that people could ensure their eternal happiness by building a tomb for the afterlife of their spirit and being mummified upon their death. There was no longer a dark fear of the spirits of the dead that had previously dominated their primitive ancestors' cults. We derive our understanding of ancient Egyptian art from the findings in ancient tombs, because very little has survived of the ancient Egyptian palaces and cities. Pyramids and temples, built to last forever, were constructed to house the tombs of kings. The Egyptian pyramids were not isolated structures; they were linked with vast funerary districts. The most elaborate such area is the district around the pyramid of Zoser created by Imhotep, the first artist whose name has been recorded in history. The oldest known image of a historic personage identified by name is that of a carved state palette of King Narmer of Egypt. As the hieroglyphic labels and rational orderliness of the design signify a new art, primitive art is left behind through this palette.

The history of ancient Greece (1200–200 B.C.) spanned several centuries. It started from the prehistoric or Doric Period, emerged into the archaic, slowly developed to full maturity in the Classical or Golden Age, and eventually declined toward the end of the Hellenistic Era. All basic art forms known today were developed during the 1,000 years of ancient Greek history, although each one of these periods was stamped with its own individual character, nature, philosophy, and functions of the arts. Architecture, sculpture, theater, music, dance, and poetry (in all their forms: epic, dramatic, and lyric) were developed in ancient Greece. In the view of numerous scholars, the exceptional development of all art forms of ancient Greece into perfection is not an isolated phenomenon that occurred miraculously. It was the result of such factors as prosperity (gained by trades and wars), organized city states (gained by democratic ideals), and religion (which gave the impetus for the development of all aspects of life, including philosophy, the arts, and sciences). Whereas the studies of ancient Greek religion, mythology, sciences, and philosophy easily reveal the ontological basis of that society, the study of the Greek arts uncovers the entire spectrum of human emotions that transform the biological being into a creative human being, striving to perfect the mind and understand the emotions. Styles such as geometric archaic, black figure, red figure, and classical characterized the paintings of the ancient Greek period. Its methodological approach permeated science, technology, philosophy, religion, and the arts, and characterizes the entire ancient Greek period. In visual arts, particularly, the central concern was the definition of objects and concepts in their proper dimensions and limits (see Fig. 7.1).

The ancient Greeks paid exceptional attention to the concepts of balance, proportion, direction, harmony, and unity, all major compositional factors creating aesthetically pleasing works of art. Sculpture was one of the major art forms. Gods, heroes, and ordinary people were created in white marble, reflecting the skill and artistry of many anonymous artists. The perfect human body—as reflected in ancient Greek sculpture—was the ideal place for the perfect human mind to reside (see Fig. 7.2).

Their perfection in architecture, buildings, landscapes, and sculpture, particularly in statues of gods, goddesses, heroes, and scenes of everyday life, was extended and found total application in ancient Greek drama. The architecture of the ancient Greek theater was exceptional in symmetry, harmony, acoustics, and location and the dramas performed in these theaters were the highest form of art ever created in the Western world (see Fig. 7.3).

The study of ancient Greek drama when performed in its natural environment (the ancient Greek theaters) could suffice in providing the students of visual communication media aesthetics with the best example of aesthetic

FIG. 7.1. The Parthenon, an architectural marvel of the Western world, was built in the Golden Age of the ancient Greek civilization.

FIG. 7.2. Hermes and Dionysus. This sculpture was created at the peak of the Golden Age of ancient Greece.

pleasure and the reasons that the study of the arts is such an important factor in the development of aesthetics.

Aristotle's book, *Poetics* (Ferguson, 1961), which analyzes ancient Greek theater as an art form and provides the basic rules for the perfect play and its aesthetically pleasing production, is still the most valuable source to students of visual communication media aesthetics (see Fig. 7.4).

The Roman Period that lasted roughly 600 years (300 B.C.–300 A.D.) succeeded the Hellenistic Era. Although the Romans conquered the ancient Greek world and imposed their political dominance as warriors, they in turn were conquered by Greek arts, sciences, religion, technology, philosophies, and so on. Because Roman art is so decisively influenced by Greek art, it becomes difficult to distinguish Roman style in fine arts. The Romans reproduced and imported by the thousands Greek originals of earlier days. Furthermore, artifacts produced under Roman auspices did not distinctively differ from Greek art. The Roman Empire was an open cosmopolitan society that absorbed material or regional traits into a common, all-Roman pattern that was homogeneous and diverse at the same time. The unique characteristics of the Roman arts are found in this complex pattern rather than in a single and consistent quality of form.

FIG. 7.3. The Theatre of Epidaurus.

FIG. 7.4. Ancient Greek drama. The performances of the comedy *Peace*, by Aristophanes, at the ancient Greek Theatre of Epidaurus, Greece.

The Roman cosmopolitan society created a thirst for the spectacular and the grandiose, the elaborate festivals and gatherings that characterized the autonomy of the Romans in their public and private life. This reflects in their visual arts, particularly architecture and theater. Greek models of architecture no longer sufficed as the sheer numbers of the population demanded larger buildings and gathering places. Thus, radical new forms had to be invented and cheaper materials and quicker methods had to be used. The most obvious example is the Colosseum, which could seat up to 50,000 spectators. Greek models of theater, also, could not serve the purpose for which the Romans attended them. First, the basic structure of the theater had to be changed to separate and protect the spectator from the orchestra and the actions (events) on stage. Second, the themes, myths, and plots of ancient Greek drama were modified for the needs of contemporary Roman spectators. Violent bloody scenes and spectacular war confrontations were common happenings on the Roman theater stages. Lastly, toward the end of the Roman period, ancient Greek theaters were turned into arenas where wild beasts feasted on early Christians in front of the Roman spectators. Nevertheless, the Roman period managed to preserve the Greek art forms and in some instances to develop them.

The decline of the Roman Empire came after Constantine I, the Great Roman Emperor, in 330 A.D. divided the Empire into eastern and western, with Constantinople and Rome as the two capitals, respectively, destined to carry the Orthodox and Catholic faiths. The decay of the western half of the Roman Empire under the impact of invasions by Germanic tribes, the rise of Islam, and the development of the Byzantine Empire began the separation of the age of Classical Antiquity and the Middle Ages.

The Middle Ages

Christian dogma dominated all aspects of life of the Middle Ages, as it is reflected in all art forms created during this long historical period. With the Middle Ages, the center of European civilization shifted from what had been the northern boundaries of the Roman world; the Mediterranean basin was no longer the epicenter of cultural exchange. Art of the Middle Ages is classified as Early Christian, Byzantine, Medieval, Romanesque, and Gothic.

There is no defined style that characterizes Early Christian art that refers to all art forms produced by or for Christians during the first 400 years of its existence before the separation of the Catholic and Orthodox Churches. With Christianity as the state religion under Constantine I, society changed from a polytheistic to a monotheistic order. The religious soul took over and the human soul was no longer important. The burial rite and safeguarding of the tomb was of prime concern to the early Christians whose faith rested on the hope of eternal life in paradise. Symbolic content prevailed over the need to make a specific event look real. The Old Testament prohibited carved images. The Christian aesthetic was to abolish sculpture, reducing forms to an unreal flatness of surface. Drawings lost perspective and depth and pictorial representation became flat. Frontal and profile views prevailed and artists deliberately avoided any expression of movement that could be interpreted as imitating life. Above all, this particular period took advantage of the powerful influence of visual communication media, and particularly painting, to narrate, propagate, and promote the Christian dogma.

A specific quality of style is found in the visual communication media arts of the Eastern Roman Empire, the so-called period of the Byzantine Empire. A compassionate quality is evident in the works of the late Byzantine Period. Compassionate gestures and facial expressions also characterize the religious artifacts of the so-called Second Golden Age of the Byzantine Period, as illustrated by the famous Crucifixion Mosaic in the church of the Daphne Monastery in Greece.

The architecture of the Byzantine churches and their interior decorations of mosaics, icons, and wall paintings (all visually documenting Christianity), were constructed to offer the most striking environment in which the dramas of Christ, His birth, His miracles, His crucifixion, and His resurrection were performed by impressively dressed monks, priests, and bishops.

The predominant art forms of the Medieval Period, which covers roughly 400 years of history (400–800 A.D.), are illustrated manuscripts, mostly gospels and lives of saints. Some Medieval society scholars suggested that the development of feudal and seigniorial systems that dominated the social, political, and economic lives of the people of the Middle Ages living in castles and towns or villages, respectively, hindered the development of great works of art. However, Christian religious arts and Gothic architecture dominated the arts of this period.

In the regions of Northern Europe and in Italy, another movement of the arts, the Romanesque, emerged. This movement produced art forms mostly in architecture, sculpture, and painting, of a large variety, somewhat similar to the Classical Period art, yet different. In architecture, the characteristics of this style are the use of round barrel vaults with large expanses of wall pierced by slit windows and often a wall decoration imitating the classical orders, as well as acanthus friezes and inhabited scrolls. In large-scale sculptures the figures took on an antique style of elegance as compared to the dumpy, earlier medieval figures.

The centralization of governments in Northern, Central, and Western Europe and the establishment of more orderly feudal societies in England, Germany, and France created the so-called Gothic Movement of the arts. This movement was most evident in the building of churches, cathedrals, castles, and so on. The Gothic movement signified two important concepts: a taste for decoration rather than plainness and a firm belief that the kingdom of God is located upward, as pointed out by the vertically oriented buildings.

The Romantic Era

Whereas the early 18th century marked the Rococo period of the arts, which placed emphasis on ornaments and decorations in all their art forms, in the late 18th century and throughout the 19th Romanticism blossomed. Although Romantic artists reached their peak from 1750 to 1850 A.D., during the reign of Louis XIV, Louis XV, and Louis XVI of France, Romanticism is a phenomenon that cannot be confined to a particular period or country. The spirit of Romanticism has been with us all along as it is generated by a basic human need. The movement reached its peak during the reign of the above French rulers. It is a way of looking at things, a certain vision found simultaneously or not in the most widely different spheres of arts, philosophy, and literature. It is characterized by restlessness, yearning, the idea of growth, self-identification with nature, infinite distance, solitude, the tragedy of existence, and the inaccessibility of the ideal by the sublime and the picturesque. Romanticism worshiped emotion as an end to itself and presumed that earth was made for man to enjoy rather than serve or obey.

The central concern of the Romantic artists was to produce the total work of art; a work that would appeal simultaneously to all the senses, the sensibilities, the emotions, and the intelligence. For the artists of this movement, the pictorial element never was an end in itself. Romanticism demands that everything should appeal to all perceptions. The Romantic spirit assumes that emotions are incomplete unless aroused by all the senses even if the work fails to live up to this expectation. Therefore, to get the most out of a painting, to appreciate it fully, it is never enough to simply note its pictorial qualities. This is one of the key elements of Romanticism and one of the major reasons for the movement's tremendous impact on the evolution of the arts in the Western world (Brion, 1960).

The Renaissance Era

Renaissance, or rebirth, is an intellectual movement that revived the letters and the arts and marked the transition from medieval to contemporary history. Among the principle components reflected in the Renaissance arts are "a revival of the classical form originally developed by the ancient Greeks and Romans, and renewed vitality and spirit in art, in which the individual, human qualities of man are emphasized" (Funk & Wagnalls New Encyclopedia, 1972, p. 221).

When people, mostly of Central Europe, realized that neither scholasticism and feudalism, nor Christianity and the Church could provide adequate causes for a meaningful existence, they turned to nationalism and individualism. People thought of themselves as the center of the universe and created new trends of individual spirit. The basis of Renaissance art was drawn from the philosophy of ancient Greece; it was characterized by recognition of rights and reason of specific topics and theories of art. The notion of a sense of beauty assuming various names gained attention in 18th century aesthetics. A three-dimensional perspective emerged for the first time in the history of the arts.

The first examples of Renaissance arts, primarily in architecture and sculpture, appear to have been greatly influenced by the Gothic arts spread throughout Europe. Some believe that the first Renaissance painter was Giotto de Bontone (c. 1276–1337). A century later, a second revolution occurred under which Renaissance visual arts—mostly painting—were born. This revolution occurred independently both in Italy and the Netherlands. A common trend linked the movement: the conquest of the visible world beyond the limits of the international Gothic style. As far as architecture, sculpture, and paintings are concerned, there is no doubt that the Renaissance began in Florence around 1400 A.D. and reached its peak with the famous Florentine multilevel, multifaceted artists, Leonardo da Vinci and Michelangelo.

The Contemporary Movements in the Visual Arts

The period in art history that refers to the Modern Era covers roughly the 19th and 20th centuries. During this period the appreciation of art for art's sake found its full application. As is evident by the arts created during these two centuries, they express the concern of the artists. The arts, no longer linked to the church, state, or any political institution, had an autonomous function, serving the needs and reflecting the aspirations of the artists and the people rather than promoting the established institutions. For example, the arrival of photography in 1850 released painting from its role in portraits, thus leaving painting to be developed on its own. The development of theories in sciences and technology documents the notion that seeing should not mean believing and common sense is not always what it seems to be.

An important factor in the study of the history of the Modern Era is that during its relatively short period of time a plethora of artistic movements were created stemming from various ideas, theories, and political ideologists such as realism (1840), impressionism (1860), symbolism (1880), feminism (1903), cubism (1907), expressionism (1908), futurism (1908), vorticism (1912), mono-objectivism (1912), neoplasticism (1916), Dadaism (1916), surrealism (1920), neorealism (1920), and existentialism (1940; Funk & Wagnalls New Encyclopedia, 1972). Of all these artistic movements, no one alone characterizes the arts of the Modern Era. However, these movements were strongly identifiable and have collectively nourished the concept of art for art's sake. Art found a mass audience, liberating artists from these artistic periods, and provided a freedom of vision to the artists unparalleled by any previous historical period of the arts of the Western world. Above all, the arts generated the revolution of the contemporary visual communication media art products of photography, film, television, holography, and computer graphics.

PHILOSOPHY, NATURE, AND CHARACTERISTICS OF THE ARTS

The study of the evolution of the arts of the cultures of the Western world provides a basic understanding of the ways societies function. It does not explain, however, the meaning of the arts and their significance in shaping the foundations of society. To properly understand the significance of the arts, it is necessary to examine the philosophies that have been used to explain, evaluate, and interpret the arts; it is also important to obtain a clear understanding of the nature of the arts and their various characteristics. Once examined, the three elements—philosophy, nature, and character—reveal a certain pattern that helps us to identify more readily the major movements, theories, and messages carried by the arts.

A striking example from the prehistoric era is the Venus of Willendorf, a primitive statue with intricate carvings of an overweight woman with exaggerated curves. It is believed that this artifact symbolizes the cult of the Earth Mother. The characteristics attributed to the worship of this female figure go beyond a matriarchal structure of the people that created it to an understanding of them as worshipers of the moon. To follow the Earth Mother is to explore a certain mysticism. It is to enjoy, live in, and admire nature. Emotion and intuition draw her flock to worship her emotive icon (see Fig. 7.5).

The rise of ancient Greek civilization heralded the age of reason. People sought to explain their life, not merely to experience it. The cult of Apollo and the Sky Father replaced the Earth Mother cult. As people withdrew from the forests and nature and started building cities and states, their tools were no longer their feelings and intuition, but logic and reason. Their philosophical approaches changed. At the peak of ancient Greek civilization, with such philosophers as Plato and Aristotle, linear logic and rationality became the standards for beauty and perfection. As evidenced by the Parthenon, in the Acropolis of Athens, lines, planes, and angles replaced the curves and circles that were previously the ideal forms in the arts (see Fig. 7.1).

The Sky Father still dominates the culture of the Western world where logic and urban landscapes still rule, yet the cult of Earth Mother is also present, creating a serious tension in our culture, evident by the rising feminist liberation mystique. These two contradictory beliefs and the tensions they create are deeply rooted in the culture and the arts of the Western world. When we look at the different movements of the arts we begin to detect a continuous swing between the austere, calculated perfection of classical Greek tradition and the less serious, free, and expansive forms representative of the cult of the Earth Mother.

FIG. 7.5. Venus of Willendorf.

The Philosophy of Art

Another important factor in the study of composition is the philosophy of the arts. The history and the philosophy of the arts collectively form the interdisciplinary field of aesthetics, although each one has grown from its own roots. As Detels (1993) suggested:

> Each of these pursuits springs from the same quintessential human need to "know thyself." With art, we seek knowledge of ourselves and our surrounding world through engagement with the sensual domain of symbols and perception. With philosophy we seek knowledge through the process of questioning and defining ourselves and the world. With history, we seek knowledge through preserving and studying the past, including the art. (p. 363)

A brief review of the major philosophical bases on which the arts of the Western world were created underlines the importance of the philosophy of the arts in the study of composition and aesthetics.

For the ancient Greeks, peoples' proportions and their power of rational thought were heralded as the ultimate test of beauty and truth. Protagoras of Abdera (c. 480–411 B.C.) was the first Greek philosopher who theorized that man is the measure of all things. It was not the human body itself that exerted beauty, but its perfect proportions (Barash, 1985). Logic and scale became the measuring sticks by which craftsmanship was elevated to artistry. The philosophy of the Greeks of that time was that art must be pure and rational. This notion, also held during the Hellenistic Era, dictated that all sculptures should consist of proportions and measurements of the human body. They were less concerned with finding meaning in beauty and more interested in finding beauty in form. The austere and linear architecture of the ancient Greek and Roman temples also indicates the basic philosophy of beauty in the form; although these were geometrically beautiful, they were not user friendly. Gods were worshiped through their structural form, through their functional human qualities. The ancient Greek philosophers in particular believed that art's meaning lay strictly in the beauty of its form. They were more concerned with explaining art's mandatory components than exploring the philosophies that govern the arts. Art was not an end in itself but a means to understand the ultimate truth. The detailed account of the rules governing all three forms of poetry—epic, dramatic, and lyric—as analyzed by Aristotle in *Poetics*, is a vivid example of what the ancient Greek philosophers thought about art. Some art historians (Huyghe, 1962; Novitz, 1990) have suggested that the ancient Greek philosophers' artistic ideals were based on works whose physical features were the transparent link to enlightenment. Beauty was to be extracted from nature, from the raw materials in which beauty is latent. With the help of reason and intellect these raw materials can release beauty. This philosophical view dominated the arts of the Western world for a long time.

Christianity and the Christian dogma that followed were based on and maintained by several Greek beliefs. As far as the meaning and the place of the arts were concerned, the early Christians believed that the arts were essentially nonutilitarian. Some scholars view early Christian art as graven and superfluous, producing tempting or even outright devilish images (Barash, 1985). An explanation for this negative view of early Christian artistry could be the fact that art soon encompassed certain characteristics attributed to the Earth Mother, thus losing, gradually, the ancient thought and its stringent rules. In its place a much more mystical art was created, not based on perfection measured by human proportions; instead, it scaled to divine heights. The immaterial and the mystical became the central object of artistic endeavor. At that time art philosophy considered the nature of the arts and its impact on the soul and some scholars (Huyghe, 1962) suggest that early Christian art was more of a schematic language in which illusion replaced imitation.

It is interesting how this opposition, the replacement of these two basic ideals of what art should express, has affected the development of the arts of the Western culture. After the Middle Ages, when art took on its spiritual characteristics and therefore was much more mystical, the Renaissance brought back its methodological, human-centered depictions. In fact, all artistic movements of the Western world can be seen as movements between these two ideals of imitation and representation to illusion and allusion. At that time, however, art was always used in a utilitarian manner and had a practical purpose. Architecture focused on the practical uses of the buildings; paintings and sculptures were decorative rather than monuments in their own right; theater and music were, for the most part, subservient elements to the Divine Liturgy of the Christian Church.

The contemporary era brought a revolution to the development of the philosophy of art. Until the 19th century, art was considered an expression of a social need—decorative, educational, and spiritual. The arts were not considered, until that time, as entities in their own rights regardless of the compositional rules established and the functions they performed. It was only with the impressionistic and expressionistic movements that the arts began to acquire a meaning of their own. Philosophically speaking, the contemporary era marked the beginning of the holistic approach of the study of the arts that considers all art objects or events as having complete entities of their own. At the end of the 19th century, art for art's sake appeared as a philosophical approach that meant that art had evolved into its own realm. Art had no ties to religion or to reason; it no longer needed to be a simple tool by which one could gain insight into greater truths; it had a truth of its own. A statue's aesthetic elements were not simply the form. They carried a message as well, a content closely connected to the form that justifies the major function it performs.

The 20th century brought yet another important revolution to the philosophy of art influenced by such scientific developments as psychoanalysis, sociopolitical theories such as Marxism, and communication explosions such as mass media, electronic media, and visual communication media. For example, the philosophical basis of criticism is to explore the canvas and even reality through two-dimensional geometry. This geometry followed the traditions of the ancient Greeks, of course, in its search for truth within perfect proportions and linearity. With the abstract movement, the philosophical basis centered on the world of feelings and emotions that was mostly aided by nonrepresentation. The emotional impact of the art on the reviewer and consumer enhanced its form and content.

Although the evolution of art in the Western world has been examined and the basic philosophies of the arts have been reviewed, the nature of the arts still needs to be explored before an outline of the specific functions they performed within the societies that created them is provided.

The Nature of Art

What is art? Art philosophers and aestheticians have written a great deal in their attempt to define art and explain its nature. Obviously, each art form, object, or event must be defined according to its own form and subject matter if it is to be understood. There is, however, some agreement among art philosophers, art analysts, and aestheticians regarding the nature of art. The brief review of the history and philosophy of arts suggests that three dominant concepts define the nature of art as an imitation of life and nature, an expression of the emotions of the artists, and the creation of beauty for its own sake.

For some aestheticians, art is the conscious use of skill, task, and creative imagination in the production of aesthetic objects or events. Here the terms skill, task, and creative imagination of the artists are the fundamental elements that stamp the nature of the art. It is a strong belief of this author that skill is performance acquired by personal experience, continuous study, and intensive observations. These are the basic elements that define and clearly explain the nature of a work of art. For contemporary philosopher Irwin Edman (1939), the nature of art is to interpret life; it is to provide a new experience of life and nature. In his book *Arts and the Man*, Edman (1939) stated that, "art is the name for the whole process of intelligence by which life, understanding its own conditions, turns them to the most interesting or exquisite account" (p. 12). Art helps to shape our understanding of the world, as it often creates it. It is a formative influence in our lives that actually brings things and states of affairs into being (Novitz, 1990).

In his book *Understanding Media: The Extensions of Man*, McLuhan (1964) provided an interesting definition of what art really means. For McLuhan it was in the nature of art to predict the future. Artists have a better grasp of the future because they are able to manipulate new media within the medium's intricate characteristics. We look at and study the works of experimental artists to grasp what will happen in the future. Artists' vision does not only interpret this world, it predicts the next one; for them it is the nature of art to prophesize.

Regardless of how one defines and therefore identifies the nature of the arts, there are three basic processes or acts all arts undertake: (a) the process of constructing the art object or event, (b) the process of presenting it, and (c) the process of responding to the presented art. This threefold process, however, emphasizes yet another aspect in the nature of the arts—communication. The nature of art, whether it is seen as an imitation of nature and life, as an expression of the artist's own emotions and thoughts, or as a creation of beauty for its own sake, is to communicate ideas, feelings, and aspirations. The communicative nature of all arts is an important aspect in the study of aesthetics in general, and television aesthetics in particular, as is discussed later in greater detail.

The Characteristics of Art

Whereas the preceding discussion of the nature of the arts provides definitions as to what is art, the discussion of the character of the arts brings into focus those key elements that contribute to transforming the creative process to an aesthetic experience. What sets art above the crafts or the skills of its practitioners is that it is, above all, an aesthetic experience consisting of feelings of harmony, taste, beauty, catharsis, balance, and unity.

Art is an expression of either the artists, the times, or the culture they live in. However, those feelings and emotions are aesthetic emotions that have been transmitted by memory and by imagination into an integral part of an imaginative creation (Chiari, 1977). Art is a coherent and imaginative representation of life, a symbolic entity embodying more or less universal aspects of truth. Even if art escaped the strict confines that the ancient Greeks placed in its meaning, it still permits itself certain of the goals the Greek philosophers gave it. For example, Aristotle maintained that true art suggests the hidden meaning of things and not their appearance. This profound truth contains the true reality of things that are not evident in their appearance (Chiari, 1977).

It is, therefore, obvious why art has been linked to religion for so many centuries. The creative nature of art demands that it examine the myths, fantasies, and dreams of the culture from which it emerges. Like religion, it speaks of the sacred and the profound. Logic and science may provide their own explanations of society, but it is art and religion that give it meaning and expression. The ancient Greek drama sprang from the worship of the deity of Dionysus. Attending the performance of a drama in ancient Greek theatre was a social as well as a religious event and involvement. Attending the Divine Liturgy in the Greek Orthodox Church today is also a social as well as a religious undertaking.

Another important characteristic of art is the meaning it conveys. The ancient Greek doctrine that the ultimate duty of art is to express truth should be enhanced with the contemporary belief that art must carry meaning that explains the inexplicable. It is an inherent characteristic of art to look at various objects, issues, events, and beliefs, and to provide new insights and new approaches.

All arts, and particularly the fine arts, are products of human action that, through craftsmanship exhibited in sensory and formal exploitation of materials, presents for interpretation a possible world segment having mimetic relationships to the actual world with significant potentiality for aesthetic contemplation to all those who receive them (Walhout, 1986). Therefore, we see that the threefold process rooted in the nature of the arts is also one of the key elements that characterizes all arts: (a) they are made by humans, (b) they use a medium to transform them, and (c) they cause or require a response.

However, an art form must be more than merely the cause of a response. That response must be of various levels and human dimensions, emotional, communicative, educational, informative, and aesthetic. The more such levels the art response reaches, the more significant are the three key elements that characterize and, indeed, value all fine arts: their significant content (or message), form (or medium), and impact on their receivers (Metallinos, 1973).

As suggested by some art analysts (Chiari, 1977; Dudek, 1990), a great work of art, in addition to these unique features, must have an identifiable entity all its own separated from morality, religion, politics, and even from human interest and drama. Fine art is an object or event on its own, from contemplation or apprehension of which one may derive an awareness of potential truth and an enriching experience. It must be a unique entity in itself, be it sculpture, painting, architecture, or poetry. The collective contribution of all these elements that make the work of art to be a work in itself, rooted in reality, expressing transmitted reality, and yet capable of transcending it, foremost characterizes the work of art (Chiari, 1977).

FUNCTIONS AND CATEGORIES OF THE ARTS

An inside view of the various functions of the arts is a prerequisite for the establishment of the criteria that examine their artistic elements. Consequently, a review of the major functions that all art forms perform, in general terms, is important before we concentrate on the particular functions of the specific category of the arts. It is emphasized, however, that as the previous review of the history of the arts overlapped with the review of the various philosophies that created them, and the discussion of the nature of the arts overlapped with that of the analysis of the character of the arts, so does the discussion of the functions performed by the arts overlap occasionally with the nature and character of the arts. Such overlapping seems to be unavoidable because these terms mean different things to different people and the literature in the field often uses these terms interchangeably. In this text, the word *function* is synonymous to the word *operate*. The functions of the arts are discussed here in terms of the ways they operate within the society.

Overlapping, also, is unavoidable in the categorization of the arts of the Western world because the boundaries that separate one art form from the other are not readily distinctive and are often misinterpreted. I have proceeded to enlist the arts under some broad genres, aware that readers may have different opinions. However, categorization does not always mean elimination. The placement of the various art forms under various homogeneous groupings was necessary. It allows a closer observation and stimulates discussion of their commonalities and differences, thus enhancing our understanding of them.

The Functions of the Arts

The literature on this subject is immense. How do the arts operate? What are their roles in society? What do they do to the artists who create them, the society that nourishes them, and the individual recipients? Are the arts necessary? These are some of the key questions that need to be answered if the functions performed by the arts are to be understood—regardless of the complexity of the task on hand. These questions touch on all fields of the arts and sciences and refer to all levels of humanities, social, and behavior sciences. For an artist, the arts communicate or externalize feelings. For the behavioral scientist the arts, among other things, help to purge the inner emotions. For the sociologist, the arts reflect the norms under which society operates, and so on.

The most interesting observation regarding the functions of the arts (closest to the present discussion) was given by the philosopher (and professor of aesthetics) Edman (1939) who stated:

> These three functions, intensification, clarification, and interpretation of experience, the arts fulfill in various degrees. For many observers the arts are simply sensuous excitements and delights. For others they are the language in which the human spirit has clarified to itself the meaning of the world. For many the arts are the sensuously enticing and emotionally moving vehicles of great total visions of experience. (p. 34)

This is, of course, the concept of contextualism of the arts, and the basis for the development of the contextualistic theory discussed in the introduction of this book.

All art forms, according to Edman (1939), follow this process of intensification, clarification, and interpretation of experience starting from the physiological sensation (as the first step), moving toward the speculative and reflective stages (as the second step), and ending up in interpreting the meaning of the phenomena (as the final step). All art forms undergo these stages to interpret the phenomena and, therefore, these three basic functions justify the role of the arts for mankind.

Herein only the communicative, social, and psychological (including persuasive and aesthetic) functions of the arts are broadly examined.

The Communicative Function of the Arts. Because all art forms operate as the catalysts for the interpretation of the complex phenomena in life, all art forms communicate. Scientists confirm that prehistoric people created the first cave paintings to send messages to their fellow people to communicate their fears of the wild animals confronting them. Regardless of the cause of the communication act (e.g., fear, joy, and hatred), the fact remains that people have always felt the need to communicate their ideas and feelings.

The previous reviews of the history of the arts, their philosophy, nature, and character indicate how important it was for humankind to create language, architecture, painting, sculpture, drama, dance, and poetry to communicate and to share ideas and emotions with others. When the pure utilitarian purpose of an artifact was fulfilled, its communicative operation took over to be later succeeded by a higher task: aesthetic appreciation.

An art form created by an artist who uses it as a medium to send messages to receivers establishes the parameter of the communication process: sender–medium–receiver (SMR). It is for this reason that communication is one of the most important functions of the arts of the Western world.

The Social Function of the Arts. It is known that the arts of a society reflect the culture and indicate the conditions that govern the society. Artists, as members of the society, reflect, in their arts, the society's beliefs, ideologies, and concerns. Sociological and anthropological studies confirm that the artists and the societies they live in are interrelated, inspiring, and that they influence each other. As Benedic (1935) stated (at the time that the field of sociology was in its fullest development), "Society in its full sense ... is never an entity separable from the individuals who compose it. No individual can arrive at the threshold of his potentialities without a culture in which he participates. Conversely, no civilization has in it any element which, in the last analysis is not the contribution of an individual" (p. 253).

The analysis, therefore, of a theatrical play, a musical synthesis, a poem, or a painting should not ignore the decisive factor of this interrelationship of the artists and their societies and the roles each of these forces play in the development of the art forms.

More than the illustration of the culture of a society, a fundamental role of the arts of a society is to project the individual artist's perceptions of various trends, to point out the existing contradictions, and to predict the outcome of both. In this respect the artists are, above all, unique individuals who maintain their freedom of expression within the confines of the society they live in. As the creation and appreciation of an art form are individual endeavors, for the most part, so is the artistic creation the result of a force that motivates human instinct. This distinction of artistic expressions and social norms is the vital force in the creation of a society's culture.

A firm supporter of this belief is Read (1966), a polymorphic scholar who merged anthropology, psychology, history, and aesthetics in his search for the functions of the arts. Read (1966) saw the social function of the arts to be the nourishing of a dialectic activity in which the arts through reason (thesis) and imagination (antithesis) result in a new unity (synthesis) that reconciles these two contradictions. Read (1966) concluded that:

> We begin by admitting that art can only develop in a favorable climate of social amenities and cultural aspirations but art is not something which can be imposed on a culture, like a certificate of responsibility. Actually, it is like a spark springing at the right moment, between two opposite poles one of which is the individual, the other the society. The individual expression is a socially valid symbol or myth. (p. 3)

Furthermore, the arts of a culture operate as the education catalysts of that society. Such has been the function of theater, poetry, painting, and so on, in all Western societies. The educational function of the arts is even more evident today with the creation of museums, art galleries, and such educational activities as art exhibits and art festivals.

In this sense, artists assume the role of educators among other things, providing ideas and a superstructure of the mind, sometimes rational, sometimes intuitive, yet always challenging and progressive. As Read (1966) stated in his discussion of the social function of the artist as a prophet and an educator, "His primary function and the only function which gives him his unique faculties, is his capacity to materialize the instinctual life of the deepest levels of the mind" (p. 95).

In summary, the social function of the arts of a society is not only to mirror the culture but expands to include the prophecies, contradictions, and beliefs of the artists who compare them.

The Psychological Function of the Arts. The most important factor that needs to be considered in the study of the compositional principles of the arts is the psychological function performed by all art forms to a greater or lesser degree. It is a vast subject that needs to be examined on various levels and from different points of view as it has been the main concern of philosophers starting with Plato (Dickie, 1971), Aristotle (Ferguson, 1961), art historians, critics, aestheticians such as Read (1966) and Edman (1939), and psychologists such as Freud (1949), Maslow (1954), and Arnheim (1966).

The basic human need that seems to be universal and eternal is to externalize and to share with others inner intuitions, thoughts, and emotions. It is the main reason human beings invented the various art forms. This fundamental human activity is purely behavioral in its nature and can be better explained by the considerably new field of study that Arnheim (1966) called psychology of art. The inner forces that drive the artists to create works of art, the numerous effects the arts have on their receivers, and the human need to vicariously purge one's emotions and to experience the beautiful are fundamental behavioral activities involving the artists as creators, the society as receivers, and the media as carriers and as institutions.

It is beyond the scope of the present discussion to examine these areas in relation to their psychological functions. Briefly, however, it must be pointed out that on the issue regarding the psychology of the artists, Freud (1949) provided adequate psychoanalysis of the behavior of the artists. Concerning the behavior of the receivers of a society, Read (1966), among others, provided adequate discussion of the subject. On the issue of the art forms as media or carriers of the aspirations and the inspirations of the arts, Arnheim (1969a) provided a thorough analysis to the extent that visual communication media arts are concerned. Here, the discussion centers on the following four main psychological functions of the arts: to persuade, to purge the emotions, to satisfy or fulfill fundamental human needs, and to provide aesthetic experience.

The power of the arts to persuade or to convince and often to impose on the receivers certain beliefs is one of their oldest and most powerful psychological functions. Plato was the first to recognize the seductive power of the arts and for this reason he excluded both the artists (as irrational persuaders) and the arts (as suspicious modes of emotional expressions) from his ideal republic.

Throughout the history of the arts we have striking examples of their persuasive power in generating religious beliefs, as was true with Christianity and the Christian dogma, or forming political ideologies as was the case with the Roman and Byzantine Empires early on and the formation of Communism in the Eastern Bloc and imperialism in the countries of the Western world later.

The persuasive power of the arts is indisputable as was also shown by Brown (1963) and O'Keefe (1990). In his book *Techniques of Persuasion*, Brown (1963) equated persuasion with propaganda that expands to cover communication, politics, religion, commerce, and even science. He emphasized the power of the various art forms produced by modern people's media of television, radio, cinema, newspapers, paperback books, and magazines, to influence the minds and reach the psyche of their viewers or readers to the point of total indoctrination and brainwashing by certain persuasive techniques. On the other hand O'Keefe (1990), in his book *Persuasion: Theory and Research*, provided the means, the medicine to cure the bad influence of persuasion in general, suggesting that attitudes and beliefs can change through various systematic techniques of persuasion.

Another significant psychological function of the arts is to involve receivers emotionally by allowing them to evolve their emotions vicariously. Aristotle was the first philosopher and art analyst who recognized this significant function of the arts. In his book *Poetics* (Ferguson, 1961), Aristotle discussed the three types of poetry—the epic, dramatic, and lyric—and examined primarily dramatic poetry (both in comedies and tragedies). In his definition of tragedy, Aristotle (Ferguson, 1961) specifically pointed out the therapeutic (purgatory) function of tragedy for the spectators when he stated that, "Tragedy, then, is an imitation of action that is serious, complete, and of certain magnitude; in language embellished with each kind of artistic ornament, the several kinds of being found in separate parts of the play; in the form of action, not of narrative; through pity and fear effecting the proper purgation of these emotions" (p. 7).

Various forms of art, particularly comedy, storytelling, and more recently situation comedies abundantly found in today's television programming, evoke laughter that unquestionably has a therapeutic (in the Aristotelian sense) purpose. Laughter releases hidden feelings of sorrow, anger, hostility, and desperation. The arts can evoke these emotions when the spectator vicariously lives fictitious situations.

Indisputable, also, is the psychological function of the arts regarding the fulfillment of several fundamental human needs, motives, and desires. The theory that all art forms, some more, some less, are created by artists who live in a particular cultural environment to satisfy some basic needs and desires of their fellow beings was first formalized by Maslow (1954) in his book *Motivation and Personality* and later verified by his students Aronoff (1967) and Goble (1971).

In his book *Psychological Needs and Cultural Systems: A Case Study*, Aronoff (1967) examined Maslow's general theory and considered it a basic factor in the study of the organization of social and psychological systems and stated that, "It can be demonstrated that the organization of both social and psychological systems is the final product of these independent factors: environment, institutional determinants, and organismically based psychological needs" (p. v). This statement is significant because it demonstrates how central the psychological functions of the arts are for the development of a society. Furthermore, it shows how significant Maslow's concepts of basic human needs (physiological, safety, love and belongingness, self-esteem, and self-actualization) were for the study of the arts in general. Maslow's theory of basic needs was more fully analyzed, discussed, and developed by Goble (1971) in his book *The Third Force*, which provides specific examples drawn from known art forms to support this theory. It is for this particular reason that this source is used here, rather than Maslow's (1954) original book, which does not have sufficient empirical data to support this very significant theory.

By examining the theories of various art forms of the Western world, we can see how numerous and how important these terms were for the development of civilization. For example, a person's basic need to see evil punished and virtue rewarded; the need to reminisce about the good old days; the need to communicate with others; the need to create fictional characters; the need to see authority figures exonerated or diminished, depending on their actions; the need to idealize the mundane; the need for emotional outlet, and so on. These are a handful of cases and only a few examples of the basic human needs fulfilled by the various forms of art. This concept was further developed by Hyde (1970) in the syllabus of his course *History and Analysis of the Public Arts*.

However, the most important function of the arts, from a psychological point of view, is to provide an aesthetic experience to both the artist or creator and the receiver. In fact, some critics of the arts suggest that the process of creating a work of art should bring a delight, an inner satisfaction, and an aesthetic pleasure to its creator. Equally, the outcome and the exposure of that product and that process to the receivers should create these emotions. In support of the aesthetic pleasures the arts fulfill, Edman (1939) stated: "Art is another name for intelligence, which in an ordered Society would function over the whole of men's concerns, as it functions happily now in those scattered works we call beautiful, in those happy moments we call aesthetic pleasure" (p. 35).

Maslow's theory of the psychological needs fulfilled by the arts goes as far as to suggest that beauty helps one to feel better, healthier, and happier (Goble, 1971). Here we see that the psychological state of the mind acts on the biological state of the body and supports the notion mentioned previously that all human senses are at work in the processes of perception, recognition, and aesthetic appreciation resulting from our encounter with the various art forms; it is a total human involvement.

In summary, the most significant function of the arts is the psychological, and among the various psychological functions of the arts, the persuasive, therapeutic, or emotive, the fulfillment of basic human needs and desires, and the aesthetic experience are the most important.

The Categories of the Arts

The vast development of the arts of Western civilization during the last 3,000 years makes the classification of the arts very difficult. Political movements, religious beliefs, scientific discoveries, traveling explorations, industrial developments, and information communication technology explosions have caused the development of a vast number of art forms that are as difficult to categorize as they are to define. Furthermore, the art classification task becomes even more difficult today due to the rapid developments of media technologies. This section provides a broad classification of the arts, distinguishes the various forms of popular arts, and briefly examines the visual communication media arts, specifically the various television genres.

A Broad Classification of the Arts. The discussion of the characteristics of the arts suggest that an art form is characterized by a threefold process: the act of creating the art form, the art of presenting it, and the art of responding to it. Although in some art forms like painting, theater, and music, this process can occur simultaneously, there are nevertheless three distinct stages that must be taken and three different agents involved in this process: the artist(s), the medium, and the receiver(s). Furthermore, it was stated that to consider an event or an object significantly artistic it must surpass the ordinary and provide uniqueness and significance in its message (content), in its medium (form), and for its audience (impact). Equally important (before any general classification of the arts is made), is to discuss their various functions, whether they are communicative, utilitarian, social, psychological, and so on.

On the basis of these parameters the arts fall into two major categories: fine arts and applied arts. Whereas fine arts such as architecture, painting, sculpture, poetry, music, theater, photography, and film have been defined as art created primarily as an aesthetic expression to be contemplated and enjoyed for its own sake, applied art such as decorative designs of manufactured items, advertising, commercial art, and plastic art is defined as utilitarian. It is used as an instrument for other activities (such as decoration), which remain subservient to the function of the objects, media, and events they promote. All popular commercial and industrial arts are applied arts. The significance of the applied artist's version is limited to the media, the product, or the industrial needs it encompasses. Fine arts, on the other hand, are broader in the intellectual, emotional, and aesthetic scopes extending their significance to all three areas: their message, medium, and recipients.

It is, of course, obvious that the distinction between fine arts and applied arts remains a line that is difficult to draw. There are some applied art objects or events that occasionally meet the requirements of the fine arts and vice versa; the fine arts appeal to a small and elite public, whereas the applied arts appeal to a large, broader, and more general public.

The Popular Arts. The advent of mass media (or media of mass communication) such as newspapers, magazines, comic books, radio, and television created the phenomenon of a mass society and a mass culture (particularly in North America) and this, in turn, marked the genesis of the so-called popular arts, public arts, pop arts, and electronic media arts. They are placed under the broader umbrella of applied arts as these art forms, for the most part, are subservient to the particular media, agents, industry, or interest groups that generate and carry them.

Popular arts are art objects or events that have been brought to the attention of the general public, the vast majority of the people of a society, by way of the mass media. Risoner (1977) believed that it is the mass media that make the popular arts popular, and indeed possible. In this sense, any fine art becomes popular as long as it is presented through a medium like television, which reaches a vast population as it has happened with many so-called classic art forms from the paintings of the great masters (Rembrandt, van Gogh, da Vinci, Michelangelo) to the plays of Shakespeare, Chekhov, Moliére, and Ibsen.

Public arts are art objects or events that have been publicly exposed and have become readily available to the general public. Seldes (1957) explained their major characteristics, stating that, "The Public Arts are popular to the extent of being almost universally acceptable. They tend to be more and more professionalized, less and less to be practiced privately. The public arts are offered to the public as a whole, not to any segment of it" (pp. 557–561).

It is obvious that such arts are all those art events, for the most part, presented through the medium of television, bringing to the general public literary art forms such as poetry, performing art events such as theatrical plays, music concerts, and art exhibits.

Pop arts are art objects or events derived from commercial art forms or even commercial motives and are characterized by outsized replicas of items of mass culture such as comic strip panels, food and popular brand names, and in the case of musical performances the pop artists that appeal to massive audiences. The paintings of Andy Warhol and the concerts of Michael Jackson are considered the finest examples of pop arts.

The Visual Communication Media Arts. This term refers to those art forms that communicate primarily with pictures, although the elements of sound (audio) and motion are equally present in most of them. Depending on the media that produce them and their degree of satisfaction, some of the visual communication media arts fall under the category of the fine arts (painting, sculpture, architecture, photography, motion pictures); others, such as television, holography, video, and computer arts, fall under the category of applied arts.

The recently formed academic fields of visual literacy and media aesthetics deal with the study of visual images in general, and media images in particular. They have given us many empirical research studies on the visual communication media, particularly television.

The visual communication media most popular today are television (in both of its forms, conventional or network television, and video arts), computer art, and holography. These three visual communication media are referred to briefly and the different categories of television genres are examined in the following.

Holography is an interesting visual communication medium that is still in the developing stage and almost totally subservient to commercial use. It is more an example of a three-dimensional image-making medium than a pure art object. However, it has the potential to develop into a unique form of fine art as soon as it is liberated from its commercial usage, succeeds in advancing its technology so that its holographic images become more refined, and manages to expand its usage to other media such as television, creating holographic television, a promising, three-dimensional medium of the future as it is proposed by the three-dimensional television researchers at MIT (Brand, 1987).

Computer art is a visual communication media art generated by computers and projected either through the computer's own screen or through television. It has been in existence since 1956 and has marked its presence in many public displays (electronic, three-dimensional, synthetic image). Computer art is subservient to the appropriate computer program required and its commercial use, particularly in advertising. Although there exist admirable examples of computer drawings, lettering, and images in computer genres, some of which are extremely imaginative, computer art remains synthetic and mechanical, unable yet to arouse the interest and to stimulate the aesthetic curiosity of the average viewer.

Television, as a visual communication medium, is one of the most powerful media ever invented and one of the most popular worldwide. The images produced by television and the subsequent events, shows, or programs presented combine all three elements: sight (vision), sound (audio), and motion (kinesis). Because television as a medium presents many different kinds of programs we must distinguish television from radio and network television programs from video art.

Television is thought of as the conventional broadcast industry medium that provides a variety of programs for mass consumption (Metallinos, 1985a). Socioeconomic factors during the early years of North American television have formed this attitude toward television. Consequently, television is thought of as a commercial broadcasting medium whose goals are to maximize its profit by providing low-level information, entertainment, and educational programs to the masses. The basis on which various commercial television programs was founded are advertisements and commercials.

Video, on the other hand, is exactly the opposite. The basis on which video was founded was to counterattack the low-quality programming of conventional television and to use the creative potentials of the medium. As Price (1972) suggested:

> Unlike educational TV, video is made (1) by anyone, not just those who have financial control over the airwaves; (2) by individuals rather than committees or corporations formed when lots of cast is involved; and (3) for personal reasons, art, therapy, or learning, not as a pretext for nationwide bursts of ads. Most video also exploits the unique capabilities of the medium, rather than uses it to imitate other forms. (p. 9)

These two different camps created a vast variety of programs that fall under one or the other of these two categories. Any discussion of the artistic potential and the possible aesthetic merits of these programs must not ignore these two different points of view on which they have been created.

Another distinction that needs to be made before underlining and enlisting the various categories of television programs is the existence of the Public Broadcasting System in North America. It was created by the U.S. government and consumer protection groups in order to (a) break the monopolistic trend of commercial broadcasting of low-quality, low-budget programming; (b) provide alternative programming free from commercial interruptions in such needed areas as children's programs, documentary shows, and the performing arts such as theater productions; and (c) provide the forum for experimentation and artistic expression through and by the use of the television medium. Any analysis of the artistic potential and the aesthetic merits of a television program should consider its educational broadcasting origin.

On the basis, therefore, of the three broader categories of television programming we can enlist the various television genres developed over the last 70 years with the understanding that some of these categories often overlap.

1. *Conventional or network television programs developed (including Public Broadcasting Service).* The bulk of network television programming is centered on entertainment and information and less time is devoted to education. Education has become a province of noncommercial television (public broadcasting). In the entertainment category there are the following general genres (Summers & Summers, 1966, p. 218):

- Soap operas, both daytime and nighttime (e.g., *General Hospital* or *Dallas*).
- Detective stories, police- and crime-oriented programs (e.g., *The Untouchables*, *Hill Street Blues*, *Law and Order*).
- Situation comedies or comedy variety shows (e.g., *The Cosby Show*, *The Carol Burnett Show*).
- Variety shows (e.g., *The Ed Sullivan Show*).
- Talk shows (e.g., *The Tonight Show*).
- Adventure, suspense programs (e.g., *Young Indiana Jones*).
- Science fiction programs (e.g., *Star Trek*, *Seaquest DSV*).
- Musical variety shows (e.g., *The Lawrence Welk Show*).
- General or anthology drama shows (e.g., *Dr. Quinn, Medicine Woman*).
- Westerns (e.g., *Gunsmoke, Bonanza*).
- Game shows (e.g., *Wheel of Fortune, Jeopardy*).
- Specials or personality shows (e.g., *The Bob Hope Special*).
- Theatrical feature films and movies made for television (e.g., *Movies of the Week*).

2. *Information.* In the information category, commercial television has developed the following types of programs:

- News: Regular broadcast day and evening news, news magazine shows such as *60 Minutes* and *20/20*, and news specials.
- Public affairs: Panel discussions with various personalities, interviews, and documentaries.
- Sports: Regular sportscasts, event sportscasts, sports commentaries, interviews, and panel discussion shows.

It should be emphasized that some news, public affairs, and sports programs lean more toward entertainment than information. In fact, today, for some observers, sports no longer belong to the information television genre, but to the entertainment genre (Head & Sterling, 1990). This is generally true with most conventional television programs whose motives are to maximize profits at all costs.

3. *Education*. In the educational category, conventional television does not have many programs to offer, particularly after the strong presence of the Public Broadcasting Service, pay and closed-circuit television, and video art. Nevertheless, the following types of programs were developed:

- Children's television programs: This includes a great variety of programs that touch on all areas of education, entertainment, and information for children (e.g., animated cartoons, *Sesame Street*).
- Documentary programs: This also assumes many different forms depending on the subject matter exposed or the production techniques they employed (e.g., *The World of War*, *Civil War*).
- Docudramas or semidocumentary programs: This category uses both genres, drama and documentary, to present the contribution of great historical figures (e.g., *Abraham Lincoln*) and at the same time to entertain the viewers.
- Instructional and/or educational programs: This is a large category of television programs, mostly produced by Educational Television (ETV), covering both pure instructional or how-to kinds of programs (e.g., cooking shows, building houses shows, teaching of language) and educational programs dealing with history, theater, art analysis, teaching animal shows, and natural phenomena (e.g., *The National Geographic Specials*, *Nature*, *Cosmos*).
- Religious programs: This category, developed primarily by various religious groups or televangelists, is broadcast primarily on Sundays on either network, pay, or private broadcasting stations. These programs assume various forms such as religious interviews, talk shows, direct broadcasting of religious ceremonies, and sermons of known televangelists.
- Performing arts shows: This form of educational television programming is also developed by the Public Broadcasting System (PBS) in the United States, the British Broadcasting Corporation (BBC) in England, and the Canadian Broadcasting Corporation (CBC) in Canada, to broadcast and promote the great performances of theatrical plays, classical music concerts, operas, and ballets. All three networks either plainly broadcast great performances (e.g., *Live From the Kennedy Center*) or adopt and reproduce for the medium of television the works of famous playwrights (e.g., the Shakespearean plays produced by the BBC).

Although the entertaining and often the information nature of these educational television programs are overwhelming, it should be pointed out that the educational aspects of these programs are the concern of the producers, and indeed, the basic philosophy of the broadcasting networks that present them.

4. *Video Art Category.* Literary sources available on the subject suggest that the potentials of the medium of television to produce and present programs of aesthetic merit were found in video art. In less than 20 years, video art has become a medium in which a youngster competent in high technology can define a complex personality with surprising originality (Price, 1972).

The expressive potential of video art is unlimited and has shown that it can reach high levels of appreciation. As Price (1972) stated, "Because the apparatus offers hundreds of pictorial techniques that can be combined with an unpredictable subject and sound, to produce a nearly infinite number of combinations, it has great expressive potential" (p. 91).

The basic assumptions that spark the development of video art, identify their nature, and outline their major characteristics are as follows: (a) video art is an extension of the visual communication media arts of the past (traditional) and the present (television); (b) video art is a self-expression of the artists who create it, and who, in some cases are also the performers and the subjects of their art; and (c) video art is a unique art form that uses the features of the medium that carries it. As Price (1972) suggested, "Reducing TV to mere light levels, flowing electrons, blur, and continual change, artists have gradually narrowed down the areas that seem uniquely video. It is here that the best art takes place, our culture suggests. Not imitation film, but genuine video, not theatrical photographs, but live videos" (p. 93). (d) Video art is an electronic art created by a flowing metamorphosis of images rather than mechanically static changes; (e) video art can be either an event, as it is presented in a video program, or an object, as is the case with the television sets creating an art exhibit; and (f) the ultimate objective of video art is to provide an everlasting aesthetic experience rather than to provoke temporary emotional reaction.

It is impossible to provide an accurate classification of the existing video arts not only because of their enormous varieties, but also because of the great overlap among them. Furthermore, the creative process constantly shifts its central emphasis from the art's subject matter to the medium's particular use. Whereas some pioneer video artists experiment with the aspect of time in their video artistry (Paik, 1976), others emphasize space as the element of artistic exploration (Reich, 1976). Certain video artists such as Tatti (1976) use current electronic technology and traditional materials and equipment to produce their video art forms. Some video art is surrealistic in its appearance, mostly due to overuse of special video effects (Schneider & Korot, 1976), and computer-generated images with video special effects (Downey, 1976). Music Television (MTV) uses music and music personalities to promote records, combining striking special effects, colors, camera angles, and editing techniques.

Video art is a growing visual communication media genre with promising future developments and great aesthetic potential, particularly for those using images generated by computers with the unique features of television technology.

In summary, the discussion of the various visual communication media arts, particularly those art forms generated by television (both conventional and video) provides a starting point to the study and the understanding of their basic compositional structure. In building the field of television aesthetics, the basic understanding of the various categories of visual communication media arts is warranted.

8

▼▼▼▼▼▼▼

Introduction to Criticism

Knowledge of the historical and philosophical developments of the arts of the Western world and an understanding of their nature, character, functions, and categories provide the necessary background information and suggest the relevant nomenclature to examine the subject of art criticism. Furthermore, the discussions on the nature, character, functions, and categories of the visual communication media arts provide the basic materials for the building of the foundation of criticism of the visual communication media in general, and television criticism in particular, which is precisely the purpose of this chapter.

Criticism encompasses a vast area of human interaction and activity. Therefore, the discussion in this chapter is selective. The connection of literary and art criticism to criticism of the visual communication media arts constitutes the necessary bridge between the aural or linear mode of expression and the visual or vertical mode of expression in the evaluation of visual messages, two concepts that are further developed here.

The history of criticism divides into literary criticism and art criticism, both of which started with Aristotle's *Poetics*, a comprehensive treatise that discloses the imitative nature of dramatic and epic poetry (both of which are literary forms) and the unity of dramatic action necessary to tragedy (a performing or visual art form; Ferguson, 1961). It is, therefore, only natural that the development of the criteria of visual communication media arts could not ignore their dual roots of literary criticism (linear) and visual art criticism (vertical).

The first section of this chapter further explains this duality of literary and art criticisms and points out the areas in which they are connected by examining the nature, the role, and the functions of art criticism.

162

The second section discusses the various approaches to criticism in general, and art criticism in particular. It provides an overall view of the development of the various schools of criticism of the arts depending on their nature, character, and the functions they perform, the ideology they represent, and the particular discipline that examines them.

The last section looks at the existing movements toward the establishment of visual communication media arts criticism, examines the developed critical approaches to various television genres, and applies the established criteria to existing television programs.

THE NATURE, ROLE, AND FUNCTIONS OF ART CRITICISM

This section centers on the following questions: What is the nature of critical inquiry? What is the role (or the objective) of art criticism? Which functions (or purposes) does art criticism perform?

There is a coherent sequence and hierarchy in the discussion of these three terms as they relate to the subject of art criticism. For example, the nature of art criticism defines the terms, provides the elements, and underlines the key factors that constitute art criticism. The role of art criticism outlines the purpose and discusses the character assumed by art criticism. The function of art criticism concerns itself with the objective and the scope of art criticism and explains how it operates as an academic discourse.

The Nature of Art Criticism

The intrinsic characteristic and form of art criticism (in short the nature of art criticism), is to describe, analyze, evaluate, and interpret works of literature and art. The nature of critical inquiry, particularly art criticism, is to investigate through the elaborate process of analysis, evaluation, and interpretation, whether all the elements that constitute a work of art are in place.

This threefold process of art criticism presents a continuous and progressive conflict in each of these stages. For example, if it is the nature of art criticism to analyze (describe) the structure of an art form, what specific form should the analysis take? Furthermore, if the nature of art criticism is to evaluate (judge) a work of art, on what specific judgment should the evaluation be made? Finally, because the premise of art criticism is to interpret the particular art form, who will provide the interpretation? How can subjective comments become objective suggestions? In short, is it the nature of art criticism to provide objective interpretation to a subjective evaluation?

This important issue has caused considerable discussion among art critics, aestheticians, and philosophers. Beardsley (1958), for example, recognized this conflict and argued that:

The fact that critics do often give objective reasons for their critical evaluations is noteworthy, for it shows that they think of their evaluations as the sort of thing reasons can and should be given for. But, this fact does not by itself settle philosophical probes about normative criticism; indeed, it creates them. For to give a reason for a statement is to claim that anyone who accepts the reason ought to accept the statement, or at least be inclined to accept it. And the justice of this claim must always rest upon some underlying principle of reasoning. (p. 470)

Beardsley (1958) went on to develop specific theories stemming from the nature of critical argumentation such as the "performative theory of critical argument" (pp. 473–474), the "emotive theory" (pp. 474–478), "relativism" (pp. 478–483), and the "argument for inflexibility" (pp. 487–489), which go beyond the scope of the present discussion because they refer to the nature of all critical arguments, not art criticism in particular.

The nature of art criticism is to provide appropriate arguments for each form of art it evaluates. This presupposes that art criticism should have a specific structure. However, there are two views that conflict over whether art criticism should have a specific structure. The first view, as supported by Kostelanetz (1985), dismisses having strict, implemented guidelines from which to evaluate an artwork because, as he stated: "Criticism must seek its values through particular instances—works, artists, and art movements— rather than through the application of rules formulated by criticism in advance of the works" (p. 194). Such criticism tends to be more subjective in its evaluation of the artwork and thrives in democratically ruled societies that allow freedom of expression.

On the other hand, the traditional school of thought embraces the more stringent concept of having a set of criteria, a sort of rulebook, a canon that would outline how a work of art should be evaluated. The basic position of this view is that art must be evaluated according to specific critical rules in an objectively formulated manner. Such criticism of the arts presents a serious problem in totalitarian societies in which the rules are dictated by the state itself. As Eagleton (1984) stated: "You can criticize with assurance as long as the critical institution itself is thought to be problematic. Once that institution is thrown into question, then one would expect individual acts of criticism to become self-doubting and mottled" (p. 37).

To be able to rely on an already formulated means of evaluation might be reassuring—as the modern mind is tempted to end its suspense by affirm- ing systems of value, including aesthetic systems—but it is equally dangerous. In a totalitarian society where the future course of events is already decided and charted, standards of judgment are imposed on artworks to serve the society's political agenda, thus using art as a means of propaganda, as ex- perienced in the arts produced by Stalin's Soviet Union or Hitler's Third Reich. It is, therefore, dangerous to rely on rulebooks as to what is acceptable or deemed worthy because it lessens one's ability to judge for oneself, undermining the presence of original and innovative critical ideas.

However, it is equally dangerous (and often detrimental to the creative process) if uncertainty and instability characterize the society and the institutions that produce artworks. The criteria that evaluate art forms are influenced by the society's state of affairs, contaminating the critical process.

Another important issue concerning the nature of critical inquiry, and art criticism in particular, is the role of language, known also as the grammar of criticism. Art criticism, for the most part, consists of language. It is linear, always in written form, starting with the writings of literary critics. Although it extends to full-fledged written critiques of all fine and performing arts, it is still limited as to the use of language. This presents a serious conflict to the development of criticism of the visual communication arts (and particularly television criticism), because words are limited in describing visuals and it is almost impossible to grasp the essence of the artistic fact with plain words (Isenberg, 1973).

The use of language displays the ultimate facility of critical analysis to any art form and it is, for the time being, the cornerstone of critical expression. Language is the instrument that enables critics to voice their reactions to a work of art. Thus, by analyzing, evaluating, and interpreting the art, they not only introduce it, but foremost provide points of view and insights that are not readily recognizable to the reader or viewer. This is particularly significant to the development of the discipline of aesthetics because the scientific explanation of aesthetic experiences can be mainly accomplished by descriptive terminology and the use of an appropriate nomenclature for a brief explanation of a specific aesthetic experience.

The development of the appropriate grammar, or nomenclature, for the discussion, evaluation, and interpretation of each art form is the natural basis of art criticism. Before an art form can be understood to its fullest, the receiver must have a background knowledge and a vocabulary (or grammar) from which to draw inferences to express a response. The need, therefore, for the development of a critical language for each of the existing art forms is evident. Because many of the visual communication media arts are presently in the developing stage, they borrow the vocabulary and use various grammatical and syntactical terms from media that have similar qualities. This is a logical evolution in the field of criticism, as it is in the evolution of the arts.

Television, among all other visual communication media arts, being in the developing stage of its criticism, is presently borrowing heavily from the grammar of other media arts with similar qualities such as painting, photography, film, and theater. Although television has its own idiosyncrasies and distinct qualities (Adler & Cater, 1975; Metallinos, 1985a; Millerson, 1972; Toogood, 1978; Zettl, 1978), its visual grammar can gain a great deal from the already established visual communication media arts (Greenberg, 1977). Recognition of its uniqueness, limits, and potentials, and the adaptation of pre-existing visual communication arts critical vocabulary should be the natural basis for the development of television criticism, and from that, the academic discipline of television aesthetics. For, as stated in the next section, the development of the appropriate language is fundamental to the establishment of the various approaches to art criticism, and particularly to television criticism.

The Role of Art Criticism

This section briefly discusses the role of art criticism in general, and examines the role of visual communication media arts in particular.

The development of literature and the arts of the Western world owe much to the academic discourses of literary and art criticisms. Each needed and often depended on the other for its growth because it was through critical discourse that we learned the real meaning, the ultimate purpose, and the value of the literary works and artworks. A responsible critique of a novel, a poem, a painting, or a theatrical performance not only describes in detail the message intended by the art form, but compares it with similar ones, evaluates it, and provides explanations about the art and the artist, interpreting the artist's motives and outlining his or her goals.

The significant role of literary and art criticisms is to act as an objective judge, an inspector whose purpose is to make sure that the standards of the art form have been presented. It is not the role of criticism to hold in contempt, to devalue, or to provide only negative comments on the work of art. Instead, a responsible critique provides both the positive and the negative elements of the form under consideration. Some critics overlook this important role and provide one-sided, negative comments on the arts they evaluate. This type of criticism hinders the development of art and should not be a common academic practice.

Another important purpose of criticism of the arts and literature is to convey the message expressed by the particular art forms to the general context and the key issues of the society. In short, it is the role of art criticism to relate the art to the innovations and happenings of the society. As Allen (1987) suggested, "In order to be relevant art criticism today must maintain continuing sensitivity to major characteristics particular to the modern epoch that effects the situation of art including the outlook, rituals, and objectives of those who created it" (p. 45).

Foremost, the role of critical inquiry is to analyze, evaluate, and interpret the particular literary and art forms and bring into focus their idiosyncratic nature and specific merits. As such, criticism must be related and refer only to the particular category of art it discusses. This brings us to the main concern of this study, the discussion of the role of criticism of visual communication media arts.

Visual communication media arts such as painting, photography, film, theater, holography, television, and computer arts each have their own form, elements, and idiosyncrasies, as discussed previously. The role of the visual communication critic is, therefore, to separate, identify, and bring into focus the unique elements of the particular art forms, identified by Tarroni (1979) as *instruments*, *materials*, and *techniques*, and from these unique elements to draw the value judgment for the discussion, evaluation, and interpretation of the particular visual art form.

The literature that identifies these unique elements is vast, covering the entire spectrum (perceptual, cognitive, and aesthetic) of these art forms. Arnheim (1969a, 1969b), in his books *Art and Visual Perception* and *Visual Thinking*, was among the first visual communication media arts analysts to point out how we perceive, recognize, and compose visual arts, suggesting that the elements of balance, shape, form, growth, space, light, color, movement, tension, and expression are fundamental ingredients of all visual communication media art forms. McKim (1980), in his book *Experiences in Visual Thinking*, and Dondis (1973), in her book *A Primer of Visual Literacy*, underlined the unique characteristics of the visual communication media arts falling under the broad categories of representation, abstraction, or symbolism, and synthesized according to such established rules and guidelines as balance, symmetry, regularity, simplicity, and unity. Moholy-Nagy (1969), in his book *Vision in Motion*, and Kepes (1969), in his book *Language of Vision*, were among the first scholars to recognize motion and vision as the fundamental elements expressing the visual communication media arts. Contemporary media scholars such as Millerson (1972) and Zettl (1990) have emphasized the roles of sight (light and color), sound (audio and sound techniques), and motion (in both edited and live media presentations) as unique structural elements of visual communication media arts, and particularly television programs. It is beyond the scope of this discussion to underline the unique elements of each visual communication media art form. What is important and needs emphasis is that a major role and a significant purpose of the visual communication media arts criticism is to discover and bring into focus the unique elements that characterize these media products.

The Functions of Art Criticism

The term *function* is used here to describe the objectives that literary and art criticisms accomplish by virtue of their constitution. The objectives of art criticism are synonymous with the mission, goals, and scope of both criticism and the art critic. The discussion centers on the functions of criticism of visual communication media arts, starting with a general reference to art criticism.

There is an educational function performed by literary and art criticisms in that the critique provides pertinent information about the work. All parts of the critique, but primarily the description and the analysis, usually provide valuable insights with significant educational value. For example, a critique of the theatrical performance of Shakespeare's *Hamlet* usually provides an overview of the psychological, historical, and social issues that led to the writing of the play. This presupposes, of course, that the critic must be knowledgeable in the fields of psychology, history, and social sciences. The educational function of literary and art criticisms is warranted.

A responsible critique of a literary work or an art form assumes, also, an important social function. It must describe how the particular work serves society and what society will gain from the analysis of the particular art form. The critique must expose to the society at large the messages and meanings conveyed by the art form so that those benefiting the society will be applauded and the destructive ones condemned. This makes the mission and the responsibility of the artist very serious and makes the art critic an important social benefactor who helps to preserve cultural standards.

Criticism of the visual communication media arts performs a multitude of additional functions in our complex contemporary society. All visual communication media arts appeal to the masses, and, as such, critics function as the spokespersons of the society. In the past, criticism of the arts served the useful function of stimulating education and learning and maintaining cultural standards. Because the audience for the visual communication media arts was generally smaller and more homogeneous, social commentary was criticism's function. However, with the information explosion brought on by the most powerful of all visual communication media, television, the function of criticism has expanded to serve as a sort of safeguard or barrier. Because the audience is large and heterogeneous, the need is greater than ever to preserve and to create standards of quality and taste. This is a need that has not been fulfilled successfully by contemporary television critics.

The function and one of the main objectives of television criticism is to interpret the society in which the viewer is immersed, not in a quick manner, but with an understanding of the evolution of the human race. In this light, the critique should be able to provide explanations as to why certain trends are popular and others fade away. The television critic, by surveying trends and types of programming, is able to analyze the content of different programs and provide comparative evaluations. The critic also can suggest relationships between these changing forms and the world outside the television screen. If this is done, the public can understand the facts and be in the position to know what causes our viewing habits rather than to accept them blindly. This, however, demands from the television critics vast knowledge of various fields and their function becomes that of educators. As Littlejohn (1975) suggested, "I take it as axiomatic that the good critic of a particular field, a) knows more about the field than most of his readers, b) attends more closely than they do to particular events, and c) is better able to articulate his response" (p. 167).

In all visual communication media arts criticism, the critic's main function is threefold. First, the critic must identify the unique characteristics of the art object or event under investigation. In locating the major characteristics, the critic discusses what specific instruments, materials, and techniques identify the art. This presupposes general knowledge and understanding of the medium that carries the art. Second, the critic must discuss the internal workings of the art form including the analysis of the message, the examination of the technical aspects of the medium, and the intended effect on the receiving end, the audience. Third, the critic must create a system of judging the art by selecting specific criteria stemming from the previous discussion. By performance of these tasks, critic's function, mission, and objectives are accurately met.

In summary, an essential part of the critical process is to know and understand what the nature, role, and functions of art criticism are in general, and visual communication media arts in particular. By having a basic knowledge of these elements, the critic's process of inquiry becomes better organized, more precise, and effective. Rather than simply reacting to a work of art or accepting a critical analysis of an art form as being truthful and responsible, knowing the nature, role, and functions of art criticism provides the student and the viewer of the visual communication media arts with a broader spectrum of these media and the programs they produce.

APPROACHES TO ART CRITICISM

The various schools of thought regarding art criticism, formed over the years as distinct academic discourses, concern this section, which provides a brief review of existing approaches to art criticism, stressing their basic concepts and the critical questions that identify them. It deals with the various approaches to art criticism and bypasses the detailed discussion of the developed categories of art criticism because they are recorded in the literature of art criticism. The purpose of this section is to build the basis on which the visual communication media arts criticism is developed. The categories of criticism of the visual communication media arts are further examined in the next section.

There are as many approaches to art criticism as there are opinions of the art critics who express their own predispositions, backgrounds, disciplines, and objectives. The nature of the critical inquiry (questions raised by art critics) determines the critical approach that decides on what basis the value judgments of the art were formed. Some of the key questions that need to be raised are: Who made the statement? What was the statement? How was the statement made and presented? When was the statement made and to whom was it addressed? Answers to these and other similar questions underline the specific approaches of the critical inquiry and provide the standards of art criticism.

The reason for the selection of such approaches to art criticism as philosophical, anthropological, historical, semiological, sociological, psychological, rhetorical, narrative, and cultural is threefold. First, they are all traditional and academic; they have existed in literature and literary criticism for generations, shaping the culture of the Western world. Second, they are applicable to both criticism and art criticism, thus forming the necessary link that connects literature with the arts. Finally, they have resulted from scientific investigation, verification, and, for the most part, vigorous research undertakings.

The Philosophical Approach to Art Criticism

Using judgments of a philosophical nature, this approach to art criticism stems primarily from the study of philosophy. It is closely related to skepticism and dogmatism and draws from a variety of other academic disciplines such as religion, history, political science, and sociology.

Most of the questions that concern humankind lie in the way in which society looks at its own understanding of certain events. Philosophical critics of the arts draw on such disciplines as, for example, psychology when they wish to make a distinction between actual experience and actual knowledge, and religion when they wish to make a distinction between the real and the idealized.

Among the great philosophers who established the field and formed the philosophical types of questions in art criticism are Plato, Aristotle, Kant, Bergson, Marx, and McLuhan (all discussed in the introduction of this book). An example of a philosophical statement concerning art criticism could be the proverb "Nothing is new under the sun."

The Anthropological Approach to Art Criticism

The anthropological approach stems from the science of anthropology, the study of the physical and cultural characteristics of people and the societies they live in. Whether they connote the principles of physical or cultural anthropology, anthropological archaeology, linguistic or applied anthropology, the anthropological judgments and critical statements are distinct in their approach and necessary for the development of art criticism.

This approach is closely connected to the philosophical as well as sociological approaches in that it also bases its interpretations on the society and its culture. Anthropological critics base much of their rationalization on their knowledge of a specific culture or on the way of life of the people living in that culture; they provide the necessary link between the physical and the cultural characteristics of people of the past with people of the present.

Some famous anthropologists who have contributed, directly or indirectly, to the establishment of art criticism as an academic discourse are David Hume (1711–1776), Lewis Morgan (1816–1881), Leslie White (1910–1972), Julian Stuart (1901–1978), and Margaret Mead (1901–1990). An example of an anthropological statement regarding art could be the proverb, "Man is the measurement of all things."

The Historical Approach to Art Criticism

The historical approach to art criticism is among the older schools of thought and centers on the historic events that caused the development of the particular art forms. The basis of criticism of the arts is drawn from history, the discipline that systematically studies past events that affect nations, institutions, arts, and sciences. Past events that cause the development of a particular art form are central to the development of the historical approach to art criticism. This approach is considered synonymous with sociological or conventional art criticism (Scodari & Thorpe, 1992) because history and the events of the past, the institutions and their structures, and the presence of the arts are all interrelated. Historical circumstances that helped the different art forms to develop are the standards for the evaluation of the arts of the historical approach.

Among the great historians who assisted in the development of this particular approach to art criticism are Herodotus, Thucydides, Horace, and Julius Caesar during the ancient Greek and Roman civilizations; the Italian Giovani Batista of the Age of the Enlightenment; the Briton Edward Gibbon; the Frenchman Voltaire; the Scotsman David Hume; the German Oswald Spengler; and the American Arthur Meier Schlesinger, to mention only a few. The art historian uses statements that reflect history such as, "The play is a record of the disaster that occurred at . . . such and such a time" or "The painting belongs to the Romantic Era."

The Semiological Approach to Art Criticism

The semiological approach to art criticism is created from semiotics, the scientific study of signs that refers to how meanings are created and communicated within a culture and examines the laws and conditions under which signs and symbols (including words) assume their meaning. Purely a scientific approach to art criticism, it is mainly concerned with the development of knowledge about language to increase its influences in scientific as well as artistic works.

Developed originally by the Swiss philologist Ferdinand de Saussure (1857–1913), semiotics created the branches of pragmatics, syntactic, and semiotic semantics, the last of which generated the distinct field of general semantics with the pioneering works of the British philologist Stephan Ullman (1914–1980). Among the contemporary proponents of the semiological approach to criticism are Eco (1976) and Hayakawa (1964) and of the semiological approach to media arts criticism Fiske (1987) and Scodari and Thorpe (1992).

The basic premise of this approach to art criticism is that the more one understands the sign system of one's culture, the more easily one perceives their meaning in society. Limiting the meaning of specific signs involves many constraints and this modifies the meanings of special signs. Because all art forms are symbolic, this approach is both scientific in its scope and fundamental for the development of criticism of the visual communication media arts. A semiologist critic of the arts asks such questions as, "What is the ideology behind the use of black and white instead of color in this particular picture?"

The Sociological Approach to Art Criticism

The sociological approach to art criticism is the most widely used and well-established approach that examines the arts through a framework of social relations and functions. Sociological critics often concern themselves with changes and assimilations that take place in society and point out how various institutions are affected by the arts. The basis for their concerns lies in classes, roles, status, and races and may combine stereotypes and particular lifestyles that may be considered taboo. It is the concern of the sociological critic of the arts to point out to what extent the arts express the society's basic ideology and the degree to which the arts gratify the needs and wants of the citizens.

Sociology has a long history of development, interconnected with philosophy, history, psychology, political science, and art. Among the key figures in the development of the discipline were the French philosopher Augustine Comte (1798–1857), the British philosopher Herbert Spencer (1820–1903), the German political philosopher Karl Marx (1818–1883), the German sociologist Max Weber (1881–1961), and the French sociologist Emile Durkheim (1858–1917). The major issues confronting these sociologists were the interrelationships of changes in the economic structure, political organization, kinship system, and moral basis; and the causes, consequences, and interrelationships between such phenomena as industrialization, capitalism, science, technological change, bureaucracy, democracy, extended family structures, and the most recent phenomenon of the transformation of communities into mass societies (Funk & Wagnalls New Encyclopedia, 1972). From these issues and phenomena, the sociological critic of the arts draws the standards of criticism. An example of a sociological statement of an art critic of this approach is, "Does the architecture of City Hall reflect the austere government of the state?"

The Psychological Approach to Art Criticism

This school of thought is fundamental to the construction of judgments for the analysis of the arts and refers to the psychological impact (overt or covert) the arts have on society and individuals alike. Stemming from the behavioral sciences, the psychological approach to art criticism assumes different forms such as psychoanalysis (referring to the emotional states of the individual), social psychology (concerning the relationships of the individual and the society), the Maslowean or motivational psychology (referring to the basic human needs, wants, and desires the arts fulfill), and perceptual and cognitive psychologies. The basic issues concerning all forms of this approach to art criticism are feeling, emotions, learning, perception, cognition, motivation, needs, memory, and thinking. These and other similar issues form the standards of criticism of the psychological approach of the arts.

The enormous psychological impact of the arts on individuals and their institutions was first pointed out by Plato in *The Republic* and Aristotle in the *Poetics*, and later by the father of psychology and the founder of psychoanalysis, Sigmund Freud (1856–1939), and his pupils and followers Carl Jung (1875–1961), Alfred Adler (1870–1937), Otto Rank (1884–1939), and Abraham Maslow (1954), to point out only those directly related to this discussion. The powerful impact of the arts on individuals and society has generated the ethical and the aesthetic approaches of art criticism in which the standards of criticism are based, heavily, on ethics and taste of the art forms (Scodari & Thorpe, 1992). An art critic who approaches the evaluation and interpretation of the art form from the psychological point of view usually asks questions regarding the emotional effects of the art such as, "What causes the melancholic behavior of Hamlet?"

The Rhetorical Approach to Art Criticism

Used first by Protagoras and Aristotle, who created rhetoric as an art form in public speaking (oratory), modified, reformed, and continuously used through the centuries, this approach to art criticism has been widely adopted by the various media art forms starting with speech and storytelling in the fine arts category and expanding to cover such art forms as film and television (Rybacki & Rybacki, 1991). It is the most traditional of the critiques of the arts and the most descriptive because it draws its standards from such traditional rhetorical schemata or techniques of persuasion as *ethos*, or ethical standards, *pathos*, or truth, and *logos*, or narrative standards, regardless of the art and the medium that carries it. Foremost, the rhetorical approach includes all the protagonists involved in the act of creating, transforming, and responding to the art such as the sender, the medium, and the receiver.

This approach is also closely related to and is considered synonymous with persuasion in that they both attempt to use the threefold process to draw the attention, consideration, and involvement of their audiences at all costs, ethical or aesthetic. Although rhetoric as a formal study of oratory gained great success during the ancient Greek and Roman civilizations, the Middle Ages, and the Renaissance (when the subject of rhetoric was among the first three to be taught—the other two being grammar and logic), it drastically declined as a scientific study in subsequent years until it found its broad application in semantics and other visual communication media arts, as discussed in the next section. The rhetorical critic of the arts imposes mostly personal question such as, "Why did the music of the Beatles appeal to the baby boomers?"

The Narrative Approach to Art Criticism

The narrative approach to criticism draws the major standards for the analysis, evaluation, and interpretation of an artwork from the way the story is told. The narrative approach, however, goes beyond the fundamental communicative purpose of the arts to tell a story. It combines the artistry of narrating with that of persuasion to discover the truth. The reaffirmation of existing ideas and images, their revitalization or reinforcement, the purification of ideas and images, and their evisceration are, according to Fisher (1987), the goals of the narrative approach to criticism. Being a by-product of the rhetorical approach, this approach uses the rhetorical structure of discourse and storytelling to evaluate the art form. However, the narrative approach considers the message, the story's content, separate from the form, the medium of discourse (Rybacki & Rybacki, 1991).

The origins of the narrative form of criticism of the arts are found in Aristotle's *Poetics*, in which the three forms of poetry are analyzed and the characteristics of epic and dramatic narration (or plot) are described (Ferguson, 1961). It maintained its presence in art criticism mostly under the auspices of the rhetorical approach to criticism and arrived at the 20th century revitalized, defined, and established as a separate discourse by such proponents as Fisher (1987), Chatman (1978), Deming (1985), Lewis (1987), Martin (1986), and Smith (1988), all of whom acknowledge its appropriate application to all visual communication media arts, and particularly film and television programs. An example of a critical statement of this approach to art criticism could be, "Was the story of the show as truthful as it was believable?"

The Cultural Approach to Art Criticism

The cultural approach to art criticism was rather recently developed as a means to explain the impact of mass communication media in creating popular culture and forming the meanings of contemporary society. As Rybacki and Rybacki (1991) stated: "Cultural approaches to criticism examine the creation and distribution of meaning in contemporary society" (p. 131).

Critics of this approach form their standards of interpretation from observed trends and movements such as civil rights, antinuclear and environmental movements, and even from products of such communication media as film, television, music, books, magazines, and newspapers (Rybacki & Rybacki, 1991). Because the criteria are drawn from a great variety of cultural observations and mass media programs, the cultural approach to art criticism is divided into various schools stemming from the specific cultural phenomena, ideologies, movements, or issues such as the feminist approach, the Marxist approach, the capitalist approach, the audience-centered approach, and the Jungian/psychological approach (Bywater & Sobchack, 1989; Rybacki & Rybacki, 1991; Scodari & Thorpe, 1992). Each of these separate schools develops a model that represents the values and ideologies (feminist, Marxist, capitalist) inherent in them. This way, practically all art forms and primarily all television programs can be discussed, analyzed, evaluated, and interpreted by the critics of this approach. An example of a question that identifies the value judgments of this approach could be, "What philosophical and/or ideological forces generated the feminist movement?" Among the founders and proponents of the cultural approach to art criticism are Allen (1987), Davies, Farrell, and Mathews (1982), Stewart, Smith, and Denton (1984), and Rybacki and Rybacki (1991).

In summary, the discussion of the existing approaches to art criticism helps to build the foundations for the establishment of the various distinct categories of art criticism; it provides the theoretical basis necessary for the development of the visual communication media arts criticism that follows.

VISUAL COMMUNICATION MEDIA ARTS CRITICISM

This section examines the movements toward the establishment of visual communication media arts criticism stemming from the previous discussion of the approaches to art criticism as the necessary link between these two art categories. Specifically, this section reviews the major characteristics of the visual communication media arts and the criteria for their evaluation, examines the developed critical approaches to existing television genres, and attempts an application of the critical approaches to the existing television genres.

Standards for the Evaluation of Visual Communication Media Art Forms

Any meaningful discussion as to what constitutes the standards for the evaluation of a particular film or television program must start first with an understanding of the generic terms *media, media program, communication media,* and *visual arts media*, to mention only the most commonly used terms in media criticism. The responsible critic or evaluator of such commonly produced visual communication media art forms as film and television programs should obtain solid background information on these terms in all their ramifications. Because these terms have been defined and discussed earlier in this book, the basic concepts of these terms are reviewed as they relate to the creation of the standards for media criticism.

It is commonly accepted that the term *media* "generally refers to channels that convey messages for mass audience, as well as to the primary electronic channels that mediate communication in other context" (Scodari & Thorpe, 1992, p. 4). The television medium, therefore, that concerns us here, is a mass audience-oriented medium, mediating or communicating messages to a vast audience. This factor is crucial for the development of television criticism, as discussed later.

Media programs such as films and television programs are the products produced by the media of film and television. The threefold process of producing, transmitting, and presenting television programs involves a vast number of institutions, people, and activities that must be considered. For example, the production process of television programs involves the establishment of powerful corporate television networks and media institutions with people working in the business, technology, and creative areas of the medium. Knowledge and understanding of the production units and the laws that govern them as institutions are necessary in media criticism. The transmission process of television programs decides the means by which they reach the viewers (e.g., regular broadcast cable television, closed-circuit and pay television, or satellite direct broadcasting), and this, in turn, decides the nature and the content of the programs in relation to their intended audience. The presentation process of the televised program is yet another key factor that media criticism must consider because it decides the scheduling of the particular program, which, in turn, determines the very nature of it.

The generic term *communication media* in the context of this discussion refers to the ultimate purpose of all media, and particularly television, to mediate or communicate messages to a vast audience. The communicative purpose of the medium, therefore, is unquestionable. It is emphasized that the mass media, and particularly television, are susceptible to a greater number of obstacles that interfere and hinder the communication process. For example, it could be that the cause of the breakdown of smooth and effective communication occurs in the sender or message, in cases in which the issues are not clearly presented. It could be that the images, technologically and artistically, are not clear representations of the intended message, in which case it is the medium that causes the breakdown of the communication act. Or perhaps the audience, at the receiving end of the communication process, were not ready or capable of receiving the mediated message and, therefore, remained unmotivated by the program. However, the most significant factor that should not be ignored is the indirect feedback communicated by television viewers, which often results in switching of the channels, anger, or disappointment, all of which cause the breakdown of the communication process. The features shown in the visual communication media model illustrate the areas in which the communication process is vulnerable and can easily interfere as destructive noise (see Fig. 8.1).

The television program is a visual communication media artifact that incorporates images, sounds, and motion. The popular visual (sight) communication media of film and television, for the most part, consist of live (moving) images enhanced with voices (sound), three elements unique to these two media that constitute the basis for the critical evaluation of the programs they produce. Visual images tell the story; depending on the way they are presented on the screen (e.g., long shots, close-ups, zoom ins) and the sequence they follow, pictures constitute the narrative aspect of the program. The television program critics must be aware of both the technology and the artistry involved in the production of the images of the program. The narrative text, known as *script*, with other natural or added sounds, supports the visual images to tell the story; they assist in the development of the characters and help to establish the atmosphere of the program. Naturally, television program critics must have knowledge of script writing, story and character developments, the functions performed by various sounds, and the technology and artistry involved in the production of the program. The motion of the image creates the scene of liveliness and reality on the screen and gives depth to the pictures. Critics must explain how motion helps to create the program, technologically and artistically, and they must acknowledge the overall importance of motion in the perception, recognition, and artistic success of the television program.

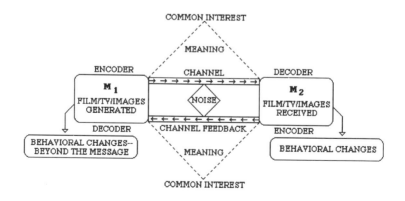

FIG. 8.1. A model of the visual communication.

In summary, the definitions of the generic terms of media, media programs, communication media, and visual media arts are able to provide the basic critical standards for the evaluation of the products of the visual communication media.

Approaches to Television Criticism

Television criticism emerged from the traditional studies of art communications, mass media, popular or public arts such as video and film. Although not fully developed, one can find in today's literature a great variety of sources discussing television critical methods, inquiry techniques, reviews, reports, and commentaries that are termed, collectively, approaches to television criticism.

The serious efforts during the last 50 years of a number of television scholars (critics, observers, researchers, and communicators such as Adler & Cater, 1975a, 1975b; Fiske, 1987; Hadas, 1962; McLuhan, 1964; Newcomb, 1974, 1987a; Rybacki & Rybacki, 1991; Scodari & Thorpe, 1992; Seldes, 1956, 1961; Shayon, 1962, 1971; Smith, 1980; Vande Berg & Wenner, 1991) have resulted in the formation of the many television criticism methods summarized and reviewed in the following. They are approaches, rather than genuine critical methods in three ways: (a) they assume their names mainly through the analysis of the message or content of the programs; (b) they attempt to include all types, forms, and categories of television programs—from television commercials to television spots and game shows—a task that is often superfluous; and (c) they briefly, if at all, refer to the medium of television as a form that uses various artistic techniques such as lighting, framing, editing, and audio to shape the content of the message. Unless the emphasis of television criticism shifts from its present horizontal or content orientation to a vertical one, television criticism as an academic discourse will not be achieved. We can talk about existing approaches to television criticism but we cannot, and we should not, yet, talk about fully developed television criticism as we do film and theater criticisms.

The Journalistic Approach to Television Criticism. The journalistic approach to television criticism, is the oldest approach to television criticism consisting of reviews, commentaries, reports, opinions, and short essays on various kinds of television programs. The major characteristics of the journalistic approach to visual communication media arts in general, and to television in particular, are as follows: (a) they are not traditional literary critiques but mostly subjective opinions, reviews, and comments; (b) they are addressed and tailored to the mass audience and readers of the major newspapers, or popular magazines in which they appear mostly to entertain; and (c) they are concerned mainly with the sociological aspects of the program message and seldom, if at all, refer to its artistic merits.

Examples of the journalistic approach to television criticism can be found in popular North American newspapers such as *The New York Times*, *The Washington Post*, *The Saturday Review*, *The Los Angeles Times*, and *The Globe and Mail* and magazines like *The New Yorker*, *TV Guide*, *Variety*, *Newsweek*, *Maclean's*, and *Time*.

Although the overall contribution of journalists to the development of television criticism is for the most part positive (Himmelstein, 1981), the journalistic approach to television criticism still leaves out important elements of critical inquiry that hinder its development as a responsible academic discourse. As Vande Berg and Wenner (1991) concluded, "Today, however, where there are serious attempts by journalistic writers to do television criticism, the average journalistic critic probably comes closer to meeting the ideal. In general, though, most journalistic writing falls somewhat short of what television criticism should be" (p. 8).

A striking example of how journalistic writing does not meet the standards of critical inquiry is Wolfe's (1985) book *Jolts: The TV Wasteland and the Canadian Oasis*. Wolfe, a Canadian journalistic television critic, attempted to analyze the content of U.S. and Canadian television genres, across the board, resulting in a series of unsupported opinions on the social context of the popular television programs of the two countries (Metallinos, 1991a).

The Sociological Approach to Television Criticism. This approach to television criticism is among the most popular and the most traditional in that it concerns itself with the conventional sociological analysis of the content or message of different television programs. It derives its origins from the sociological approach to literature and art criticisms discussed earlier; it refers to the various social issues, rules, relationships, and procedures contained in the film and television scripts; it interprets the effects of the programs' social issues on the viewers (Vande Berg & Wenner, 1991). In its broader adaptation and use, this approach to television criticism considers television programming (particularly the popular ones in prime time, situation comedies, and detective stories) as the catalyst of the socialization process of the mass society and the one that influences the social, occupational, economic, and other types of behavior occurrences of individual viewers (Berger, 1982; McQuail, 1969; Sklar, 1980).

The sociological approach to television criticism is an important one in that it deals with the significant issues of the society and it often predicts the effects the program's content will have on the individual viewers, thus stimulating serious, exciting, and effective public debates. However, this approach is limited in its scope because it (a) centers its efforts primarily on issues that refer to society, stripping the content to its minimum; (b) omits discussions on production techniques used, thus ignoring the role of the medium in mediating the message; and (c) downplays the role of the medium as a vehicle with any potential artistic and aesthetic merits.

The Historical Approach to Television Criticism. From the various literary sources that acknowledge the historical approach to television criticism and discuss its objectives, there are three that have a special significance to this discussion. Newcomb (1987b), in his analysis of the elements that may contribute to the development of the aesthetics of television, suggested history to be one and stated that, "We should examine the common elements that enable television to be seen as something more than a transmission device for other forms. Three elements seem to be highly developed in this process and unite, in varying degrees, other aspects of the television aesthetics. They are intimacy, continuity, and history" (p. 614).

Scodari and Thorpe (1992) believed that historical television criticism is an area that is equal to and the same as social criticism in that all historic events occur within a social context and they explained that:

> The social/historical track is one that examines critical objects from the perspective of how they might contribute to the comprehension of ourselves and our society. In this instance, the critic might examine the changes or benchmarks that have occurred over a period of time—the historical events that can be documented as part of this network's culture, particularly as they might reflect the larger culture. (p. 18)

Vande Berg and Wenner (1991) acknowledged the importance of the historical approach to television criticism, discussed its various functions, and underlined its domains. They maintained that, "Historical analyses attempt to assess the roles that technological, economic, political, legal, regulatory, and aesthetic factors have played in the creation, reception, and impact of television texts in a particular society. Historical analyses, then, examine the intersection of producers, texts, and society" (p. 31).

The connection, therefore, of the sociological approach to television criticism with that of the historical is imminent and unavoidable because one crosses over to the domain of the other. As suggested by certain television scholars (Chesebro, 1987; Marc, 1984), it is at this point that the historical approach to television criticism is often confused and limited. As with the historical and sociological approaches to art criticism, the art criteria for each of these approaches are derived from distinct disciplines that carry centuries-old traditions. The historical approach to television criticism that does not maintain such distinctions is bound to be a weak and insufficient discourse.

The Rhetorical Approach to Television Criticism. The rhetorical approach to television criticism is a relatively new one although it is one of the oldest and most traditional among the approaches to literary and art criticisms as previously discussed. Its adaptation to media and particularly to television criticism is rather recent, stemming from the works of communication, rhetoric, and media scholars starting with Burke (1950) and continuing today with the works of Farrell (1989), Foss (1989), Medhurst and Benson (1984), and Smith (1980). Critical studies that examine how media messages are structured to influence audiences belong to this approach (Scodari & Thorpe, 1992). The persuasive aspect of the mediated event is the main concern of the rhetorical approach to television criticism, and it is for this reason that emphasis is given to the way the mediated event, the television program, is structured to achieve maximum persuasive results. As Scodari and Thorpe (1992) explained, "Central to rhetorical analysis of television programs is the examination of television texts as essentially or importantly persuasive—that is, rhetorical, whether the text was intended or not intended to persuade viewers to respond to it by feeling, thinking, or acting in a specific manner" (p. 33).

The rhetorical approach to television criticism is both useful and effective in that: (a) it draws the criteria for the analysis, evaluation, and interpretation of television programs from the structural analysis of the text, and the way by which the media mediates and presents the event, the television message; (b) it is applicable to all forms of television and all formats of television programming; and (c) this approach comes closer to an accepted academic critical discourse, recognized and accepted by all scholars seriously concerned with the development of visual communication media arts criticism in general, and television in particular (Rybacki & Rybacki, 1991).

The Semiological Approach to Television Criticism.   Developed in film studies as a language of cinema, the semiological approach to television criticism looks at the ways the television script is created; it examines the program's structure; it evaluates its effectiveness to communicate the intended meanings. The standards for this approach to television criticism are the codes, metaphors, signs, and syntagmatic structures of the program, all of which derive their origins from the academic discourses of structuralism and semiotics. The symbolic representation of meaning inherent in television pictures is analyzed and evaluated by the semiological approach to television criticism that Vande Berg and Wenner (1991) categorized as a metacritical approach due to its dual origin from structuralism and semiotics.

Although its application to film criticism is both extensive and effective (Bywater & Sobchack, 1989), when adopted by television critics, the semiological approach is limited and ineffective. The reasons for this are: (a) The development of the fiction film scripts exceed, by far, the development of fictional television programs. Therefore, the creation of the language or text of the television program cannot be readily achieved with semiotic analysis. (b) The lack of conventional iconic, indexical, and symbolic signs—in the vast land of television programming—does not, as yet, permit the use of semiotics to evaluate them, as it is easily possible with the established conventional signs and codes of the medium of film. (c) The general low quality of television programming—dictated by its mass entertaining objectives—does not warrant, at this time, evaluation standards as complicated and sophisticated as those proposed by the semiological approach. An indication, perhaps, that television has matured as an art form will come when such an approach is widely adopted and commonly used by television critics.

The Cultural Studies Approach to Television Criticism. There is general agreement among scholars of cultural studies criticism of media arts that this approach is widely spread and covers various disciplines and areas of studies that have developed their own unique theoretical bases. Rybacki and Rybacki (1991), for example, argued that, "Cultural approaches to criticism are most organic methods of communication criticism because they do not depend on a single theory base. Because there are so many possibilities for doing cultural criticism, no single approach can be identified as the cultural approach" (p. 132). So did Vande Berg and Wenner (1991), who pointed out the numerous other areas covered under the broader umbrella of cultural approach to media criticism and stated:

> This approach assumes that ideology, economic structures, and culture are inseparable. This critical perspective is rooted in a combination of neo-Marxist political-economic theory, structuralism and semiotics, and Freudian psychoanalytical theory. This approach examines class, race, and gender issues in television programs by invoking ideology, hegemony, and discourse as central critical constructs. (p. 27)

Scodari and Thorpe (1992) generally agreed on the wide application of the cultural studies approach to media criticism and explained that, "Cultural studies is a broad framework for interpreted research with roots in fields such as anthropology and literature [Carey; Fiske; Hall]. It considers all types of discourse, artifacts, myths, and rituals as texts, through which a shared culture is created, modified, and transformed [Carey, 41–43]" (p. 48). It is precisely for this reason that this approach to criticism is one of the most appropriate and the most applicable ones. It gathers evaluative judgment standards from a great variety of academic disciplines, theories, and cultural movements that strengthen the analysis and validate the critics' interpretation of the program. It covers a vast number of issues (e.g., political, economic, social, ideological, and cultural) found in all television genres today. Finally, this approach to criticism considers equally the significance of the message and the importance of the medium in shaping the message, a concept based on McLuhan's (1964) theory that the presence of the medium creates the message and establishes that the cultural studies approach is the most appropriate and most applicable approach to television criticism.

The Genre Approach to Television Criticism. This approach to television criticism is defined as the inquiry or analysis of television programs with similar formats that have the same central characteristics, themes, and objectives. The standards formed for the analysis, evaluation, and interpretation of television genres are derived from the structural similarities found in the particular format, the comparisons of the program's texts, and the identification of the common elements found in particular television genres such as soap operas, situation comedies, and detective stories (Bywater & Sobchack, 1989; Scodari & Thorpe, 1992; Vande Berg & Wenner, 1991).

Although the roots of this approach are found in literature and film, it has found its wider application and is mainly effective in television program analyses for the following reasons: (a) categorizing and classifying the great variety of television programs created and broadcasted yearly helps the television genre critic to look closer at the shared conventions of the programs, which often are indicators of changes, movements, trends, and other modifications that take place in society; (b) searching for similarities among the various television programs, the genre approach critic provides valuable information on the motives and objectives of the industry and the producer or director who created the program; and (c) this approach to television criticism is intertextual in that the analysis of one text is based on and refers to another (Scodari & Thorpe, 1992).

The Producer's Approach to Television Criticism. This approach to television criticism considers the producer, director, writer, and generally the creators of a particular program to be the basis for the critical inquiry. It is derived from the conventional film analysis known as the *auteurist approach* to film criticism (Bywater & Sobchack, 1989; Scodari & Thorpe, 1992; Vande Berg & Wenner, 1991). The producer's approach is closely related to the genre approach to television criticism in that the same producer, director, and writers of successful television program formats create a series of spin-offs of similar programs. Norman Lear's situation comedies and David Victor's action and adventure shows are examples of the similarities and relationships of these two approaches (Newcomb & Alley, 1983). Today, there are enough network and educational television program producers, directors, and writers who apply their personal approaches to the programs they produce that we can talk of a producer's approach to television criticism because it is mainly the producers who assume the responsibility for the final appearance of the program by hiring the cast, the writers, the director, and the set designers (Newcomb & Alley, 1983; Shanks, 1976).

The purpose of the producer's approach to television criticism, which Vande Berg and Wenner (1991) called "auteur criticism" (p. 31), goes beyond the semantic and syntactic analysis of the similarities of the texts of the television genre under investigation. It extends its purpose to "identify the formal stylistic and thematic signature of a single creator artist—the director, the producer, the writer, the writer-producer" (Vande Berg & Wenner, 1991, p. 3). This, however, presupposes that the producer's approach to television criticism must look for such other traits as the producers' concepts and the development of their personalities, political and social ideologies and beliefs, educational backgrounds, artistic competencies, and involvements. It is an important approach to television criticism that will aid, significantly, the development of television as an art form.

The Narrative Approach to Television Criticism.   The central concern of the television critics of the narrative approach is the analysis, evaluation, and interpretation of the program's story as it is narrated by the text, visuals, and sounds. Because the various narrative elements that constitute a program's storytelling can be drawn from myths, social situations, political figures, dramatic heroes, and a plethora of other circumstances, this approach to television criticism is called narrative to incorporate such other related critical methods found in the literature of criticism as the mythical (Vande Berg & Wenner, 1991), the dramatistic, and the aesthetic (Scodari & Thorpe, 1992).

As stated earlier, the narrative approach to visual communication media arts looks not only at the ways the story is told, but also examines the characters involved, the action, the setting in which the action occurs, the television signs used, the archetypal models of the society, and many other similar elements on which the standards for discussion, analysis, and interpretation are based. They are drawn, according to Vande Berg and Wenner (1991), from such critical questions as:

> What world view—cultural or archetypal models of social identity, values, actions, and structuring is affirmed, in the narrative? What abstract ideas, values, roles, and beliefs are presented as good or evil, heroic or villainous, or natural or unnatural in this narrative? What other opposing characters, settings, and actions are present? In what other environment or past forms has this story been presented? (p. 30)

The overemphasis of this approach to the textual analysis of the content of the program; its general rather than particular look at the television program's plot, characters, and symbolisms; and the conspicuous absence of any meaningful discussion of the production techniques of the program are some of the main drawbacks of this approach to television criticism.

The Ideological Approach to Television Criticism.   The ideological approach to television criticism is built on the ideology inherent in the program's text and on the issues concerning the particular program. As such, this approach draws its standards to perform its particular tasks from a variety of issues such as the (a) *neo-Marxist's ideology* (with emphasis on hegemony of media in society), (b) *hermeneutic ideology* (with emphasis on exegesis, or interpretation of the issues in the program), (c) *structuralistic ideology* (which emphasizes philosophical and anthropological codes inherent in the program), (d) *gender ideology* (which deals with the treatment of gender in the program), (e) *dialogic ideology* (which refers to the dialogic conflict that exists in the text of the program), and (f) *discourse ideology* (which refers to the social and ideological dimensions of the language of the text; Vande Berg & Wenner, 1991).

The existing literary sources on media criticism consider each of these ideologies to constitute a unique critical method, distinct and complete on its own merits. However, this is far too great an ambition on the part of these media criticism scholars. It is unsubstantiated for several reasons: These ideologies are applicable approaches to literary and art criticisms and to such visual communication media arts as photography, film, and theater. However, they cannot apply, as yet, to commercial television programs. These ideologies are found only sporadically in issues discussed in television programming, although their application is warranted when they refer to the television medium as an institution. Finally, none of these ideologies concern themselves with the production aspects, the artistic conventions, and the aesthetic merits of the particular television program.

The ideological approach to television criticism could be an effective means of analysis as long as it draws the criteria for the analysis and evaluation of television programs from more than one of these ideologies.

The Psychological Approach to Television Criticism. The psychological approach to television criticism concerns itself with the psychological impact of the program. Psychological impacts, also called effects or results, are behavioral constructs that are caused by a variety of appeals such as persuasion, change of attitude, morality, perception, motivation, cognition, interpretation, artistic appeal, and a host of others (Scodari & Thorpe, 1992).

Whereas the psychological approach to art criticism is one of the oldest and widely used, the psychological approach to television criticism does not exist as an autonomous critical method in the literature of communication media criticism. Possible explanations for the delay of its full development are the following: (a) The Freudian psychoanalysis of the unidimensional and often shallow characters of the majority of regular television programs such as soap operas, situation comedies, and dramas do not appeal to television analysts who seem to be preoccupied with the role of the medium as an institution in a mass society rather than its potentials as an art form, (b) the various behavioral schools of thought that have been adopted by communication media criticism, such as the Freudian, the Jungian, the Maslowean, and such additional approaches to art criticism as semiological and dramatic, all of which are related closely to the psychological approach, confuse rather than assist and hinder rather than contribute toward the autonomous development of television criticism; and (c) the psychological approach to television criticism must derive its standards for the analysis, evaluation, and interpretation of the program from a great number of psychological constructs. To be ready to discuss a program in terms of its perceptual, cognitive, artistic, motivational, and persuasive elements is a serious undertaking that television critics today are not ready or equipped to assume.

The psychological approach to television criticism should be embraced wholeheartedly by contemporary television critics to assist the medium to achieve its status as a genuine visual communication media art form.

The Visual Literacy Approach to Television Criticism.   The visual literacy approach to film and television criticism stems from the visual communication media arts approach to criticism and centers on the various principles governing media arts such as film and television programs. Visual literacy refers to the area of study that concerns itself with the development of a language and consequently a body of literature with which individuals can communicate and discuss visual signs, symbols, images, and pictures with motion and sounds (Debes & Williams, 1970, 1978; Dondis, 1973). Individuals who learn to read or interpret visual images, who are able to communicate with visual images, or who have developed the ability to search for and to evaluate visual information in the visual communication media arts are said to be visually literate.

Television critics who draw their value judgments for the program from such visual literacy-related constructs as lighting, color, depth, size, framing, focusing, zooming, dissolving, cutting, and fading and the use of analytical, sequential, and sectional editing techniques, and such sound-related constructs as thematic, tonal, historical, or structural techniques, employ the visual literacy approach to television criticism. The main emphasis on (a) the synthesis of visual images, (b) the detailed analysis of the visual image production techniques, and (c) the perceptual, cognitive, and aesthetic effects and impressions of visual images are the main characteristics of the visual literacy approach to television criticism. This approach brings the critique closer to a vertical approach (most appropriate for visual communication media arts), rather than the horizontal content stemming from the linear literacy approach to criticism.

In summary, the approaches to television criticism discussed here constitute the cornerstone for the development of television programs of artistic merits. Some of these approaches are strong and are already being used, as we see next, whereas others are just beginning to emerge. Their effective application to the appropriate television genres will be the ultimate test of their value.

APPLICATION OF CRITICAL APPROACHES
TO TELEVISION GENRES: QUESTIONS
AND ANSWERS

The aforementioned approaches to television criticism have been applied to numerous television programs, sometimes with great success and other times with disappointing results. As expected, this is attributed to the fact that the sources in which television program critiques are published such as newspapers, magazines, journals, academic papers, and books are diversified and the form of presentation or critical style such as reviews, opinions, commentaries, reports, genuine critical analyses, and academic studies is not isomorphic.

From the existing literary sources (books, chapters in books, articles in academic journals that publish academically refereed television program critiques that have adopted a particular approach, as described earlier) included here are critiques representing each of the television genres reported in the literature. This is only a review of the programs and the critical approaches to establish the nature of critical inquiry most suitable for the analysis of the particular television picture. It simply states the particular genre, provides examples, poses the critical questions, and identifies the critical approach most suitable for the analysis of the genre. Certain drawbacks of this analysis are the following: (a) the great overlapping in television program formats carries over and influences the classification of television genres (e.g., the children's program *Sesame Street* is found in both the educational and/or instructional television and in children's television genres); (b) because the issues examined in one program are equally discussed in another, there is an overlapping of themes found in numerous genres that results in applying the same critical approach to more than one genre (e.g., a feminist issue examined by an episode of a soap opera may also be examined by a situation comedy dictating the ideological approach to criticism for the analysis of both genres); and (c) a great number of television genres cannot be considered for academic television criticism because they are not artifacts, they are television events (e.g., talk shows, game shows, religious programs, newscasts, sportscasts, and commercials are information pieces or recordings of events and advertisements), rather than art products with aesthetic merits.

The need, however, to identify the critical approaches most appropriate to each of the existing television genres in general, and its importance for the development of television criticism overrides these drawbacks.

The genres reviewed here are: soap operas and drama series; situation comedies; crime dramas; variety shows; music, music variety, and MTV shows; science fiction, adventure, and horror programs; general or anthology drama shows; specials and personality shows; westerns; theater feature films and movies made for television (miniseries); documentaries and docudramas; educational and instructional television programs; children's television; and televised events such as talk shows, game and quiz shows, religious programs, newscasts, news magazine shows, public affairs programs, sportscasts, and advertisements and commercials.

Soap Operas and Drama Series

Soap operas broadcast during the day or drama series televised in the evening are among the oldest types of programs in network television broadcasting that have assumed their distinct character, established their unique objectives, and gained a central position of dominance in the television programming of North America (Kaminsky & Mahan, 1985).

Examples of daytime soap operas are *All My Children*, *General Hospital*, and *Days of Our Lives*, and of evening and prime time dramas, *Dallas*, *Dynasty*, and *Hotel*.

The basic critical questions for the analysis of the soaps are as follows: (a) Questions regarding the issues explored (e.g., What was the central theme in this week's episode of *Dallas* and how effectively was it approached?), (b) questions regarding the production techniques employed that refer to the use of the medium (e.g., How does the extensive use of *close-up* framing in *Days of Our Lives* affect the building of the program's characters?), and (c) questions regarding the effect of the program on the viewers (e.g., What visual and narrative means did the series *Dallas* use to attract its weekly viewers?).

In addition to the genre approach the visual literacy approach is also appropriate for the analysis, evaluation, and interpretation of all soap operas and drama series. This is because the visual literacy approach equally considers the significance of the issues explored, the production approach in explaining the theme, and the effects of the programs on its specific viewers (Allan, 1987; Timberg, 1987).

Situation Comedies

In North American television programming, situation comedies (sitcoms) have gained a dominant position in prime time on all networks and television stations and rate among the top television programs. Like the drama series, sitcoms constitute one of the oldest and most generic of television genres, keeping their nature, characteristics, and categories intact. However, they have undergone certain changes in their various formats following the social changes in North American societies (Horowitz, 1987).

Examples of situation comedies that held the longest runs and gained enormous popularity in the past are *I Love Lucy*, *All in the Family*, *M.A.S.H.*, *The Mary Tyler Moore Show*, *The Cosby Show*, and *Cheers*, and more recently *Empty Nest*, *Nurses*, *Mad About You*, and *Family Matters*.

The basic critical questions for the analysis of the situation comedies are as follows: (a) questions based on the issues presented in each particular sitcom program category or episode (e.g., How is the issue of gender examined in *Cheers*?), (b) questions based on the videotaping techniques concerning the medium (e.g., How did the placement of Archie Bunker's chair in the center of the living room affect the behavior of his character?), and (c) questions referring to the sitcom audience (e.g., How did the longest running sitcom, *I Love Lucy*, influence its viewers?).

In addition to the genre approach the critical approach also appropriate for the sitcom genre is the ideological one in all of is numerous forms such as *gender*, *discourse*, *ethnographic*, and *hermeneutic* criticism. Such an approach considers the complex nature, the numerous characteristics, and the functions of situation comedies and projects the hidden ideologies of the sitcoms (Deming & Jenkins, 1991).

Crime Dramas

The various detective, police, courtroom, law, and crime-oriented programs are called, collectively, crime dramas (Head & Sterling, 1990); they constitute a unique and popular television genre in existence since the invention of network television programming. Although the central theme is crime and its punishment, this genre appears in different program formats such as crime mysteries, courtroom debates, and police and detective stories investigating criminals as regular, weekly series with tragic, comic, or melodramatic plots.

Examples of such crime drama shows are *Dragnet*, *Perry Mason*, and *The Untouchables* in the past, and more recently *Hill Street Blues*, *Cagney and Lacey*, *The Equalizer*, *L. A. Law*, *Miami Vice*, *Murder She Wrote*, and *Law and Order*.

The basic critical questions for the analysis of crime dramas are as follows: (a) questions regarding the subject matter of the particular show (e.g., How faithfully does *Law and Order* dramatize reality in courtroom debates?), (b) questions regarding the use of the medium to narrate the story (e.g., In what ways do the camera angle placement and subsequent framing help to dramatize the court debates in *L. A. Law*?), and (c) questions regarding the impact of the crime show on the viewers (e.g., What particular elements of the program *The Untouchables* maintained viewers' curiosity for such a long time?).

The critical approach most appropriate for the crime drama genre, in addition to the genre approach (Turner & Sprague, 1991; Vande Berg & Wenner, 1991), is the producer's approach (Thompson, 1991) because most of the crime dramas are spinoffs created and produced by popular television industry personalities.

Variety Shows

Variety shows have a long tradition in the world of North American entertainment starting with the vaudeville theater. Variety shows were adopted by radio, and are carried on by television. All those television programs that include appearances of a great variety of artists and other entertainers constitute the variety show genre that is also among the oldest in television programming. This genre takes on many different forms depending on the television personality that acts as host of the program or on the star of the variety show who performs the various acts of the comic or melodramatic character of the particular show.

Examples of variety shows are the *Ed Sullivan Show*, *The Milton Berle Show*, *The Jack Benny Show*, *The Smothers Brothers*, and *Laugh-In* early on, and recently *The Carol Burnett Show* and *Saturday Night Live*.

The basic critical questions for the analysis of the genre approach are: (a) questions regarding the message or the issues presented in the program (e.g., Other than its entertaining value, what does one learn from *The Ed Sullivan Show*?), (b) questions regarding the use of the television medium (e.g., Why did Ed Sullivan use a real theater to radiotape his program? In what ways did it help the production?), and (c) questions regarding the audience (e.g., Did the live audience of *The Carol Burnett Show* contribute to the success of the show and if so, in what ways?).

The critical approach most appropriate for the analysis of the variety show genre is, of course, the genre approach itself (Ferner, 1991), but the narrative or the producer's approach can also be used effectively; the former because it helps to analyze the structure of the individual arts and the latter because it centers, for the most part, on the creators of the program and on the main characters, hosts, and hostesses.

Music, Music Variety, and MTV Shows

Although some of its programs fall under the variety show genre, some under the great performances specials, and some under the personality shows, the music variety and MTV shows constitute a unique genre. Its main emphasis is music for entertainment and its main objective is to introduce the music or songs of an entertainer, a group of singers, or a music company.

Examples of this genre are the *Boston Pops*, *The Lawrence Welk Show*, *Live From The Kennedy Center*, *The Bing Crosby Show*, and various MTV shows featuring pop and rock singers.

The critical questions and the critical approaches most appropriate for this particular genre are the same as for the variety shows discussed previously. For MTV shows in particular, some suggest that rhetorical criticism could also be employed (Morse, 1991).

Science Fiction, Adventure, and Horror Programs

There is a great variety of television programs with emphasis on science fiction, science fiction and adventure, or science fiction and horror, mystery, and suspense. Collectively these programs constitute the science fiction and horror genre (Kaminsky & Mahan, 1985). The specific subject matter (scientific field), the particular setting in which the mystery takes place (gothic castles, old cellars, dark attics, and cemeteries), and the producer's intent (entertainment, information, or education) all are factors that determine the formats of many science fiction, adventure, and horror programs that have gained enormous popularity and success in network television programming.

Examples of this genre are *Star Trek*, *The Munsters*, *Dr. Who*, *The Incredible Hulk*, and the more recently developed *Star Trek: Deep Space Nine* and *Seaquest DSV*.

The basic critical questions for the analysis of the science fiction adventure and horror genre are: (a) questions referring to the story or message (e.g., What is the overall message of the show *Star Trek: Deep Space Nine?*), (b) questions regarding the medium (e.g., What special effects used in *The Incredible Hulk* metamorphosized the main character from a person to a monster?), and (c) questions regarding the impact of the programs on the viewers (e.g., Why do viewers of science fiction, adventure, and horror programs like to be horrified and emotionally motivated to such extremes?).

The critical approach most appropriate for this genre (in addition to the genre approach to criticism itself), is the psychological approach and specifically what Kaminsky and Mahan (1985) called the "Jungian Approach" (p. 15) because of the enormous psychological impact of the programs of this genre on their viewers.

General or Anthology Drama Shows

The general or anthology drama shows form is an old and well-established genre that some scholars classify as the cultural programs genre because of the generic theatrical performances this genre presents. It originated in Great Britain from the British Broadcasting Corporation with television productions of Shakespearean plays and in the United States with the development of such series as *Play House 90* and continues today with the dramas presented mainly by the Public Broadcasting Systems.

Examples of general or anthology drama shows are *The BBC Theater Presents*, the *Play House 90* series, *Masterpiece Theater*, and *Great Performances*.

The basic critical questions for the analysis of this genre are: (a) questions regarding the topic presented by the program (e.g., What key issues did the *Masterpiece Theater* program *Macbeth* address?), (b) questions referring to the medium usage by the producers and/or directors (e.g., What lighting technique was used in *Hamlet's* scene with the ghost?), and (c) questions regarding the effects of the program on the viewers (e.g., How did the audience respond to the violent nature and the evil attitude of *Richard the Third?*).

The critical approach most appropriate for this genre, in addition to the genre approach, is the psychological and particularly the Maslowean psychological approach that refers to emotional outlet and the aesthetic fulfillment these programs offer to their viewers (Bywater & Sobchack, 1989).

Specials and Personality Shows

This category of television programming refers to the occasional programs that network broadcasting industries have created to attract a vast number of viewers using annual and special events and personalities from the entertainment world as the basis. Their common characteristics and frequent appearance in television programming have given them the status of a separate television genre (Head & Sterling, 1990). In many respects, the special and personality shows are similar to variety programs. Therefore the critical questions that critics of these programs ask are on the same line with those of the variety shows and so are the approaches to criticism most appropriate for the analysis and evaluation of this genre.

Examples of specials and personality types of programs are *The Bob Hope Specials*, *The Miss America Pageant*, *The Academy Awards*, *The Emmy Awards*, and *Charlie Brown's Christmas Special*.

Westerns

In both film and television, western movies and television programs held a predominant place in North American network television programming. They created a unique genre characterized by the struggles of the first settlers of the new world to establish their lives in the rough and hostile frontier. Adventure, war, and cowboy and Indian conflicts are among the numerous subjects of the western programs that dominated the programming of network broadcasting for many years.

Examples of such programs in television are *Gunsmoke*, *Wanted—Dead or Alive*, *Wagon Train*, *Maverick*, and *Bonanza*.

The basic critical questions regarding this genre are: (a) questions regarding the theme or message (e.g., What was the basic issue in the western *Gunsmoke*?), (b) questions regarding the medium (e.g., What shooting setup—camera, lights, microphone—was used on the set of the Ponderosa ranch in *Bonanza*?), and (c) questions regarding the impact of the westerns on their viewers (e.g., Why do viewers around the world enjoy westerns?).

The critical approach most appropriate to westerns, in addition to the genre approach to criticism (Bywater & Sobchack, 1989), is the ideological approach that includes the structural analysis of the text of the show that is deeply rooted in the myths of the West (Write, 1975).

Theater Feature Films, Movies Made for Television, and Miniseries

The adaptation of film and television is more evident with the creation of the television programming genre known as movies and miniseries (Head & Sterling, 1990), in which feature films are shown for an extended time period on television or certain movies made for television are broadcast as feature programs on regular prime time in television.

Examples of such programs are *Roots*, *War and Remembrance*, and *Lonesome Dove*. Due to their similarities with the westerns genre, this genre's basic critical questions and approaches to criticism most suitable for its analysis are the ideological and the genre approaches.

Documentaries and Docudramas

Although these two terms refer to two different kinds of television programs, they are discussed here together because the critical questions and the critical approaches most appropriate for both are the same. Documentary television programs document real events, issues, and conflicts of any sociopolitical or sociocultural nature to the general public (Bluem, 1965), and fall into two major categories: thematic and anthology (Rybacki & Rybacki, 1991). Docudramas, on the other hand, are dramatizations of factual events and of the lives of historic figures (Hoffer & Nelson, 1980). In both of these types of television programming, the documentation, the reality, the accuracy, and the producer's own interpretation are the major concerns of television critics.

Examples of documentaries and docudramas are the BBC series *Kenneth Clark's History of the Western Civilization*; James Burk's *Connections*; the PBS series written, introduced, and narrated by Carl Sagan, *Cosmos*; and the various National Geographic series such as *Inventions and Discoveries* and *The Animal World*; and from the North American television networks such thematic documentaries as *Victory at Sea* and anthologies as *See It Now*, *CBS Reports*, *Missiles of October*, *Washington Behind Closed Doors*, and *Abraham Lincoln*.

The basic questions regarding documentary and docudrama criticism are: (a) questions on the subject matter (e.g., What were the main issues of *Victory at Sea*?), (b) questions regarding the medium usage (e.g., How did the framing and camera angle placement in the debates between U.S. Senator Joseph McCarthy and anchor Edward R. Murrow during the program *See It Now* help to reveal the Senator's ill intentions?), and (c) questions regarding the impact (e.g., In what ways psychologically, socially, economically were the viewers of the program *Missiles of October* affected?).

The most appropriate critical approach for documentaries and docudramas (in addition to the genre approach) is the rhetorical approach to criticism (Rybacki & Rybacki, 1991).

Educational and Instructional Television Programs

The programs that are included in this genre are almost exclusively produced by educational television institutions such as the PBS, the BBC, and the CBC. They are free from commercial interruptions and their main purpose is to provide information of educational or instructional nature. The educational subjects and instructional topics vary, but the main objectives, functions, and characteristics of these programs are similar.

Examples of programs for this genre are (a) educational programs for children such as *Sesame Street, Electric Company*, and *Mr. Roger's Neighborhood*; (b) educational programs for the general public such as *Nova, Nature, Nature of Things*, and *National Geographic Specials*; and (c) instructional and how-to programs for adults such as *Today's Gourmet, Cooking with Master Chefs*, and *Collector's Antiques*.

The critical questions asked by critics of this genre are: (a) questions on the subject explored (e.g., What were the main issues discussed in this week's *Nova*?), (b) questions regarding the production of the program (e.g., What camera placement was used for the show *Today's Gourmet* and how effectively was the program recorded?), and (c) questions regarding the effects of the program on the viewer (e.g., Who are the viewers of the *National Geographic Specials* and what are their reactions to the program's format?).

The critical approach most appropriate for this genre (in addition to the genre approach) is the narrative approach in that these types of programs depend heavily on their educational content, which, in turn, dictates the plot (Rybacki & Rybacki, 1991).

Children's Programs

The great variety of children's television covers such areas as entertainment, instruction, and education. This constitutes a unique genre with a long history, major developments, and enormous success. Such is the degree of children's programs' sophistication that there are different programs for different ages, and within each age group one can find examples of specific entertaining, instructional, or educational programs.

Examples of children's television programs commonly found and produced by both network and educational North American television are *Sesame Street, Electric Company, Mr. Roger's Neighborhood, Bugs Bunny, Wonderland*, and *Batman*.

The basic questions regarding the analysis of the children's programming genre are: (a) questions regarding the subject matter (e.g., What, if any, is the educational value of the program *Batman*?), (b) questions concerning the use of the medium (e.g., Why do cartoons visually attract young children?), and (c) questions regarding the program's impact on its younger viewers (e.g., What did children find in the character of *Pinocchio* that made this cartoon program so popular?).

The most appropriate critical approach to the children's television genre is the genre approach itself for several reasons: (a) children's television programming is vast and has many different categories that could create additional unique genres such as the cartoon, the entertaining, the instructional, the fantasy, and the educational genres; (b) children's television programming differs from one age group to the next, as the understanding and comprehension of children changes with age; and (c) the enormous complexity of children's programming often requires more than one approach for critical analysis and appropriate evaluation of such programs. For some cartoon television critics, the historical approach is most appropriate (Williams, 1991), whereas for others, the sociological approach is suggested (Schrang, 1991).

Televised Events

In the context of this book, talk shows, quiz and game shows, religious programs, newscasts, news and public affairs programs, news magazines, sportscasts, and advertising and/or commercials do not constitute art forms in the Aristotelian sense. They are spectacles but not mimetic in their nature. They are presented by television yet they are information pieces, games of all sorts, round-table talks, and minidocumentaries. They have characters, but they are not fictitious characters as required by a play. They have, for the most part, straightforward narrations or simple performance genres but they do not have theatrical plots structured to involve the spectators and to release them from anxieties built up by the play. They are simply events and recordings of real-life actions that are presented via television for convenience rather than aesthetic purposes.

As such, these genres belong to a unique family of shows called *televised events* because the medium is merely the vehicle that records them in their real environment and presents them on screen. The emphasis in producing these plays is technical and functional rather than artistic and aesthetic.

Examples of televised events are as follows: (a) Talk shows (e.g., *The Today Show*, *Good Morning America*, *The Tonight Show*, *Larry King Live*, and *The Late Show*), (b) game and quiz shows (e.g., *Hollywood Squares*, *Jeopardy*, and *Wheel of Fortune*), (c) religious programs (e.g., *Divine Plan*, *Spirit Alive*, *World Tomorrow*, and *Orthodox Voice*), (d) newscasts, news and public affairs, and news magazine shows (e.g., *Nightline*, *MacNeil–Lehrer Report*, *Meet the Press*, *60 Minutes*, *W5*, and *20/20*), (e) sportscasts (e.g., *Monday Night Football*, *Wide World of Sports*, hockey, bowling, tennis, and golf), and (f) advertising and commercials, which are 5-, 10-, 20-, 30-, or 60-second spots, advertising different products or announcing various events. Commercials appear before, during, and after the regular programs and include such common products as beer, soap, toothpaste, hairspray, cars, and food. They may also announce forthcoming movies and television events.

The literature of television criticism includes critiques on all televised events that employ various critical approaches for their analysis as follows. For certain talk shows, the cultural studies approach (Buxton, 1991) and socio-logical (Banks, 1991) approaches are used; for certain game and quiz shows, the cultural studies (Fiske, 1991) and rhetorical (Williams, 1991) approaches are used; and for certain sportscasts, the ideological (hermeneutic) approach (Duncan & Brummett, 1991) and the ideological (reader response) approach (Wenner, 1991) are used. For certain newscasts and magazine shows the rhe-torical approach (Mumby & Spitzak, 1991) and ideological (mythic) approaches (Campbell, 1991) are used. For certain advertisements and commercials, the ideological (gender) approach (Kervin, 1991), and the ideological (mythic) approach (Crombeck, 1991) are used.

In summary, the applications of the critical approaches to television genres and to televised events, with the appropriate examples of critical questions and programs of genres, provide a profile of the present status of television criticism. Some of the applications are well fitted to these television genres. Televised events could be analyzed by these approaches to television criticism; however, their nature, function, and purpose go beyond the study of the visual communication media products as art forms with traditional aesthetic dimensions.

9
▼▼▼▼▼▼

Applied Rules for Composition
of Television Pictures

The review of the nature, functions, and categories of the arts in chapter 7 and the discussion of criticism's purposes, approaches, and applications to television genres in chapter 8 provide the necessary framework for the close study of the compositional principles pertaining to television. This chapter examines the major formulas (compositional rules or production techniques) that should be employed in creating television programs with unique artistic qualities and aesthetic merits. Specifically, the first section provides a brief review of the debate regarding television as an art form; the second section examines the major compositional principles of the visual communication media arts in general; the third section discusses, in greater detail, the particular rules of composition and production techniques pertaining to television and cites examples of where such techniques are applied.

TELEVISION AS AN ART FORM:
BASIC CONSIDERATIONS

The intense debate among prominent television theorists, critics, and practitioners on the issue of television as an art form and the subsequent question of whether television aesthetics is possible has generated a considerable amount of literature that distinguishes television from other media and underlines its unique features, outlines television's aesthetic potentials, recognizes certain television programs as art products, and establishes the particular compositional principles governing the medium. Therefore, a brief review of some of these debates is necessary before the discussion of the major compositional principles of visual communication media arts.

197

Among the oldest literary sources on the issue of television as an art form that supports the notion that television's unique features, by definition, establish it as an artistic medium, is the pioneer article by Tarroni (1979), *The Aesthetics of Television*. Presented first in 1962 as a conference paper at the International Meeting on Film and Television Teaching organized by UNESCO, this article later appeared in various other publications and was very influential in the support of television aesthetics. It provides the constructs that support specific theories dealing with the use of hardware of television (e.g., lights, cameras, editing, and sound equipment) and the application of software (e.g., lighting, staging/framing, editing, and audio production techniques).

According to Tarroni (1979):

> As soon as an instrument, a material, and a technique become available, man has a new art form at his disposal, at least potentially. This applies, precisely, to television.
>
> In television we have, without any possible doubt, an instrument (the camera and other technical equipment), a material (for after all, sound waves and light waves are themselves a *material*), and a technique (the artist must carry out a series of operations that are by no means identical with those carried out by a film director or the producer of a play. (p. 440)

The British Broadcasting Corporation and the Society of Film and Television Arts (SFTA) are two British institutions that extensively debated the issue of television as an art form with these general results: They developed various production techniques unique to the television medium, they produced outstanding dramatic television programs as unique television art forms, and they generated substantial and much-needed literature on television as an art and as a technique. For example, as far back as the mid-1950s, Davis (1960) of the SFTA wrote a treatise on television production rules that was later revised by his colleagues and published as a book titled *The Grammar of Television Production*, in honor of Davis, who died at the time of the preparation of its original publication. The BBC's television production director, Millerson (1991), published the book *Television Production Techniques*, which became an influential source, helped to establish television's artistic production techniques, and pointed out the medium's unique attributes such as intimacy, small size, and immediacy.

The question of whether television is an art form or merely a transmission device was also debated by a number of television critics in the United States during the 1960s and early 1970s, producing a considerable amount of literature that, in summary, challenges the artistic potentials of the medium (Shayon, 1962; Steinberg, 1974), distinguishes the medium of television from those of film, radio, and theater (Metallinos, 1985a; Toogood, 1978; Zettl, 1978), and outlines certain production techniques of television (Millerson,

1972; Wurtzel, 1983; Zettl, 1992). For example, television critics participating in debates organized by the International Radio and Television Society (IRTS) have suggested that a television aesthetic is possible as long as we recognize the distinct features that separate it from other media such as the size and location (small size, home viewing), the editing techniques it uses (interrupting the flow or maintaining continuity), that it is a visual, not an auditory medium (Steinberg, 1974), and that it is a mass medium that belongs to the public or popular arts.

Discussing the potential of television as an art form, Toogood (1978) underlined television's features in terms of intimacy, intensity, strong emotional, and, therefore, subjective viewer involvement. Zettl (1978), however, went one step further to the real nature of television and explained its uniqueness in terms of its existential media factors (light, camera, switcher, sound) and experimental media factors (time, motion, sound, sights) and suggested that, "We are now at the point where we can correlate these existential media factors with the more prevalent experimental phenomena such as the instantaneous and irrevocability of the moment, the complexity of the moment, and the multiplicity of the viewpoint" (p. 6).

In regard to television production techniques, Millerson (1972), Wurtzel (1983), and Zettl (1992) were among the first to point out the key principles of television production, suggesting the appropriate use and handling of such major production components as lighting, framing, editing, and audio in creating programs with artistic outlook.

Recently, the debate has approached a considerable climax that has resulted in new literary sources on the issues of television as an art form and television aesthetics as a potential area of study within the field of visual communication media arts. The reasons for this are as follows: The study of television has matured and has been accepted as a serious academic discourse, the areas of television production and television critical analysis have made serious strides and have reached high levels of sophistication; in many cases they are comparable to those of film, and empirical research on television composition also has increased and has produced a significant number of verified theories that support television as an art form.

For example, the anthologies on television studies by Burns and Thompson (1989) confirm how serious, advanced, and esoteric some of the studies are that are found as books, articles in refereed journals, or conference papers. Cultural studies and critical studies in either dramatic or nonfiction television are found in great number and are of great importance, directly contributing to the development of the content of television programs, and indirectly to the development of television as an art form.

Newcomb's (1974, 1987a) contribution to the debate and consequently to the development of television aesthetics is, undoubtedly, one of the most significant and is acknowledged by scholars in the field. In his widely used textbooks *Television: The Most Popular Art* (1974) and *Television: The Critical View* (1987a), Newcomb, as author in the former and editor in the latter, gives us an in-depth analysis of the medium and outlines its artistic and aesthetic potentials with great accuracy. In his article *Towards a Television Aesthetics*, Newcomb (1987b) stated:

> In approaching an aesthetic understanding of TV the purpose should be the description and definition of the devices that work to make television one of the most popular arts. We should examine the common elements that enable television to be seen as something more than a transmission device for other forms. Three elements seem to be briefly developed in this process and unite in varying degrees, other aspects of the television aesthetic. They are intimacy, continuity, and history. (p. 614)

Basically a television analyst and an acclaimed television critic, Newcomb (1987a) recognized that a critical analysis requires an understanding of the unique features of the medium, and the technologies that work to make the television product. This is precisely the purpose of the study of television aesthetics: to understand, to describe, and to define the devices (the instruments, materials, and techniques) television employs, and to underline the unique aesthetic factors and compositional principles that govern it. Intimacy, continuity, and history are three television aesthetic factors that support the field of television aesthetics.

As far as empirical research findings are concerned, studies are now beginning to emerge either as well-written books or articles in journals. The pioneer books on television composition such as *The Psychology of Television Images* (Baggaley, Ferguson, & Brooks, 1980), *Sight, Sound, Motion: Applied Media Aesthetics* (Zettl, 1990), and *Transmission*, an anthology of articles edited by D'Agostino (1985) are examples of academic sources that provide theory and research findings on the aesthetic potentials of television. The journals in the field of communication such as *Critical Studies in Mass Communication, Communication Research*, and *Journal of Broadcasting and Electronic Media*, publish articles specifically dealing with the issue of television composition. These particular findings are reviewed in the discussion of the major compositional principles of television in the third section of this chapter.

In summary, the review of the debate regarding television as an art form provides the basis for the discussion of the main principles of composition that apply to all visual communication media arts, particularly film and television.

FUNDAMENTAL COMPOSITIONAL PRINCIPLES OF THE VISUAL COMMUNICATION MEDIA ARTS

Art design and the studies of art history, art philosophy, and art criticism have always supported the development of art composition and aesthetics. In fact, the basic rules of composition of the arts stem from the skills and techniques of the artists. This is also true of the products of the visual communication media of film and television. The composition of film and television images stems from the producer's and/or director's expertise, craftsmanship, and techniques that they have developed and enhanced with such additional cumulative elements as observation, knowledge, sensitivity, intelligence, and understanding.

Mentioned in general terms, composition is defined as the act or process of composing. However, when it refers to the arts, it is defined as the act of arranging various elements into proper proportions, relations, or artistic forms (Webster's Ninth New Collegiate Dictionary, 1989). Even more accurately, art composition is the process of making a work of art (an art object or an art event) whose elements are structured according to the art's own specific rules of composition. Such a composition's end process is an art form. Although each art form is structured according to its own compositional rules and processes, literature suggests that there are a number of principles common to all visual communication media arts.

This section examines the fundamental and most commonly found rules of composition in visual communication media art. This is because the specific compositional principles that govern the medium of television—examined in the third section—derive from the traditional compositional rules found in other arts. This review, therefore, provides a better understanding of television composition and television production techniques. Specifically, such fundamental rules of composition as direction, proportion, balance, space, shape and form, level of sophistication, light and color, time and motion, tension, expression, and point of view are discussed.

Direction

Direction is a universal rule that applies equally to all art forms—literary, fine, performing, and applied. It refers to the specific orientation that directs the art reader, listener, and viewer and decides where the action starts, how it progresses, and where it ends. Direction orients us in space and time and helps us to follow the logical evolution of events. It is not, necessarily, linear; it can go forward or backward, it can go down or up, and so on. Usually, direction is provided by vectors (indicators) that lead the eyes or the ears to a particular location, regardless of whether such vectors are visually present or implied. For example, a novel has a starting point and obliges the reader to follow the events as they develop, thus providing direction and orientation. Buildings and pictures are either horizontally oriented (directing the eyes to the horizontal lines and action), vertically oriented (directing the eyes upward or downward), or even diagonally oriented (directing the eyes in a slant or diagonal upward or downward orientation; see Fig. 9.1).

In all visual communication media arts, direction plays a fundamental role in the construction and subsequent understanding and appreciation of

FIG. 9.1. Screen directions. Three overlapping directions/orientations: (a) horizontal, (b) vertical, and (c) diagonal.

a particular art. The direction of a film or television picture is indicated by the flow, the sequence of events within the visual field by its various index, graphic, or motion vectors, by zooming in or zooming out, and, generally, by the logical progression of the actions on the screen.

Although it is obvious that lack of direction and orientation in a film or television program hinder the communication purpose, directors occasionally confuse viewers' orientation with purposefully staged unspecified directions. Dream episodes, madness, or mental illness scenes often lack direction so that they can reinforce a sense of disorientation. These cases, however, are the exceptions to the rule that dictates that a good composition should have a clearly stated direction and a specified orientation.

Proportions

Proportional harmony in the arts has been a central concern of all artists from ancient times to modern days. It refers to the ways by which an artist distributes the art's various elements. All works of art and literature divide their domains into smaller entities and smaller sections, thus distributing them either symmetrically or asymmetrically. An architect divides an architectural structure into smaller units that make up the building. A novelist divides the novel into parts or chapters, thus dividing the novel into units that have a proportional relationship with each other and with the entire novel. A playwright divides, proportionally, the play into acts. A painter divides the visual elements within the frame either symmetrically (given even visual space) or asymmetrically (placing the visual emphasis on either side of the painting).

The architectural buildings of the ancient Greeks were built on the basis of the *golden section* that was considered a harmonious division of the parts of the buildings. According to the golden section on proportional division, the smaller section is to the greater what the greater is to the whole (see Fig. 9.2).

Art forms that are proportionally divided asymmetrically are considered to be dynamic and more interesting than those that are perfectly evenly divided and structured completely symmetrically. Furthermore, art forms such as novels, poems, theatrical plays, paintings, and film or television pictures whose parts are proportionally divided according to the golden section seem to be more harmonious and preferable. For example, if the important visual elements of a television picture are proportionally constructed according to the golden section (asymmetrically), the greater part will be placed in the left visual field whereas the smaller one will be placed in the right visual field. This is consistent with studies found in both the fields of neurophysiology (Ornstein, 1972) and communication (Fletcher, 1979; Metallinos & Tiemens, 1977).

Visual communication media artists should be free to find their divine or perfect cutting points that proportionally divide the visual elements of the film or television pictures. However, empirical evidence of the left and right brain cognitive functions and the left and right picture orientation suggest that the golden section area of composition within the visual fields of film and television screens is more acceptable and appropriate.

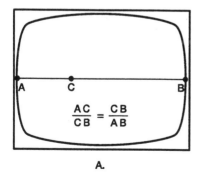

A.

B.

FIG. 9.2. The Golden Section or Golden Mean. This asymmetrical placement of visual elements within the television field (b) is based on the ancient Greek principle known as Golden Mean or Golden Section (a).

Balance

Balance, as a compositional principle, is universal to all art forms, literary or otherwise. It is defined as the point at which all elements, visual or otherwise, come to an equilibrium, a starting point, in harmony or in perfect proportions. According to Arnheim (1969a), "Balance is the state of distribution in which everything has come to a standstill. In a balanced composition all such factors as shape, direction, and location are mutually determined by each other in such a way that no change seems possible, and the whole assumes the character of 'necessity' in all its parts. An unbalanced composition looks accidental, transitory, and therefore invalid" (p. 12).

In all art forms, and particularly in the visual communication media art products, balance determines, to varying degrees, the artistic value of the artifact. For example, an unbalanced frame looks unprofessional and accidental, and therefore improper. A balanced picture could be stable (totally symmetrically structured dividing evenly all visual elements within the visual field), neutral (the visual elements are asymmetrically structured, dividing them unevenly), or unstable (the visual elements are not only asymmetrically structured but also pushed to their extremes, creating tension, instability, uneasiness, and imbalance; see Fig. 9.3).

All human beings, and moreso visual media artists, have the innate sense to see things balanced out. We try to harmonize the forces that pull in one direction or another the visual elements such as lights, colors, vectors, framing, sequencing of events, and arrangements of sounds. This innate characteristic of artists has been challenged repeatedly. The applications of either stable, unstable, or neutral balances in structuring visual images can produce excellent compositions and interesting expressions. The communication content, the message one wishes to convey, can be enhanced if assisted by the application of mutual stability or unstable balance. As Zettl (1990) suggested:

> Whether the balance should be stable, neutral, or labile is largely a matter of communication *content*. If you want to communicate extreme excitement, tension, or instability in relation to the event at hand, then the pictorial equilibrium should reflect this instability. You may do well to choose a labile picture balance. On the other hand, if you want to communicate authority, permanence, and stability, the pictorial arrangement, should, once again, reinforce and intensify this by means of a stable balance. (pp. 140–141)

Space

For the visual communication media of film and television, the manipulation of space is a major compositional factor. The concentrated space, shown in the camera's viewfinder and on the film and television screens, constitutes the canvas on which the directors compose the pictures. The bounded screens

FIG. 9.3. The three stages of balance.

are, for the film and television directors, what the stage is for the theater directors: an area to stage theatrical events. However, whereas the theater space, the stage, is three dimensional, film and television screens are flat. Consequently, visual communication media directors must manipulate the screen space so that the pictures appear real, as though they have depth and are three-dimensional. A series of perceptual, cognitive, and compositional laws are at work here that help the directors to construct realistic, three-dimensional (in appearance only) pictures.

Concentrated Space: Film and Television Screens. The directors of film and television compose visual images in a limited space; this limitation has its advantages and disadvantages, both of which can be manipulated for the benefit of the visual message. For example, the limited space of the television screen forces the director to intensify the events and to direct the viewer's

FIG. 9.4. Film and television screens.

attention to the important parts of the scene. The directors of visual communication media of film and television should not ignore this principle (see Fig. 9.4).

Equally important in visual composition is the awareness and understanding of the differences between the visual world and the visual field as described by Arnheim (1969a), Gibson (1950), Metallinos (1979), and Zettl (1990).

Aspect Ratio. The film and television screens are both horizontally oriented with an approximate aspect ratio of 3:4 (3 units width, 4 units length). This type of space not only offers a greater flexibility in centering the action within it, but it is based on the biological fact that our binocular vision ratio, in its extremes, is 180°:150° (150° vertical vision—top to bottom and 180° horizontal vision—from extreme left to extreme right). This space factor is very important for the composition of film and television pictures and it can be used to the advantage of the total synthesis of the visual image (Stone & Collius, 1965; see Fig. 9.5).

Illusionary Depth. The manipulation of screen space to increase the illusion of depth is a great challenge for visual communication media art artists. The successful directors and composers of visual images consider such depth principles as positive and negative space interplay, hierarchy of ground perception, figure–ground relationships, and z-axis space manipulation.

Television screen

Television picture

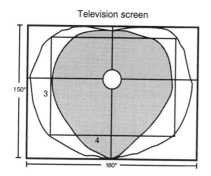

FIG. 9.5. The binocular visual field and television screens. The television screen matches the dimensions of the binocular visual field, which comes close to the 3:4 aspect ratio.

In film and television productions, the directors have to record the events that occur in the studio or field. The empty space between the camera and the objects (props, scenery, studio walls, etc.) or the subjects is the *negative space* that has to be considered in filming or videotaping. The occupied space by the objects and subjects is the *positive space* that provides the main images, often as figures, in the foreground. This space duality—its economic use and proper handling by the directors—is an important factor in creating the illusion of depth and should be always considered by film and television media artists (see Fig. 9.6).

The creation of the illusion of depth in pictures also depends on the perceptual principle of gradual ground deterioration with distance. It states, in effect, that objects in the foreground are clearer than those in the middle ground, which are clearer than those in the background. This hierarchy of ground perception, if reproduced properly in film and television staging, provides excellent depth cues and creates an illusion of real depth in film and television pictures (see Fig. 9.7).

The hierarchy of the ground perception principle has been commonly used and successfully applied by master painters and photographers and has generated a number of techniques of creating the illusion of depth in two-dimensional pictures such as overlapping planes, relative size, linear perspective, aerial perspective, height in plane, light, shadows, and color saturation, which Zettl (1990) called "graphic depth factors" (p. 162) and he recommended very strongly their careful consideration and application in television programs.

The psychological principle known as the figure–ground relationship, in which we assign certain elements to be the grounds on which the figures are placed, not only is an excellent depth factor, but is, foremost, a key compositional principle in the construction of film and television pictures. Used

FIG. 9.6. Positive and negative space. The space occupied by the furniture, subjects, cameras, and so on, is positive space. The empty space between the props is negative space.

FIG. 9.7. Hierarchy of ground perception. The trees (foreground), the mountain (middle ground), and the snow-covered mountains (background) in the far distance.

extensively in painting, sculpture, photography, and film and television, it is considered one of the most basic compositional principles in both literature and the arts. As the stage constitutes the ground on which the actors perform, so do the frames of film and television pictures constitute the background where the visuals are structured (see Fig. 9.8).

Maintaining this hierarchy of figure–ground produces clear, easily distinguishable, and realistic pictures. However, when intentionally violated or ignored, it produces serious anomalies in picture composition (Metallinos, 1989).

To increase the illusion of depth in film and television pictures, directors employ what Zettl (1990) called "z-axis blocking" (p. 199), in which the action and motion of the events are vertical (screen inward or outward) rather than horizontal (screen motion from left to right or right to left). If we consider the picture's height to be the x axis and its length to be the y axis, the picture's depth constitutes its z-axis or depth dimension. Placing the visual elements—and consequently the entire scene's action—on the z-axis space increases the illusion of depth and provides great flexibility of motion. As discussed in the third section, this staging technique that derives its origins from theater and film has been widely adopted by television directors and has become the most effective staging technique for television production (see Fig. 9.9).

Screen Space Forces

As previously stated, film and television screens constitute a concentrated, limited, and framed-in space that the directors must learn to manipulate to create images that communicate clearly the intended message, and at the same time to be dynamic, interesting, and aesthetically pleasing. Along with these space factors, directors must consider the established rules and guide-

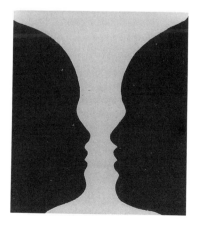

FIG. 9.8. Figure-ground interchange. The ground constitutes the basis, the frame on which the figure is placed. However, when alternated, they create perceptual tension and curiosity.

FIG. 9.9.   Depth axis space. The vertical (or inward) vector direction creates
the depth axis space, most appropriate for staging the action (framing) in
television.

lines known in television arts as the *field forces* (Arnheim, 1969a; Gibson, 1950; Zettl, 1990). According to the field forces theory, within the concentrated space of the film and television screen, a dynamic interplay takes place between the visual and auditory elements. This has stimulated media researchers to examine these elements and to identify the particular agents that cause their interplay. The specific elements, or constructs, of the field forces theory are magnetism of the frame, main direction, asymmetry of the screen, attraction of mass, figure–ground relationship, psychological closure or gestalt, and vectors (Metallinos, 1979; Zettl, 1990). Each of these forces operates independently and in cooperation with the others, and requires close attention and careful consideration in film and television composition (Herbener, Van Tubergen, & Whitlow, 1979). They are excellent aesthetic agents that help to manipulate the concentrated film and television screen space for the benefit of the composition of film and television pictures (see Fig. 9.10).

FIG. 9.10. Screen space forces. The empty field is lifeless (a), whereas the occupied field is alive and exerts considerable visual energy and attention (b).

In summary, the external and internal space factors constitute an important compositional principle regarding space manipulation of the visual communication media of film and television, which can become an excellent tool in the hands of visual images constructors.

Shape and Form

As a compositional principle of the visual communication media arts, the two terms *shape* and *form* refer to the specific configuration, construction, or appearance of the images within the picture field—the film and television screens. It deals with the particular ways by which the constructors of visual images record images so that they appear to have certain shapes or forms that are unique to the individual producer and/or director. For example, a director's decision to film or videotape an entire program predominantly with medium shots (MS) or with extreme close-ups (XCU) constitutes the particular compositional form, the directing style—as it is sometimes referred to—or approach. In general, the large screen of film offers a different compositional form than the small vista of the common television set that demands different configurations such as close-ups (CU).

Shape and form are not the same when discussed in reference to visual perception processes. Shape refers to the external structure of an object, whereas form refers to the specific content, the particular meaning, and format exerted by the shape or configuration. According to Arnheim (1969a), "Shape is one of the essential characteristics of objects grasped by the eyes. It refers to the spatial aspects of things, excepting location and orientation. That is, shape does not tell us where an object is and whether it lies upside down or right side up. It concerns, first of all of the boundaries of masses" (p. 37).

Form, on the other hand, is the agent that tells us about both location and orientation and provides the context for the discussion and understanding of

(a)

(b)

Shape (a) provides information about the nature of things through their external appearance and *Form* (b) concentrates on the way things are shaped and structured, their essential nature, distinguished from their materials.

FIG. 9.11. Shape and form.

the shape. In distinguishing the two terms, Arnheim (1969a) stated, "Actually there is a difference of meaning between the two terms. The preceding chapter dealt with the spatial aspects of appearance. But no visual pattern is only itself. It always represents something beyond its own individual existence which is like saying that all shape is the form of some content" (p. 82). Whereas in the process of visual perception it is the shape that provides the codes for the interpretation of the art form, in the study of composition of visual images both terms are considered synonymous. They identify the structure, configuration, and style of the images. The constructors of visual images should acknowledge the powers and the key roles of shape and form manipulation in the composition of pictures (see Fig. 9.11).

Level of Sophistication: Growth

In the construction of visual images an artist's level of sophistication is an important factor. It determines how good the images are compositionally and artistically. However, how does a producer or director of film and television obtain a level of sophistication, an understanding of visual image composition? What steps should be followed to reach the necessary level of sharp observation, knowledge, and the ability to understand visual complexity in the manipulation and construction of visual images with artistic considerations? Art philosophers, psychologists, designers, historians, and communicators reviewed earlier have provided some answers to this question although they have given different terms to this principle.

For perceptual psychologists of the visual arts such as Arnheim (1969a), the level of sophistication is termed *growth* and is achieved by constant observation and systematic study of visual perception. The degree to which visual media artists do not simply copy reality but modify it, enhance it, and add new elements to it suggests the level of growth of the artists. According to Arnheim (1969a), "At best, the artist is able to 'improve' reality or to enrich it with creating a fantasy by learning art, or adding details, selecting suitable examples, rearranging the given order of things" (p. 155). For art philosophers and aestheticians such as Edman (1939), artists achieve a desirable level of sophistication when they compose art forms by following the threefold process of clarification (distinguishing the object or event to be reproduced among its various other similar ones), intensification (exaggerating, modifying, or enriching the image representing the object or event), and interpretation (providing a meaning, a new context, to the art product).

According to visual arts designers such as Taylor (1964), sophistication, growth, and understanding in composing visual images are key compositional principles achieved through the systematic study of artistic designs and are measured by the artist's ability to abstract the unnecessary, to maintain the essential, and to enhance the important representation, whether that is a building, a tree, a figure, or anything else. As Taylor (1964) suggested, "But the artist in his proper capacity is as little concerned with imaging the actual relations which he discovers in nature as the architect. His business is to provide a system of scaled relations, not to copy one, to produce a vision of order, not to reproduce it" (p. 194).

The compositional principle of the visual communication media arts that we have called level of sophistication can be applied to these media successfully after media producers or directors study and experience the idiosyncratic nature of the media (see Fig. 9.12).

Light and Color: Colored Light

Light and color are the most profound aesthetic agents of all visual communication media arts but moreso of the media of film and television. Light and color, of course, are two different components and, as such, they are treated separately by media theorists, artists, and analysts. The dichotomy between light and color should always be maintained when we study them as aesthetic agents in producing visual communication media images. Colorless light that produces black and white images has a different aesthetic quality than colored light as shown in the next section. However, because today's media of film and television almost exclusively produce films and television programs in color, these two aesthetic agents are considered as colored light here and are discussed together.

FIG. 9.12.   Level of sophistication: Growth. The evolution of ancient pottery, from the simplest form to the more sophisticated. Reproduced with permission from Arnheim, R. (1969). *Art and visual perception: A psychology of the creative eye* (p. 206). Berkeley, CA: The University of California Press. Copyright © 1974 The Regents of the University of California.

For film and television producers and/or directors, light and color are what paint is for the painter. They are the materials that directors use to compose film and television pictures. As fundamental components in the construction of images, light and color require a detailed study of the instruments that produce them (the hardware of the media of film and television) and the techniques employed (the software of these media).

The instruments that produce colored lights in film and television are basically two types—the directional lights and the diffused lights. Directional lights are instruments that are used as the main light sources, are intense, and produce noticeable cast and attached shadows. Diffused light instruments produce soft colored lights; they are mainly used to fill in light in unlit areas, to eliminate the shadows produced by the directional lights, and, therefore, to even the lighting.

The colored lighting techniques established and widely used in the media of film and television fall under two major categories: overall illumination and lighting for volume. Overall illumination, known also as Notan (Millerson, 1972), or flat (Zettl, 1990), is used to provide a basic, overall illumination of a scene without any real concern for the creation of depth or cast and attached shadows. It is used simply to provide visibility to objects or events in the scene. According to Millerson (1972), the Notan technique "Depicts surface detail; outline; generalized tonal areas; but it is little concerned with tonal gradiation as such. Tonal pattern rather than form dominates. The effect is flat, two-dimensional. Photographically, Notan effect comes from high-key (i.e., low-contrast, reduced back-light, absence of modeling light" (p. 78).

The lighting for volume technique, known also as *chiaroscuro* (due to the sharp dark and white areas it creates), is the technique that uses the lighting instruments to generate predominant cast and attached shadows, which, in turn, create depth and volume in the scene. This technique subdivides into three separate forms of chiaroscuro lighting: the Rembrandt technique, the cameo technique, and the silhouette technique" (see Fig. 9.13).

The *Rembrandt* lighting technique, named after the Dutch master painter, emphasizes only selected areas of a scene and leaves the rest dark. It creates pools of light that illuminate only highly specified areas that are contrasted with the darker areas in a scene. The *cameo* technique, named after the cameo stone ornaments, is a chiaroscuro illumination in which the background remains totally dark and only the figures in front are illuminated. The *silhouette* technique is exactly the opposite of cameo in that it is the background of a scene that is lighted and the foreground remains totally dark, thus creating only a contour, or silhouette, of the figures in the foreground.

All visual communication media arts can, potentially, use either one or all of these techniques to create a certain mood and atmosphere, to provide volume or depth to images, and, generally, to produce pictures with artistic qualities. Lighting and color are the most fundamental compositional guidelines for the construction of images in visual communication media arts that the directors of these media should study and master.

Time and Motion

As light and color, time and motion are two distinct aesthetic agents that are involved in the compositional principles of visual communication media known as timing and movement. However, they are considered here as one for the following reasons: Time generates motion, and motion is measured by time units in all visual arts; the elements of time and motion are the basic ingredients that generate the principal of movement in the composition of visual media arts; and these two aesthetic agents cooperate for the creation of the unique compositional principle of editing in the visual communication media of film and television (see Fig. 9.14).

As film and television time differ considerably, so does motion. The constructors of visual images use them interchangeably to achieve certain desirable effects, to involve the spectators in certain ways, and to convey specific messages. Both are powerful tools of composition of moving images but they are not unique to film and television.

In fact, Arnheim (1969a) suggested that time and sequence that result in movement have a universal application to both the static and moving arts, including architecture and theater, or painting and dance, and he stated that:

a. Rembrandt   b. Cameo

c. Silhouette

FIG. 9.13.   Chiaroscuro lighting techniques.

The essential difference between the two kinds of artistic media is not that the one is based on time and the other on space but that the sequence in which the parts of a composition are to be related to each other is presented by the work itself in the dance or play whereas it is not in a work of painting or architecture. The temporal order of our perception is not a part of the composition when we look at sculpture or painting, whereas it is when we look at a dance. (p. 363)

The temporal order or motion that characterize the media of film and television involve even more the agents of time and motion and epitomize the uniqueness of these media that are known as moving images (cinema-

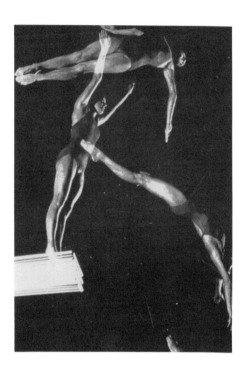

FIG. 9.14. Time, motion, and sequence. Frozen moments of sequential motion.

tography or television) media. As such, these two media follow their own rules of composition in their use of timing and movement. The common time and motion elements found in both media and the specific principles under which each of these aesthetic agents operate are described in detail in a later section.

Tension

As a compositional principal of the visual arts, tension is synonymous to dynamic composition and concerns the vibrant and vigorous structure of all art forms to arouse spectators' attention and involvement in the content of the art, the mediated message. Although all parts of an art form must generate the feeling of tension to be effective, it is the final structure, the end product, that characterizes an art form as a dynamic composition.

Tension, in the visual communication media arts of film and television, is both more readily created than in still pictures and more intense for obvious reasons. Tension is achieved by motion, and film and television images are moving images. Motion vectors created in the visual field provide the raw materials for the synthesis of dynamic and tension-arousing pictures. However, they must be controlled so that the balance, proportions, depth, shape, and form of the moving images are maintained. Unlike painters and sculptors, who create a sense of motion in paintings and sculptures, film and television directors have to create dynamic compositions of images in motion, a task that is difficult to achieve without adequate knowledge and experimentation, starting with the composition of still pictures and gradually learning to compose moving images. Tilting the horizon, shooting from above or below eye level, zooming in and out quickly, panning gradually, and increasing the speed are examples of tension-arousing composition, which, when done properly, produce vibrant, forceful, and dynamic composition of moving images. As this compositional principle has been an excellent guide to the masters of still visual arts, so it can be an effective technique when it is studied adequately and applied carefully by film and television directors (see Fig. 9.15).

Expression

Expression is the compositional principle that visual communication media artists use to communicate, in their own unique ways, their inner thoughts, feelings, emotions, and aspirations. It refers to the ways artists of the visual media, painters, or film and television directors, shape the art forms to convey their feelings and thoughts. Just as a person's face expresses anger, sorrow, or happiness, so can a sculpture or any other visual image be made to express

FIG. 9.15. Tension is created when a character demonstrates anger, hostility, hatred.

the artists' own ways of presenting—or rather representing—their aspirations. Expression is the creator's artistry.

In the visual media of film and television, the producers or directors express their feelings and thoughts through moving images that record and represent events in the visual field. Therefore, their expressions must be conveyed both artistically and symbolically; artistically because the specific instruments, materials, and techniques of the film and television media must be exclusively used, and symbolically because all art is symbolic to economize time and space and to avoid repetition. For example, to express the sadness of death, scenes recorded in funeral homes are usually in chiaroscuro lighting (low key, dark and white areas, predominant cast shadows); the Rembrandt lighting technique seems to express the atmosphere of the scene artistically. On the other hand, the mood of the funeral scene can be expressed symbolically if, for example, we add Antonio Vivaldi's (1678–1741) musical piece *Winter, Largo* from his famous symphony *The Four Seasons*.

Expression, as a compositional principle in visual communication media arts, is achieved with the close collaboration of the body and mind. The artist's body becomes the instrument, the vehicle that brings out the thoughts of the mind. Skill and imagination are at work when artists create works of art to express themselves. The proper cultivation of both is a prerequisite for artistic expression that visual communication media artists must acquire through systematic study and extensive experimentation.

Points of View

How visual communication media artists use each one of the aforementioned compositional principles provides an indication of how artists look at things, in general, and the media they serve, in particular. For example, the more curious and concerned artists are about an issue, the more subjective and involved they become and vice-versa. In all visual communication media arts, the point of view is a fundamental compositional principle with deep roots in other forms of art and literature as well. Basically, in life we can decide to become only objective observers of events and issues, take a closer look at the issues and to become more curious and interested, or become involved and take a stand and help to find a solution. The same attitude and practice can be taken by visual communication media artists when they compose visual images. They have the opportunity to use three distinct methods to structure the visual images, to tell a story, or to explore an issue.

The Objective Point of View. Visual media artists who compose according to this principle remain primarily observers of the events. They simply look at the events from a distance and remain indifferent to what they record. This point of view, compositionally, is achieved by long shots (see Fig. 9.16).

FIG. 9.16. Objective point of view. The long shot indicates that we are looking, objectively, at an event.

The Subjective Point of View. Artists who compose according to this principle usually are curious and tend to look at things closely and subjectively, providing more details. This point of view, compositionally, is achieved by close-ups and detailed pictures (see Fig. 9.17).

The Creative Point of View. Artists who adopt this principle of composition of images become totally submerged in the event they record and use the medium's instruments, materials, and techniques to restructure and change the event, creating a new one. This point of view, compositionally, is achieved by visual effects pertinent only to the specific medium such as superimpositions, fades, dissolves, chromakeys, video feedbacks, and many other such visual effects found in film and television media (see Fig. 9.18).

It is only natural that when making a film or recording a television program, directors use these three approaches interchangeably. However, if they choose to, they can employ any one of these principles in composing their pictures. Zettl (1990) suggested this, and stated that:

When working with television or film—or any other photographic medium for that matter—we need to decide on a basic way of looking at an event. We can, for example, merely observe an event and report it as faithfully as possible,

FIG. 9.17. Subjective point of view. The close-up indicates that we are looking, subjectively, into the event.

FIG. 9.18. The creative point of view. The medium itself has created the events.

or else we can look into an event and try to communicate its complexity and psychological implications. We can also choose to use the technical potentials of the medium to create an image that can only exist on the screen. (p. 211)

In summary, visual communication media artists have at their disposal well-established compositional guidelines that they can use to create visual images with artistic potential. These fundamental compositional principles are the techniques for the creation of visual art forms.

TELEVISION PRODUCTION TECHNIQUES: PRINCIPLES AND APPLICATIONS

The review of the idiosyncratic nature of television in the first section and the subsequent discussion of the major compositional principles of visual communication media arts in the second section provided the necessary framework for the examination of the different production techniques adopted by television that indicate the specific compositional guidelines pertaining to the medium of television.

The examination of the television production techniques employed by both commercial and educational television producers and directors today presupposes a basic understanding of the nature, functions, and control of the medium's hardware. This is the domain of television production that students and theorists of the medium must learn before attempting to direct television programs or before theorizing about the artistic potentials of the medium. The more we know about the nature of each of the television instruments (how they work and how they can be manipulated to maximize their potentials) the easier it is for us to master the software and to learn to construct and produce pictures based on artistic values. Knowledge of the television hardware is a prerequisite for the study of its software. The latter is an extension of the former.

Television production techniques fall under four major categories based on the processes involved in producing a program. These are: (a) staging, blocking, and recording the scene (involving mostly camera and scenery operations and manipulations); (b) lighting the scene (involving mostly the proper handling and placement of lighting instruments); (c) sound and audio arrangements (involving mostly the setting of microphones and arrangements of sound sources for the program); and (d) editing (which takes place during the recording, or after—as postproduction editing). This section examines the existing production techniques that are used constructively in television and are accepted as compositional guidelines in each of the four major categories.

The decision to divide the production processes according to the hardware involved in recording a television program was made for the following reasons:

1. There are three known stages, three levels of activity that occur in television production. These are (a) preproduction planning, (b) production recording, and (c) postproduction editing. Considerable effort and activity take place in all three stages. Only the live production recording is considered in the analysis that follows, although the importance and value of the other two are acknowledged. For example, television scriptwriting and storyboard are both based on artistic rules known as the visualization and picturization processes (Zettl, 1990). They both occur before the production recording, as does preproduction editing in which various editing principles are employed to create the artistic outlook of the program. Students of television aesthetics must study scriptwriting, scenery design, techniques of matching pictures with sounds, and generally all the key principles of sequencing pictures to tell a story, known as editing (Millerson, 1972).

2. The production techniques discussed here are not generated by one person or one artist, but are the results of the cooperative efforts of the television production team. Coordinated by the television producer, guided by the television director, and with the work of the crew (floor manager, lighting engineers, camera operators, audio engineers, microphone operators, switching operators, etc.), the various production techniques in lighting, framing, editing, and sound are achieved. This is a crucial factor in television production that has profound consequences for the synthesis of television images and the creative outcome of the television program. The television production principles are generated by the cooperative effort of the television production crew and are unique to the medium.

3. There is a considerable overlapping of duties and much cross-reference that occurs during the recording of a television production that poses a serious challenge to the television production crew, and the director in particular. For example, the lighting engineer must work closely with the microphone operator, the camera person, and other crew members in setting the lights for the scene; the camera person must know where the boom operator will be staged throughout the recording of the program. In short, the television production crew members must be knowledgeable of the duties and functions of the other crew members. Each crew member works in cooperation with the others, supporting and complementing the television production outcome. Only such an understanding among the production crew can create the artistic outcome of the television program.

4. The television medium, as all electronic media today, consists of highly complicated, sophisticated, and sensitive technologies. Practically all televi-

sion hardware is electronically run and computerized. Lights and lighting control systems like dimmers are computerized and so are the cameras, switchers, audio consoles, editing facilities, and so on. Not only are these technologies complicated, but they are constantly changing with astonishing speed, causing considerable drawbacks in the development of the permanent rules of television composition. This poses a great challenge for today's television production teams and for the theorists of the medium. The production techniques, stemming from the specific use of the medium's own instruments, are technology dependent and therefore constantly changing. Old ones need to be modified and others rapidly emerge as new television technology becomes available. This is an important factor, a serious phenomenon that must not be ignored and must always be considered (Metallinos, 1988).

The discussion of the major television production techniques that follows considers these four important factors.

Television Staging Techniques

In television production terminology, staging is the entire process involved in placing the sets and props in the appropriate areas of the studio floor (always according to the floor plan designed during the preproduction planning stages), placing the actors (cast) and directing their movements within the set, and blocking the scene with the cameras and actors, marking the various positions occupied by both. In short, staging for a studio television production is the process of manipulating the positive and negative space of the television studio to enhance the illusion of depth of the two-dimensional television pictures and to maximize the realistic approach of the images. Consequently, when placing the sets, directing the movements of the actors, and blocking the cameras and cast, the television production team must consider the key compositional principle of ground hierarchy, discussed previously, in which the distinctions between the background, middle ground, and foreground objects in the studio floor are maintained in the televised pictures. It should be noted that while these activities take place in the studio, the lighting and microphone engineers are setting the lights and microphones according to the lighting and microphone designs prepared during the preproduction planning stages.

Obviously, the event to be staged and videotaped often dictates the particular staging technique most appropriate for the situation. However, there are a number of television staging techniques that are applicable to all television productions. These are the subjective camera technique, interview technique, below and above eye level shooting technique, point of view, or shot value, staging technique, and depth axis staging technique.

The Subjective Camera Technique. As a television production technique, the subjective camera refers to the use of one camera to record an event that occurs in the field (mostly in news gathering), or an event staged in the television studio (mostly in newscasts). Throughout the process of videotaping the event, the camera replaces the spectators' eyes and practically becomes the spectator. Viewers' involvement is total. They are no longer just observers of the action shown, but become subjectively involved, feeling that they are a part of the event and totally submerged in it. This technique of television production was adopted from film, in which it was extremely successful, mostly in running or chasing, and generally in scenes in which the camera singles out a person, a car, an animal, or an airplane, and follows the action to its completion.

In television production this is a very effective and convenient staging technique that can be applied to different situations, summarized by Zettl (1990) as follows:

> Subjective camera [technique] means that the camera no longer observes an event but participates in it. One subjective camera technique is to have the camera temporarily *assume the point of view* of one of the *screen characters.* Under certain conditions, the viewer, will, then, identify with the screen character. Another type of subjective camera is when the *viewer is discovered* by one of the screen characters (the camera). The attention and action of the character is then aimed directly at the viewer (the camera), thus forcing the viewer to participate in the screen event. The *direct address* method, in which a television performer or actor speaks directly to the viewer (the camera), is another form of subjective camera technique. (p. 219)

Today's television producers and directors have at their disposal these various forms of subjective camera techniques to assist them in staging the events and creating meaningful and artistic television programs of all types (see Fig. 9.19).

The Interview Technique. The interview technique is one of the oldest in television production and is used extensively in newscasts, magazine programs, and talk shows. It refers to the staging of two or three people (usually a host and one or two guests) in conversation. The main objective of this technique is to bring the people closer to the viewer so that viewer interest in the conversation will increase rather than decrease. To achieve this objective, directors use minimum space and sets, vary the shots and the angles of shooting, maintain a coherent flow of the direction of the event, and overlap the figures to increase depth (Lewis, 1968).

Due to its many applications, this technique has assumed different forms in the literature of television production such as "ABC rolling" and "interview technique" (Zettl, 1990, pp. 344–345), "over the shoulder" and "straightfor-

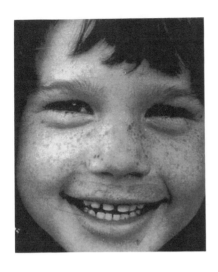

FIG. 9.19. The subjective camera technique. The camera assumes the role of the eyes of the subject; it looks at the spectators.

ward" (Zettl, 1990, pp. 223–225), and "Two persons united in a conversation" technique (Lewis, 1968, p. 60). The most commonly used forms of the interview technique are the interplay of straightforward, over the shoulder, and cross-shooting. The straightforward is the so-called person shot in which two people, usually the host and the guest, appear in a medium shot, taken by a camera positioned directly in front of the people (see Fig. 9.20).

The over the shoulder is when the camera takes a shot in which one person is facing the camera and the other is shot from behind and over the person's shoulder.

Cross-shooting is when the camera moves closer, to get a close-up of the person in the background after a gradual zoom in and passing of the shoulder of the person in the foreground (see Fig. 9.21).

The interview staging technique can be easily applied to any live production situation in which there is considerable dialogue between two or three persons. It is extremely useful as a compositional principle that, when used properly, can produce television images with aesthetic value.

Below and Above Eye Level Shooting Technique. The perceptual hierarchy of the phenomena in the visual world applies, also, to the construction of the phenomena in the visual field. When we look up at a tall building, we feel the power it exerts by being higher, taller, bigger, and dominant. Conversely, when we look down from the top of a tall building, things look smaller, weaker, powerless, and somewhat diminished. This innate feeling applies equally when we look at pictures. Anything shot from below eye level looks dominant and powerful, whereas objects and events shot from above eye level look diminished and powerless (see Fig. 9.22).

FIG. 9.20. Two person interview. This arrangement of camera and subjects allows for a better straightforward and over the shoulder shot.

   This technique of composition has been used effectively over the centuries in the arts of the Western world. The Egyptian pyramids were high and people looked up to see them; so were the ancient Greek temples and gods. In churches and icons, heaven is upward and hell is down. In later years, from the Renaissance to contemporary times, this principle has been applied extensively as exemplified by the paintings of El Greco and Salvador Dali, and in films such as *The Ten Commandments*. It is a strong principle deeply rooted in all people that has become a useful tool in the hands of visual communication media artists, particularly in photography, film, and television. In television production studies, in particular, several empirical research works have been generated that thoroughly examine this principle and attempt to verify it with vigorous scientific research. The studies by McCain, Chilberg, and Wakshlag (1977), Shoemaker (1964), and Tiemens (1965) early on, and later by Kepplinger and Donshach (1982), McCain and White (1980), and Walker (1987) have not produced conclusive results (mostly due to inappropriate application of experimental research designs and visual image measuring devices). However, these studies underline the significance of the technique, emphasize its universal acceptance, and review its extensive and variable application by visual communication media. Qualitative research on the issue, particularly descrip-

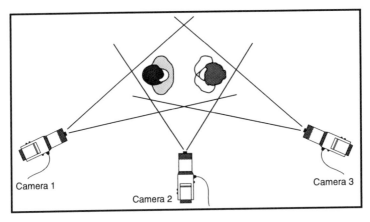

FIG. 9.21. Cross-shooting. This arrangement of cameras also allows for over the shoulder shots alternated at will.

A. Below   B. Above

FIG. 9.22. Shooting from below and above eye level. Shooting from below eye level diagonally created tension and connotes authority (A). Shooting from above eye level also creates tension, yet it diminishes the presence of the individuals (B).

tive and critical studies, supports this principle (Wurtzel, 1983; Zettl, 1990). In fact, Zettl (1990) strongly argued in favor of this technique and stated that:

> When we look up with the camera (sometimes called low-angle or a below eye-level point of view), the object or event seems more important, more powerful, more authoritative than when we look at it straight on (normal angle or eye-level point of view), or looking down on it (high angle, or above eye-level point of view). When we look down with the camera, the object generally loses somewhat in significance; it becomes less powerful, less important, than when we look at it straight on or from below. As viewers, we readily assume the camera's view point and identify with its superior high-angle position (looking down on the object or subject) and its inferior low-angle position (looking up at the subject or object. (pp. 216–219)

The placement of the camera with a normal lens, below or above eye level, in videotaping a television scene can become an effective technique of composition in the hands of television directors (see Fig. 9.23).

The Point of View Staging Technique.   The point of view staging technique of picture composition was discussed in the second section. It refers to the objective (long shot), subjective (close-up), and creative (special effects) points of view taken by the constructors of visual images. In television this

(A)   (B)

FIG. 9.23.   Shooting from above (A) and below (B) eye levels.

compositional principle is also called the shot value staging technique, and refers to the choices of shots the director has to narrate an event (Zettl, 1990). For example, the conventional long shot indicates an overall, objective point of view of the event and is often used as an established shot that identifies the event. The medium shot usually indicates a closer point of view of the event, bringing the viewer closer to the action. The close-up indicates a subjective way of presenting the event, providing both the details of the event and the director's own biases and beliefs of the event.

In addition to these three conventional points of view, the television director can create a new point of view with the use of the instruments offered by the medium, namely the camera lenses, the switcher, and the special effects generator of the switcher. For example, when staging and videotaping an event, besides the conventional shots and their variations, extreme long shots, medium close shots, or extreme close-up shots, which can be taken with normal lenses and plain switching cuts or takes, the director can record the event with additional aids. The camera lens choice could be the zoom lens that allows the director to vary the field of view of the shots starting from an extreme long shot and gradually zooming in without any interruption to the flow of action, and vice versa. This is a great advantage of the television medium: It can become an excellent compositional tool in the hands of television directors. Another aid is the switcher that helps to select the camera shots, to mix them in various ways, and to create different visual effects that extend beyond the images produced by the cameras such as superimposition, matting, chromakeying, feedback, split screens, and numerous digital video effects such as echo effects, compression expansion, stretching, rotation effect, and fly effect (Zettl, 1992).

With all of these choices available, the directors must decide which ones to use, how often to use them, and when and in what sequence to use them. The shot value, or point of view staging technique, suggests that visual continuity must first be established with the opening shot (usually a long shot of the environment where the action takes place) followed by a closer look (usually a medium shot of the event), continuing with an even closer look (usually a close-up shot), and ending with the establishing shot, to begin the process again with another point, and so on, until the event is completed. This is the basic photographic technique common to film and television. Where television directors deviate from the basic shot value technique and create their own is in the number of shots, different cameras, switching techniques, and special effects used to record the event. Directors, like painters, create their own point of view and provide their own value to the choices of shots they use to narrate an event. However, the fundamental photographic technique of the point of view staging is the starting point for the creation of the director's point of view of visual composition technique.

Depth Axis Staging Technique. The most powerful television production staging technique is along the depth axis, known also as vertical axis shooting (Toogood, 1978), or z-axis blocking (Zettl, 1990). It refers to the placement of the action (objects, subjects, movements, etc.) within the area defined by the depth or z-axis. By placing the action within the space of the z-axis, the illusion of depth increases considerably and the inward and outward motion provides flexibility of action and eliminates the camera movements that are always a problem in television production (see Fig. 9.24).

For some television production theorists, the depth axis staging technique was created because the small opening of the television screen could not allow for the lateral (also known as horizontal) staging technique. Unlike the theater stage or the large film screens, on which the horizontal movements of the actors from left to right and right to left are commonly practiced and preferred, the small television screen does not allow for such a lateral staging technique. In fact, television production practitioners and theorists alike suggest that a key difference between film and television staging and shooting techniques is the film's horizontal staging versus the vertical technique in television (Metallinos, 1985a; Toogood, 1978; Zettl, 1990). The justification for the practitioners and the advantages provided by the television depth axis staging technique is provided by Zettl (1990) who suggested that:

FIG. 9.24. Depth axis. The cars follow the street, which vanishes at the center of the picture creating depth.

When blocking action on the theater stage or the motion picture screen, we usually rely more on lateral or diagonal than up stage-down stage (z-axis) motion. In fact lateral action is generally preferred in theater because the stage is usually wider than it is deep.

But the television screen, with its highly limited picture field, cannot tolerate much lateral action without having the camera pan or truck along with it. Aside from the technical problems of keeping a fast moving object properly framed, too much lateral action can become quite distracting and disorienting. Proper blocking along the z-axis eliminates much of the camera movement and places emphasis on object (and people) motion, not on camera motion. (p. 198)

On the basis of the single depth axis staging technique, a multiple z-axis staging is possible, in which each camera projects its own depth axis action because the placement of the multiple scene action occurs in front of each camera independently. As long as the placement of the camera does not cross the line of action (and, therefore, does not violate the 180° action point), the multiple depth axis staging technique becomes very effective in eliminating camera movements and maintaining what Zettl (1990) called "shot continuity" (p. 201). See Fig. 9.25.

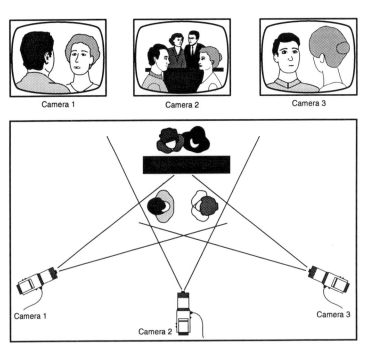

FIG. 9.25. Multiple depth axis. The placement of the camera allows flexible shooting with multiple depth axes.

In summary, the established staging techniques discussed here constitute the basic compositional factors in the artistic construction of television programs. However, they are not the only ones, as explained next.

Television Lighting and Color Techniques

The second section discussed light and color as the general aesthetic agents in the composition of visual communication media arts, primarily film and television. This section examines, in greater detail, the developed lighting and color techniques for regular television studio productions based on the fundamental compositional principles of the visual communication media arts.

It is important to consider several factors regarding the developments of these techniques and their subsequent applications: the basis on which these techniques are generated, the nature and functions of shadows in colored-lighting techniques, the types of lights used, and the differences between black-and-white and color lighting.

How are color and lighting techniques created? An answer to this question was partially given in the second section when it was explained that the development of the technique presupposes knowledge of the hardware of the medium. As it was the case with the staging techniques, so it is the case with the lighting and color techniques discussed here. There are several mechanical aspects of television lighting and color that precede the development of the technique such as the study of the nature of light and color, understanding how these two agents function, and learning the control mechanisms of these two sources. The next step is the identification of those particular aspects of the light sources that aid the development of the technique, summarized by Millerson (1972) as follows:

Its direction—the angle at which it strikes the subject relative to our environment;

Its coverage or distribution—the area lit by the source;

Its intensity, [the quantity, or amount of light available] and

Its quality—how hard or soft; whether white or colored. (p. 70)

The next step, before the development of the particular colored lighting techniques, is the consideration (by the television lighting director and production director) of the real-life experience or knowledge of the situation that justifies the purpose for which the technique was created. For example, the study and understanding of the nature of lighting and color, the functions performed by these sources, the control mechanisms that operate them, and the recognition of the unique aspects of direction, intensity, coverage, and quality, alone, cannot generate the low-key lighting technique used to create an atmosphere of an intensive arguing scene between a couple. It requires the lighting director's and the production director's sensitivity and experience of real-life situations, or at least, awareness of similar cases produced in other media such as theater or film. In short, the prerequisites for the creation of the colored lighting techniques are knowledge of and experience with the fundamental principles that govern light and color as aesthetic agents; study and experience, also, of the nature, purpose, and functions, and generally, the idiosyncrasies of lights and colors, and the lighting director's and the production director's ability to relate the created atmosphere to real-life similar, or potentially similar, situations.

Another factor that must be considered before the discussion of the television lighting and color techniques is the contribution of shadows to the development of a particular technique. The questions, therefore, that must be considered are: What is a shadow? What purpose does it serve in colored lighting? How can it be manipulated and controlled?

Shadows are defined as the images made by an observed space on a surface that cuts across it, usually representing in silhouette the form of the interposed body (Webster's Ninth New Collegiate Dictionary, 1989). The sun, the moon, and other bright sources, when they fall on objects and people, create two types of shadows, regardless of their intensity—*cast shadows* that fall outside the objects' area and are projected, and *attached shadows* that fall on the objects and are adjusted to them (see Figs. 9.26 and 9.27).

On the basis of their intensity, shadows generally divide into harsh, which Zettl (1990) termed "fast fall off" (p. 27), or smooth, which he termed "slow

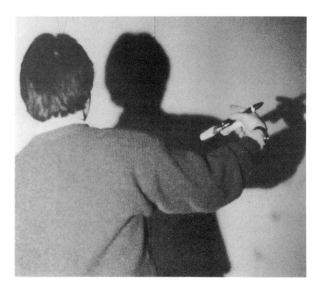

FIG. 9.26.   Cast shadows: The shadow of the man's body is cast on the wall.

FIG. 9.27.   Attached shadows. The shadow of the man's face falls on, and is attached to, his face and body.

fall off" (p. 27). The two factors that determine the intensity of the shadows and decide, therefore, the degree of their harshness or softness are the shape of objects, or subjects, and the brightness of the light source that strikes them. The sharper the objects, the more intense and harsh the shadows will be, and vice versa.

What purposes do shadows serve in color lighting? Among the key functions of shadows are: (a) the perception of shapes and forms in general, and the provision of depth of field in visual perception in particular; (b) shadows orient the viewers in space, identify the location of things, and help to identify the time (i.e., shadows were used as the first time indicators in ancient Egyptian and Greek civilizations); (c) shadows reveal the nature of surfaces and determine not only what they are but how rigid, harsh, soft, or smooth they are; and (d) shadows function as aesthetic agents used to create the mood of a scene of a television program. Cast shadows, being more distinctive, perform this function better.

Proper control and skillful manipulation of the cast and attached shadows are what television lighting is all about. To learn to control light sources in ways in which the intensities of the shadows help to emphasize the surface of an object or subject, or to de-emphasize it is the ultimate goal of the television lighting director and the production director of a program. Directional lights (usually the Fresnel spotlights) generate cast shadows, whereas the diffused or floodlights (usually the scoops) help to ease out, soften, and eventually eliminate attached shadows. Generally, the placement of the floodlights opposite the spotlights helps to soften and even eliminate unwanted shadows. In short, knowledge of the particular nature of the shadows, understanding of their purposes and functions, and learning how to control and manipulate them with the lighting instruments are important factors to consider before the creation of a particular lighting technique in television production.

The next factor to consider in developing such a technique is the type of television light to be used, environmental or electronic. As stated previously, the material, or substance, that makes the television picture is light that is generated either by the camera or by the internal workings of the electronics of the system itself. The light that is generated and creates the television picture could be called the environmental or lens light, or "external light," as it was called by Zettl (1990), who stated that, "External light is the light that is captured by the lens. It may be the light used in the studio or sunlight outdoors. External light is reflected off objects in various degrees and seen by the camera lens, similar to the eye, as light shadows. All lighting techniques concern the control of external lights" (p. 21).

Television lighting directors have at their disposal the following lighting types that can be used either in a studio production or in the field: spotlights (including Fresnel spotlights, ellipsoidal spotlights, or follow spotlights) and floodlights (including scoops, broad softlights, floodlight bank, and strip or cyc lights). For field lights when recording with portable instruments they may use spotlights (internal reflector spotlights, clip lights, portable softlights, etc.) and floodlights (Nooklight, low tote-light, Lowel V-light) and other hand-held lights (hand-held spotlights and omnilights; Zettl, 1992).

Light, on the other hand, that is generated by the manipulation of the electronics of the internal systems of television, particularly the electron beam, could be called the *control room light* or "internal light" as it was termed by Zettl (1990) who suggested that:

> When you adjust the brightness, contrast, or colors on your television set, you apply some form of internal lighting. Internal "light" is the energy necessary to produce screen images. . . . Although technically the manipulation of the electron beam results in a change of electrical energy rather than light, we nevertheless perceive these changes on the screen as shifts in the light. (pp. 49–50)

At the disposal, therefore, of the television production director is a range of electron-beam-generated light forms such as debeaming and adjusting the brightness, all of which generate distinct internal lighting techniques discussed later.

The lighting director's decision to use the lens-generated light (the external) or the control-room generated light (the internal) is a prerequisite for the development of the television lighting technique. The television lighting director and production director must examine these techniques diligently and they must consider them, seriously, in their production planning stage.

The last consideration for the development of a television lighting technique is the use of black-and-white or color pictures. Because there is a significant difference in the aesthetics of black-and-white as opposed to colored pictures, the lighting director and the television director must decide which is more appropriate for the program. The aesthetic difference between black-and-white and color pictures is discussed later. The important point that needs to be made here is that the set, costumes, props, and generally the external outlook of the scenery and the cast must be adjusted accordingly. For example, in creating a low-key lighting technique for the couple's fighting scene, mentioned earlier, de-emphasizing of the colors of the set, props, and costumes will help to darken the atmosphere and will increase the sad mood of the scene, moreso if it is shot in black-and-white and less if recorded in color. Conversely, the application of a high-key lighting technique to a happy scene such as a wedding requires emphasis and punctuation of colors, brightness, and high contrasts that will enhance the mood of the scene. This decision must be made in the planning stages of the production's lighting and is crucial for the aesthetic outcome of the production. It is unfortunate that today's television programming uses color unilaterally, which hinders the development of an aesthetic agent such as black-and-white that is often more appropriate for the creation of sad, mysterious, and moody scenes. More unfortunate is the colorization of original black-and-white films presented on television. More often than not, the colors look washed out; they are unnatural; they do not look real. Before a lighting technique is developed, the lighting director and the production director must consider what the communicative purpose of the scene is, what the atmosphere should be like, and what colors will best help to create it.

In summary, the proper consideration of all these factors provides the framework for the following review of the studio lighting techniques (such as three-point lighting, six-point lighting, multiple scene lighting, lighting from above eye level and below eye level, high-key and low-key lighting techniques, predictive lighting technique, lighting the lighting instruments), control room (or electron-beam-generated lighting techniques such as beaming and reversed polarity, video feedback, and chromakey), and various television color techniques based on color composition principles.

Studio Lighting Techniques

Three-Point Lighting Technique. This basic photographic technique of film and television is achieved with three lights: one key light in front on one side, one back light behind the area or person to be lighted, and one floodlight in front and at the opposite side of the key light (see Fig. 9.28).

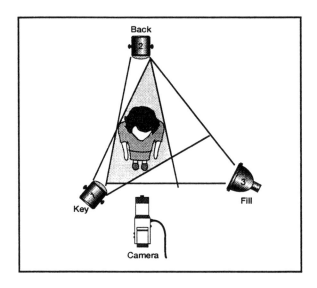

FIG. 9.28. Three-point lighting technique. The basic photographic principle
with the major light sources: key, back, and fill.

Because this lighting technique is the one that generates the different lighting approaches in television production, the principles on which this technique operates are reviewed and the functions performed by the three lights
are outlined as follows.

Placed approximately 45° above and on one side of the subject, or area to
be lighted, is an adjustable spotlight called the *key light*. This light is the main
light source and its purposes are to provide overall illumination and to reveal
the shape of the object or subject on which the light falls. Directly behind the
object to be lighted (always in relation to the camera that is placed in front),
the *back light* is placed at the same height and angle. The back light is also an
adjustable spotlight (usually a Fresnel light) that counterreacts to the key light.
Its main functions are to separate the object or subject from the background,
to reveal more of the object's shape, and to provide overall illumination in the
area behind the object. Finally, placed on the opposite side of the key light is
the *fill light* (usually a scoop floodlight) with the main functions of eliminating
the harsh shadows created by the key light and revealing more details as it
rounds up and smoothes the surface of the objects or persons to be lighted.

The degree to which the application of the three-point lighting technique
is successful depends on such factors as the proper handling of the lighting
instruments by the lighting engineers, the nature of the objects or subjects
to be lighted, the position of the camera, the movements, if any, of the sub-

jects, and the placement of the microphones. In the past, television lighting instruments were limited. Today's lighting facilities offer unlimited flexibility and accuracy in their control and manipulation, and can generally do almost anything the lighting director wishes them to do as long as the production's objectives are well-developed and clear.

Six-Point Lighting Technique. This technique is based on the three-point lighting technique. It is an extended photographic technique that applies the principle of the three-point lighting four times, interchangeably, with the use of six lights (four spotlights and two floodlights; see Fig. 9.29).

To allow greater flexibility in both the movements of the subjects in a television scene and different points of view (therefore different camera shots), the key light in one photographic shot becomes the back light in another, and so on, applying the three-point lighting four times, covering an area of 360°. The advantages of the six-point lighting technique are that it uses a minimum number of lighting instruments, leaving the rest available for multiple scenes lighting technique; it allows greater camera movement such as trucking and arcing; it allows shots from different points of view without changing the lighting set up; and it allows subjects to move freely by giving them more space for gestures.

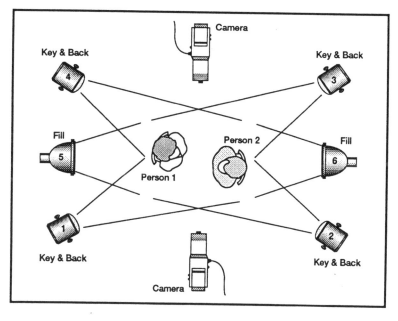

FIG. 9.29. Six-point lighting technique. The six (and more) lighting technique(s) are built on the three-point lighting principle.

Multiple Scene Lighting Technique. As its name indicates, the multiple scene lighting technique applies when there are several areas in which continuous action takes place without interruptions or changes in the environment in which the main event takes place (e.g., a kitchen scene in which the kitchen stove, table, refrigerator, sink, etc., must be lighted for action that occurs simultaneously).

This technique is a photographic technique for continuous action based on the photographic principle (or three-point lighting technique) that extends beyond the four-point lighting technique. In the multiple scene lighting technique the important things to consider are that each action or episode must be lighted separately, that the areas where the action occurs must also be lighted to cover the shots depicting the subjects' motion from one scene area to another, and that the multiple use of each of the lighting instruments must be considered very carefully by the lighting director to eliminate unnecessary production interruptions and extra work. It is a flexible television lighting technique that is common practice in today's television production (see Fig. 9.30).

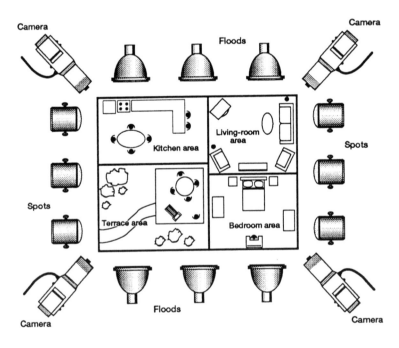

FIG. 9.30. A multiple application lighting technique. The multiple application lighting technique is also built on the principle of multiple instrument usage of the same lighting.

Above and Below Eye Level Lighting Techniques.   The aesthetic visual effects that occur when we light a scene (object or person) by placing the lighting instruments below or above eye level are considerably different (see Fig. 9.31).

A single lighting source such as a key light placed above a person, although it might create some strong and harsh shadows, still looks normal and creates a natural mood because we are experiencing the sun lighting the objects from above and the lights, at night, also above us. However, when the same light source is placed below eye level, a different scene is created, altering the atmosphere and creating mysterious, unusual, and uneasy feelings. Master painters such as Rembrandt used the below eye level technique very effectively to create mysterious and uneasy moods. Combined with the other appropriate and necessary production elements such as sounds, sets, and colors, both of these lighting techniques (but moreso the below eye level) can become an effective compositional factors in television production. As Zettl (1992) pointed out:

> Lighting from below eye level can create a mysterious mood. Because under normal conditions we experience the principle illumination as coming from above, we expect the shadows to fall below the object. A reversal of the shadows immediately suggests something unusual. If all other production elements—set design, color, sound, and actions—are in harmony with the special lighting

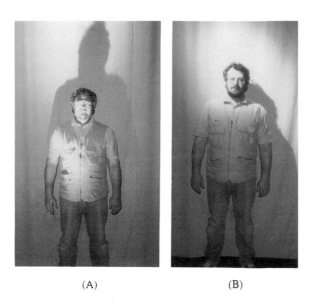

(A)   (B)

FIG. 9.31.   Lighting from above (A) and below (B) eye levels. In both cases the mood is mysterious and unusual.

effect, the mysterious mood is firmly established. Note that one production technique, such as lighting, is usually not strong enough alone to establish a feeling of normality or mystery. All production elements must work in unison to achieve the effect. (p. 181)

High-Key and Low-Key Lighting Techniques. These two techniques of lighting are generated by the placement of the key light used to illuminate the desirable scene as the main lighting source, normally above the objects, as is the case with the three-point lighting technique's setup. High-key and low-key refers to the light's high or low intensity, or quality, which generates a strong contrast between brightness (high key) and darkness (low key). It is not so much the placement of the key light that matters (although it can help), but rather the control of the amount of light that falls on the objects or the scene, and its quality. Vivid examples of high-key and low-key lighting techniques are daytime's brightness and nighttime's darkness, respectively (see Figs. 9.32 and 9.33).

By manipulating the amount of lighting (with the use of the light dimmer, barn-doors, and the flooding or spotting lighting controllers), we can create either a daytime, happy, bright, and stable mood and atmosphere (high-key lighting technique) or a nighttime, moody, dark, and mysterious type of atmosphere in a scene, other things being equal. For example, the control of

FIG. 9.32. High-key lighting technique. The set is lit with flat lights to create a daytime atmosphere. From Wurtzel, A. (1983). *Television production* (2nd ed.). New York: McGraw-Hill. Reproduced with the permission of McGraw-Hill, Inc.

FIG. 9.33. Low-key lighting technique. The same scene as in Fig. 9.32 but now the dark areas are emphasized, with directional lights strategically placed to create cast shadows and nighttime atmosphere. From Wurtzel, A. (1983). *Television production* (2nd ed.). New York: McGraw-Hill. Reproduced with the permission of McGraw-Hill, Inc.

the light intensity or the manipulation of the lighting equipment alone will not create fully the desirable mood in a scene. This requires the additional cooperation of the shadows, sets, sounds, colors, camera angles, and so on. When the low-key or high-key lighting techniques are employed in conjunction with these other production elements, it becomes a powerful and effective compositional principle in television production.

Predictive Lighting Technique.   Another effective television lighting technique that is used mostly to reinforce changes in the viewer's emotional involvement of the program is the predictive lighting technique. As its name suggests, this technique refers to the creation of a sense of suspense or for something unusual that is about to occur. It is created by an unexpected rapid change from high-key to low-key lighting. As the rainbow signals the oncoming sunlight after the rain, so does the predictive lighting technique prepare the viewers for the forthcoming change in mood and atmosphere. In black-and-white films of the past, the predictive lighting technique was effectively used to create dynamic, mysterious, and frightening moments such as storms or the appearance of monsters and vampires. In television production, this technique that is derived from basic natural phenomena can become a very effective compositional principle in the hands of the television lighting directors and production directors when combined with various other production elements.

Lighting the Lighting Instruments Technique. The lighting the lighting instruments technique has been successfully and extensively used by European filmmakers and consists simply of focusing viewer attention to particular light sources. In the United States, these are labeled *practicals*. Instantly, therefore, the lights themselves become the focus of the action, the agents that create the drama. For example, a long shot of a streetlight on a long road, a close-up of the rotating siren of a police car, or a shot of a sunset or sunrise use lighting instruments themselves in the pictures to elicit a dramatic effect. It is the placement of the lights themselves within the picture frame that creates this technique rather than the control of the light exerted by the lighting instrument (see Fig. 9.34).

Nevertheless, lighting the lighting instruments themselves is an effective and powerful technique as shown in the films *La Dolce Vita* and *8½*, directed by Federico Fellini, and in the police car chase scenes in today's network television programs.

In summary, such studio or external lighting techniques are fundamental production lighting techniques that can be used as the starting point for the development of the aesthetics of television lighting.

Control-Room-Generated Lighting Techniques

The lighting techniques that fall under this category are created, as stated earlier, internally, by special effects equipment and the manipulation of the

FIG. 9.34.   Lighting the lighting instruments, used as dramatic agents.

electron beam's intensity and direction, both of which are created by television's internal electronic system located in the control room. Except for the lighting techniques of chromakey and video feedback, all other internal lighting techniques are, in actuality, nothing more than special images (lights) created either by the manipulation of the electron beam's intensity and direction or by digital special effects equipment in the control room (such as computer-generated graphics), and through special effects functions of the television switcher. Let us consider the video feedback and chromakey first, the direction- and intensity-generated effects second, and the special effects of computer graphics and video switcher last.

Video Feedback. Video feedback, as the term indicates, is a video image that multiplies itself by feeding back its image to its image. The process of creating video feedback is both external and internal in that it requires both the environmental lighting (studio) and the electronics of television (control room equipment manipulation). In video feedback, the studio scene is lighted and picked up by the camera that is fed into the line monitor. The picture of the monitor (located on the studio floor) is picked up by another camera, thus creating an effect that is similar to the image reflected by opposite mirrors, creating an indefinite number of identical images. This is an interesting and powerful image effect that can become a useful aesthetic agent in television composition if applied properly and when needed (see Fig. 9.35).

Chromakey. Chromakey is also created by the combined techniques of external and internal lighting, and it refers to the special effects generated

FIG. 9.35. Feedback effect. In video, feedback effect is created by feeding the image produced by a camera back to itself.

by electronically keying, or matting, one picture into another. It can be created by both black-and-white and color television electronic techniques. In the first case it is called keying (or matting) and in the second it is called chromakey. Chromakey uses mostly blue color or green (chroma) as the background into which the keying of one picture into another occurs (Zettl, 1992). Anytime an event occurs in front of a blue background, the picture taken by one camera can be keyed, electronically, into the image of a second picture of a different event.

Chromakey is extensively used in television production today, particularly in broadcasting news, due to its ability to key-in the anchor person in the studio to an event that takes place in the field, sometimes live. Like feedback, keying or matting are effective compositional agents fundamental to television production, which, if used properly, produce excellent aesthetic results (see Fig. 9.36).

Manipulation of the Electron Beam.   Although the electronics that generate the debeaming effects are beyond the jurisdiction of the television director, the effects generated are within it because they can help the aesthetic outcome of the production if applied properly and when needed. According to Zettl (1973): "Since the electron beam can be manipulated with ease and reliability, internal lighting is an important aesthetic variable. You can control internal lighting by manipulating 1) the intensity, and 2) the direction of the electron beam" (p. 47).

FIG. 9.36.   Chromakey effect. This effect is achieved by keying-in one picture into another, creating a new image effect.

The manipulation of the intensity—particularly when it is reduced considerably—produces two distinct effects based on the picture's brightness. The first effect is a polarity reversal, in which the dark areas of a picture become light, or turn light, and vice versa, as is true with the positive and negative film pictures.

The manipulation of the beam's direction, on the other hand, which is achieved by altering the normal function of the scanning pattern, generates such special visual effects as keying, matting, video feedback, various forms of wipes, and other special effects patterns controlled by the television switcher and assisted by computer control changes of the direction of the electron beam.

Television's Special Effects. A unique characteristic of television is the special visual effects that are light effects generated by the electronics of the medium and controlled either by the switcher or by the special computer graphics digital video equipment.

The special effects generated and controlled by the switcher are standard effects (Zettl, 1992): the key, the chromakey, the superimposition, and the wipe. They are standard in that they are analog-generated effects and are combined with the special effects generator apparatus of the switcher that creates a variety of electronic effects, usually geometric patterns and other forms. The computer-generated, or digital, visual effects are the state of the art in video productions today. There are a great variety of such effects that fall under the categories of multi-images; image size, shape, and light; and motion (Zettl, 1992).

Regardless of the electronic ways by which the various television effects are created (analogically or digitally), they all offer enormous flexibility and can become very effective aesthetic factors in television composition as long as they are used properly, tastefully, and according to the real needs of the production. Emphasizing the need for careful handling of television's special effects, Zettl (1992) stated:

> Electronic effects are so readily available that they may tempt the inexperienced television director to substitute effect for content. Do not fall into the trap of camouflaging insignificant content or poorly shot or edited pictures with effects. As dazzling as the effects may be they cannot replace the basic message. When judiciously used, however, many effects can enhance production considerably and help greatly in clarifying and intensifying the message. (p. 337)

A brief definition of the various special effects is provided herein because it is pointless to suggest when and where such visual communication agents must be used. It remains the task of the responsible television production director to be aware of them and to learn to use them as the situation dictates.

Superimposition, as the word indicates, means that one picture is super-imposed over another. The two pictures are generated by two different video sources such as two camera shots, slides and camera shots, graphics, and studio cards.

Keying, as stated previously, means to electronically cut out a part of a picture and replace it with another. Available are not only the matte key and chromakey, but also the internal key or normal key and the external key in various forms (Zettl, 1992).

The *wipe* appears in many forms, shapes, and patterns and is created when a part of a television picture is wiped or gradually replaced by another, re-gardless of the direction it follows or its specific pattern. The most commonly available wipe types are the soft- or hard-edge wipes, the split-screen wipes, the quad-split, the spotlight effect, and the standard left to right, right to left, horizontal, vertical, or diagonal wipes.

There are two types of *multi-image digital effects*: the split-screen effects, in which the screen is divided into various equal parts—each of which shows a different image, or the echo effect, which is similar, in principle, to video feedback and produces a series of the same images repeated indefinitely.

Size, shape, and light effects are also digitally generated and appear as compression and expansion (in which the pictures actually look as though they are expanding or compressing, changing their sizes), stretching hori-zontally or vertically, positioning and point of view (in which one frame is positioned next to a basic picture usually compressed), perspective (in which pictures are distorted digitally and appear as three dimensional), mosaic (in which pictures look like they were made from small squares and resemble mosaics), and posterization and solarization (in which images look as though they are posters or negatives of the same images).

Motion digital effects refer to visual effects that create various moves and image changes such as size and position changes (in which either the size of the image or its position within the frame changes), zoom effects (in which the images look as though they expand or compress continuously giving the impression of zooming in or zooming out), and rotation and bounce effects (in which images bounce around the picture, appearing three dimensional, or rotate by revolving around the axes; Zettl, 1992).

As aesthetic agents, all of these special effects are excellent compositional factors to be considered for use in television production. However, they should not be used just because they happen to be available and only as visual gimmicks. They have an aesthetic value only when their application is dictated by compositional and artistic considerations. Because empirical research on the aesthetic value of television's special visual effects is lacking, their conser-vative, judicious, and sporadic use is warranted (Metallinos, 1988).

In summary, the control room electronically generated or internal lighting techniques reviewed here are unique television lighting techniques that constitute the fundamental compositional factors decisively contributing to the development of television aesthetics.

Television Colored Lighting Principles

Because the instruments and the mechanics or the electronics that create the substance (or material) of television are the same for black-and-white and color pictures, the procedures used to create the lighting techniques are also the same. Consequently, the lighting techniques already reviewed apply equally to colored television lighting. The fundamental principles of color as an aesthetic agent in television production are what must be reviewed. Specifically, this section examines the perception and characteristics of colors and reviews the main functions performed by color television pictures.

Perception and Characteristics of Colors. As explained in an earlier part of this book, colors are reflected lights that have been filtered by an object or liquid. The entire process of perception, as illustrated by the stimulus perception recognition model (see Fig. 4.3) is at work when we look at colors. The retina's cones are responsible for receiving the three primary colors (red, blue, and green), codifying them, and transmitting them to the brain to be decodified and interpreted. The successful decodification of colors depends on the following three main factors that must always be considered by the lighting director and the television production director.

The *quantity* and the *quality* of the lights that generate the colors of the television pictures are one of the three factors. Regardless of the sophistication of the lighting instruments, low light levels tend to distort colors and floodlights have the tendency to produce bluer colors than spotlights. The quantity and quality of the lights also influence color temperature, which always must be considered in television production, particularly if the production is recorded live. The temperature of colors is measured in degrees of Kelvin (with a maximum of 5600°K (as the highest) and a minimum of 3200°K (as the lowest amount on the scale). Generally, blue colors tend to increase temperature more than red ones. Although this seems to be contradictory to what we feel when we see colors, the fact remains that the more blue the color of an object is, the higher its color temperature is, and the more red the color is, the lower is its temperature. A rapid change from a high-key lighting to a low-key one will influence the color temperature and consequently the picture will deteriorate. A gradual change of lighting is preferred to avoid a drastic change of color temperature.

The *influence of the environment* on the perception of colors is another factor to be considered when preparing the scenery and lighting in a television production. In general, if the environment is bright—due to an abundance of light—the colors look clearly distinctive. If the scenery is dark due to the lack of white light, the colors lose their hues and intensity. The lighting of an environment reflected by the surroundings and the existing colors influence the perception of colors. For example, a low-key nighttime lighting diminishes the hues of all the surrounding colors, whereas a high-key daytime lighting brings out all the color attributes (hues, saturation, and brightness), interchangeably, and each color influences the next. In preparation of the production's scenery, props, costumes, and so on, the influence of the environment and the recognition of colors is a significant factor that must be considered.

Another key factor to consider in color television production is that the proper recognition and appreciation of colors depend on our *experience*, *familiarity*, and *memory* of color. When we have an indisputable concept of what a color is, we have the tendency to maintain it constantly and under different circumstances. For example, a red apple remains as such in our minds, and it is perceived as a red apple even from a distance, or in the dark. We relate to the color contextually because we have experienced it, we are familiar with it, and its appearance triggers our memory. The more we relate to a color due to our experience and familiarity with it, the faster its cognitive process becomes, and the more accurate is its appreciation. For the television director who acts as a mediator between the message and the audience, the fact that the internal color scale varies considerably from person to person presents a challenge. A color's constancy must be maintained unilaterally to be accurately recognized and appreciated.

Color television pictures are characterized first by their three sensations or attributes, namely their hues or the actual colors of the individual visual elements within the picture field, their saturation or the strength of their colors, and their brightness or how dark a color appears in relation to the gray scale that measures the extremes between dark and whites in a picture. The second characteristic is that the pictures consist of a variety of colors all of which are the results of mixing the primary colors. They are mixed either by adding one color to another or by removing (stripping) some color from a mixed picture. A third characteristic of colored television pictures is their dimensions. Our life experience with warm and cold environments is maintained when we produce or when we perceive colors. As previously stated, blue is a cold color and red is a warm color. This constitutes the temperature dimension of color television pictures. Another dimension that characterizes the colors of television pictures is their space, time, and weight value. All things considered, warm colors seem larger and closer than cold colors. We have the tendency to underestimate time when we are under blue light, whereas time drags on and is overestimated when we are exposed to red light. Finally, warm-colored objects seem heavier than cold-colored objects. Experimental studies in psychology have verified, empirically, the space, time, and weight dimensions of colors. Another color picture dimension is persistence or constancy, which refers to our innate ability to see colored pictures uniformly. As stated previously, this is both a perceptual and a cognitive dimension of color.

In summary, the quality and quantity of light, the influence of the environment, and the role of experience, familiarity, and memory are the main perceptual factors of color television pictures, whereas the sensation of the variations and the dimensions of colors are their main characteristics.

Functions of Colored Television Pictures

As stated earlier, color is an important aesthetic agent in television lighting that must be carefully considered and thoroughly analyzed by the lighting director and the production director. Significant consideration must be given to the various key functions performed by color when we compose color television pictures. In general, the key functions performed by colors are: (a) to communicate and/or to inform, (b) to associate and/or to symbolize, and (c) to excite and/or to dramatize events. These three traditional functions of colors apply equally to television when careful consideration is given to the basic principles of colored television lighting discussed so far.

Communication and/or Information Functions of Colored Television Pictures. Television pictures are created to narrate an event, to communicate a message, and, therefore, to inform television viewers of an issue. Yet color television pictures in particular are closer to reality; they provide a real-life appearance to the objects and persons, and they communicate more detailed information about them. For example, a colored picture of flowers reveals and communicates more details about the flowers than the same picture in black and white.

Although the communication and/or information function of color television pictures is indisputable, the fact remains that all other compositional factors such as script context, camera angle and shot, and placement of scenery and props must work cooperatively to compose the pictures. For example, color can communicate how pale a person is due to serious illness but the creation of the hospital environment and the choice of the shot are also contributory factors. Nevertheless, color television pictures, considering all other factors, communicate and inform.

Associative and/or Symbolic Functions of Colored Television Pictures. An effective compositional principle of the visual communication medium of television is the use of colors to associate and symbolize various events, feelings, and sensations. Properly manipulated, television colors can function as aesthetic agents that produce feelings of love, hatred, and joy, with which television viewers can associate. As music has the power to produce melodies to associate symbolically the listener's beliefs and concepts, so do color television pictures—as long as other television production factors work cooperatively toward that goal. For example, we can use red colors to symbolically associate passionate love in intense love scenes. Black is generally considered a symbol of evil, therefore the villain wears black. Careful consideration and proper application of the symbolic association of colors can become powerful guidelines in the construction of colored television images.

Television Colors as Dramatic Agents.   Colors are used, also, as stimulators of excitement, as dramatic agents that contribute to the establishment of the external look of the environment and the psychological (internal) mood of a scene. As aesthetic agents that create excitement, colors are extensively used in special events, sportscasts, and sunrise and sunset scenes. The multicolored decorations of the Christmas tree and the presents under the tree in television specials, the colorful uniforms of cheerleaders in television sportscasts, and the flashing lights of police cars in television detective stories are some examples of how television colors are used as dramatic agents that excite viewers. On the other hand, the sadness brought on by death in a funeral home can be reinforced by the absence of bright colors, the application of chiaroscuro lighting (particularly the Rembrandt lighting technique), and emphasis on low-key lighting that generates dark areas. With the collaboration of the other production elements, the mood of death can be effectively created.

   In summary, the key functions of color television pictures are additional color television guidelines for the creation of television pictures with artistic merits.

Television Sound and Audio Techniques

As an aesthetic component in the production of television programs, sound has been underestimated. Although equal to lighting, staging, and editing, the evolution of television's hardware and software clearly shows that the developments of both the technology and the artistry of sound in the production of television programs have had a very slow start. The reasons for this delay include the conceptual (the low-definition, small-screen television supposedly does not need good quality sound generated by expensive sophisticated sound technology), technological (the pictures and sounds are picked up simultaneously in live television productions to be more realistic and, supposedly, do not allow prerecorded sounds whose qualities could be controlled), and academic (research and theory building on television sound-related issues is not a priority for television production and research scholars; Metallinos, 1985b).

   Several developments during the last 15 years have brought considerable improvements to the technology and the artistry of television sound. The arrival of high-fidelity stereo sound (hi-fi), the development of high-definition television (HDTV), the merging of film and video that generate electronic cinematography (EC), and, generally, the enormous improvements in all other television production areas have helped to recognize the significant role of sound in the improvement of the entire production. These developments, in fact, have stimulated both the practitioners (professionals) and the theorists (academicians) of television to experiment with and to study the aesthetic potentials of television sound (Alten, 1994; Wilson, 1980; Zettl, 1992).

The basic theories of television sound—as an aesthetic component in television composition—generated from the various sound constructs, or variables, are now emerging (Alten, 1994). Unlike the staging and lighting techniques, however, generic television audio techniques are nonexistent. Consequently, we must examine the basic principles of television sounds that provide the foundations for the development of generic and genuine television audio techniques. This is precisely the ultimate purpose of this section, which examines the nature and characteristics of television sounds, outlines the functions performed by television sounds, discusses the compositional factors of television sounds, and reviews the basis on which television pictures and sounds are combined.

Nature and Characteristics of Television Sound

The physical characteristics of sound, like those of light and color, are discussed in the first part of the book. This section deals primarily with the sounds used in television to support, supplement, and supply coherence to the visuals. As is the case with all visual communication media arts, sounds used by the media can be manipulated, controlled, and skillfully adjusted for the benefit of the total outcome of the art form. Television sounds have the potential of supporting, supplementing, and supplying coherence to the pictures; they can also become powerful aesthetic agents that help to upgrade the outcome of the entire program if used systematically, cautiously, and skillfully.

Sound sources of television (such as the narrations of the cast, the supplementary music of the program, the special sound effects added to the program, and the sounds from additional video inputs), whether generated in the field or in the studio, are picked up by the numerous microphones and sound recording machines and are centralized and controlled by the television audio control console. The realistic nature of television is supported by equally real and faithful sounds that are used and recorded live and at the time of the videotaping of the television program. This is one of the main differences between film and television sound: The sounds in television production, for the most part, are picked up and recorded live, whereas in film sounds usually are edited-in after the film is shot.

By nature, television sounds differ from those of film in that the low-quality television picture, compared to the high-quality film picture, requires not only real sounds but their constant presence. Sounds, therefore, are essential for television, whereas in film the pictures carry the message and sounds are not as crucial. However, when sounds are used in film they must be of superior quality to match the high-definition film images. When HDTV is industrialized, the high quality of its pictures and the larger television screens will dictate a better quality sound such as high-fidelity stereo sound (Metallinos, 1991b). Today the application of high-fidelity stereo sound to regular television programs presents an obvious aesthetic imbalance that will no longer exist when HDTV is commercialized and universally practiced.

The gaps that exist between film and television sound are closing considerably as the merging of film and television increases. Electronic cinematography, which uses video to complete the film editing, allows also the postproduction improvement of the quality of the sound (Mathias & Patterson, 1985).

What main characteristics of the various sounds are used in television? There are several general characteristics that are found in media sounds and specific sources used primarily in television production that are reviewed herein.

According to their general application in media production, sounds are either textual or abstract. *Textual sounds* are referential sounds derived from an identifiable source, such as the voice of a particular person, the sound of an airplane, and the sound of rain falling. They identify, textually or literally, the source that originates them and are commonly found in speech as dialogues, narrations, or direct addresses (Zettl, 1992). The listener visualizes the source that generates the textual sounds.

Abstract sounds refer to those sounds that are not identifiable by the source that generates them. Abstract sounds are also called "non-literal" (Zettl, 1992, p. 338) because they are disconnected from the source that creates them and are called "non-diegetic" (Bordwell & Thompson, 1985, p. 197) in that they do not narrate (literally) the sound source. Abstract sounds describe feelings, events, or circumstances or simply exist on their own as pure structural sounds. Listeners cannot or need not visualize the source that generates the abstract sounds.   •

A common characteristic of both textual and abstract sounds is their ability to orient the listeners in space and time (e.g., night sounds or morning sounds), to involve the listeners emotionally (e.g., romantic feelings, fear, and tragic moments), and to arouse the imagination (e.g., stimulate the imagination to create images).

Among the specific characteristics of television sounds are the following: (a) they are controlled and easily manipulated; (b) their presence is necessary and essential; (c) regardless of the general category under which they fall, textual or abstract, television sounds can be used interchangeably or mixed; (d) they are equally powerful as aesthetic agents to the visuals that accompany them; and (e) they are generated live, for the most part, and occur simultaneously with the video portion of the television picture. These specific characteristics of television sounds form the basis on which the functions of television sounds are established, as explained next.

Functions of Television Sounds

The various verbal television sounds (such as dialogues, narrations, or direct addresses of the cast), the music that supplements the program (such as the theme music that identifies it), and the various sound effects (such as thunder, war sounds, and traffic sounds) perform basic functions in the program's context that are grouped under the categories of communication functions, emotional functions, and rhythmic functions. The review of these functions that follows emphasizes how powerful and significant sound is as an aesthetic agent in television composition.

Communication Function of Television Sounds.   Television sounds, like lighting and color, are used to communicate different messages, feelings, and situations. The three forms of verbal communication, as previously mentioned, are the *dialogue* or verbal communication and conversation between people, *narration* or straightforward speech during which a narrator describes the events, connecting the visuals with the story, and *direct address* or verbal communication between the person on the screen and the viewers, usually informing the viewers about issues, events, products, or circumstances.

In addition to communicating and informing viewers about the location, the environment in which events occur (on screen or off screen), they can also be used as indicators of time—daytime, nighttime, seasonal time, cultural time (e.g., Renaissance, Romantic Era, Middle Ages)—and can provide information about the magnitude of objects or events (heavy rain, strong winds, or traffic jams).

These forms of communication are sound information functions used very effectively in most television productions. Our knowledge of the communication and/or information function of television sounds provides us with the necessary guidelines for the construction of television programs.

Emotional Function of Television Sounds.   Another significant function of television sounds is the emotional, which includes the creation of mood and atmosphere; intense feelings of instability, anger, pleasure, anxiety, tranquillity; and the use of sound as predictive and symbolic agents.

Like lighting and color, television sounds function as emotional catalysts that help in the creation of a particular mood and atmosphere of a program. A funeral scene greatly intensifies with the addition of sad, heavy, moody types of sounds such as organ music and sporadic bell-ringing sounds. Conversely, a festive mood and atmosphere are created with appropriate joyful, fast-tempered, and pleasant music. An excellent example of the use of music to create the general mood and atmosphere of the seasons is provided by Vivaldi's famous composition, *The Four Seasons.*

Television sounds, whether they are textual and identifiable, or abstract and unidentifiable, have the potential to enhance the viewers' feelings of anger, anxiety, fear, instability, and their opposites, happiness, tranquillity, courage, and security. Identified, collectively, as internal conditions, Zettl (1990) described these television sounds as sounds that:

> can express a variety of internal conditions such as stable, or unstable, environment (often in conjunction with the contextual visual clue: the tilting of the horizon line) or a person who feels calm, excited, or agitated. For example, to reveal the fear and panic of sailors in the flooded engine room, you could put yet another layer of "internal fear" sounds on top of sounds that depict the squeezing of space. (p. 347)

The uses of sounds as predictive and symbolic agents are additional functions of television sound, which when used in conjunction with contextual visual clues, are powerful and effective compositional elements. As lightning predicts the forthcoming sound of thunder, so does the sound of burning bushes predict fire in the open fields. In the film *Jaws*, the forthcoming appearance of the killer shark was prepared for, predictably, by a special fast-paced, drumbeat-like, crescendo music that was used throughout the film to identify the shark. Certain music can be used symbolically to arouse the emotions and create appropriate feelings as, for example, the sounds of Christmas carols that are used to symbolize Christmas (even without the contextual visual clue of the Christmas tree) or the music of the church organ symbolizing the wedding procession toward the altar.

Rhythmic Function of Television Sounds. Another purpose of television sound is to provide rhythm in the succession of the pictures that synthesize the television program. It is an important function because rhythm provides the structural continuity necessary to connect the individual events and it unifies the entire program. Although the rhythms provided by television sounds differ from one scene to the next—and they should differ to avoid monotonous repetition of the same rhythmic structure—they help the viewers to follow the flow of action, which pictures alone often fail to do. The overall structural coordination of the television program's rhythm is the theme music known also as the "leading motif" or "leitmotiv" (Zettl, 1990, p. 346), which identifies a particular theme, story of a program, situation, action, or person. Popular films are recognized by particular leading motifs that are often used as the essential coordinate linking the rhythmic structure of the individual episodes. In television, the theme music is more effective and more essential because of the fast pace of action—many programs have to be presented in shorter periods of time—and the great variety of shots used in most commercial television programs today.

Unity, coherence, structure, continuity, and uninterrupted flow of action are among the key compositional benefits provided by the rhythms that supplement and support the images. It is an important function performed by television sound that must always be considered in television production.

In summary, the key functions of television sounds, which are to communicate with and/or inform the viewers, emotionally involve the listeners in the drama of the program, and provide the rhythmic structure essential for the coherence and the unity of the program, are additional sound guidelines for use at the discretion of the television audio directors and the production directors.

Compositional Factors of Television Sound

The discussion of the nature of sounds, their characteristics, and functions provides the necessary background information for the examination of the key compositional factors, the audio techniques of television, which, in turn, outline the aesthetics of television sound. Specifically, this section examines the preparatory stages in the selection of sounds, outlines the principles that dictate their selection, and reviews the basis on which various audio techniques are developed, stemming from the principles of which pictures and sounds are combined.

Processes of Television Sound Selection
and Audio Arrangements

The television script, which contains both audio (the sound portion of the program) and video (the pictures that accompany the text and sounds), dictates what type of audio setup is required, what types of audio effects—if any—are necessary, and what music should be used in the program. The production team carefully studies the script, analyzes each scene separately, outlines the key issues of the program, and debates the production's audio requirements. A brief review of this threefold process is deemed necessary because it provides the basis for the discussion of the principles on which the particular sounds are selected.

The first task of the television production team is to decide how many microphones are needed, the types of microphones that must be used, and where they should be placed. Some of these decisions are provided by the script (e.g., the number of people talking), the production director (as it is the director who knows where the people will be staged), and the audio director, who is solely responsible for the audio outcome of the production. Each production has its own requirements. Certain television drama and action programs demand elaborate, extensive, and complicated microphone placements, whereas others, such as interviews and newscasts, need less. Whatever the case, however, the requirements for the audio engineers are knowledge of television microphones, skill in handling and placing the microphone in the appropriate location, and basic understanding of television production processes so that they do not interfere with other activities of the production, particularly with the director's developed professional (technical) and aesthetic (artistic) responsibilities.

The second task of the television production team, and particularly the audio director and the production director, is to choose the special sound effects required in the production. These could be prerecorded sounds existing in audio libraries or sounds created during the recording of the production. Sounds of traffic, airplanes, ambulances, thunder, and a host of others are available or can be created. Often the script does not demand the use of special sound effects. However, the entire production can be improved if such sounds are used by a creative audio director with the concession of the production director. Television sound effects, whether required or invented, prerecorded or created during the production, must be carefully decided and selected. They present a challenge for the audio director and the production director.

The last step in the selection of sounds and the arrangement of the audio portion of the television production is to decide the theme music, the leading motifs of the production. The script itself provides the clues for the selection but the input of the production team is always very helpful. The issues discussed in the script usually inspire the selection process; however, other factors such as the main characters, the mood of the program, and the symbols used in the production can be the reasons for the selection of the theme music.

Because the theme music could provide the rhythmic structure of the program, as it was discussed earlier, it is necessary that the audio director and the production director consider the sounds that start and close the program. Uniformity in opening and closing with the same sound (usually a musical piece) is most effective but not always required. However, the skillful use of the program's theme music as an opening and closing of the program could be even more effective and more desirable, considering the fast pace, short duration, and nature of the average television program. This, too, presents a challenge for the audio director and the production director, who must examine the production from all other aspects before they make the final selection and arrangements of the sounds.

Applied Principles in Television Sound Selection

On what basis do we select abstract sounds, particularly music, to enrich a television program? What factors must we consider in the selection of the theme music of a television program? Are there any criteria with which the use of sounds, to enhance the program's mood and atmosphere, are analyzed and justified? These are some of the questions that must be considered in our effort to underline the principles on which the production's sounds (primarily the theme music) and the structural sounds are selected.

The importance of music as an art form was discussed earlier. What we need to emphasize here is that the power of music to arouse, to stimulate, and to influence the listener's emotions should be a serious concern to the audio director and the television production director. Ethical consideration is a key principle in the selection and application of theme and structural music in television production. For example, the selection of well-known musical motifs and their application to television commercials is a perpetual practice by many advertisers. For many people classical music used in commercials that advertise household cleaning products is not appropriate. The issues examined in the program and the main subject explored should be the basic consideration for the selection and application of the theme and the structural rhythms of abstract music. As stated previously, the script should always be the starting point in the process of the selection of television sounds. In their application, however, the underlying principle is to use abstract sounds, theme music, and rhythm compatible with and related to the key issues examined in the program. For example, it is inappropriate and tasteless to add background music to a scene of a straightforward conversation between people, as it is common practice in commercial television's soap operas. The subject matter of the conversation is pretentious because it is totally unrelated to the background music and often annoys and distracts viewers.

Another key factor in the selection and application of sounds, in general, and theme and rhythmic music in particular, of a television production is the ability (of the audio directors and production directors) to contextualize, or to relate, the picture's content with the sound's content, balancing out the sounds with the visuals. If the sounds override the visuals (particularly when they are unrelated) the pictorial composition will soften, and vice versa. The job of the audio engineer is to learn to contextualize, to relate the picture's structure with that of the sound to avoid disharmony, imbalance, and uneven reception of visuals and sounds. In fact, the greatest challenge confronting television directors is their ability to relate, contextually, the various components of the production, including sounds, to the entire program.

An important criterion, also, for the selection and application of theme music to accompany the visuals of a television program is knowledge of music as an art form. For example, when a well-known musical theme of one program is used to enhance the mood of another—with a different context— the result is confusion and disorientation. The application of the theme music of *Bonanza* to another western program will reinforce the subject of the former to the content of the latter in the minds of the spectators. This is particularly true when classical compositions are selected and applied to television programs with contemporary subject matter unrelated to the classical music composition. The audio directors and the production directors must be fairly knowledgeable of music (including history of music, appreciation, composition, and aesthetics) to succeed in their selection and application of theme music for their productions. For example, the history of music will assist the audio director and the production director in selecting the melodies of the period indicated by the script; knowledge of music appreciation will clarify and distinguish one composition from another; knowledge of music composition will allow the audio director and the production director to understand the difference of the various elements of sound (e.g., pitch, timbre, duration, and dynamics), and it will give a thorough analysis of the parts of the musical composition (e.g., allegro, crescendo, melody, homophonic, polyphonic, and harmonic compositions). The basic requirement for the selection of music to be used in a television program is to learn, study, and understand music as an art form.

In summary, the applied principles in the selection of television sounds are ethical sensitivity and consideration, the subject matter of the program, contextualism, and background knowledge of music as an art form.

Video–Audio Syntheses in Television Programs

From the preceding analyses of the processes of television sound selection and sound arrangements and the applied principles for the selection of television sounds, we now arrive at the final stage of the discussion of television sound and audio techniques in which the video and audio syntheses are examined. Specifically, this section briefly discusses the intimate relationship between pictures and sounds in regard to the perceptual factors of figure–ground, sound picture perspectives, and gestalt; outlines the criteria under which the television pictures match the television sounds; and examines the generic connection between video and audio editing.

Perceptual and Cognitive Factors in Audiovisual Composition. When we combine pictures with sounds to tell a story, by way of the media of audiovisual communication, such perceptual factors as figure–ground, visual and aural perspective and psychological closure or gestalt are mainly involved. The perceptual and the cognitive processes of these three factors were discussed in the first and second parts of this book. Herein is a brief review of their roles as aesthetic agents in structuring the audio with the visuals in television programs.

The perceptual principle of figure–ground when it applies to picture–sound combinations in television performs a dual function. First, the figure–ground dichotomy and distinction are maintained in the visual elements of the picture. In this case, the picture divides into those dominant figures in the front ground (i.e., a person walking in a living room environment) and those visual elements that comprise the background, the environment within which the figure exists (i.e., the walls, furniture, and chairs of the living room). Cognitively, in this case we consider the environmental sounds as background sounds and the narrative sounds (i.e., speech or walking sounds) of the person in the living room as foreground sounds. In short, the perception and the cognition of visuals and sounds correlate; they match, coherently and harmonically, as we would have expected. This is the first function performed by the picture–sound combination in television programs.

There is, however, a second one, namely the figure–ground audiovisual counterreaction (or exchange) in which the sounds of the environment (e.g., the music and traffic sounds) take over and overshadow the figure (and the sounds) of the foreground. In this case neither the visuals or the sounds match. Instead we experience two different components of the television picture—audio and visuals—changing places as figures and as backgrounds in the picture's final synthesis.

In visual and aural perspective combinations we tend to assign louder sounds to visuals that are closer and less loud sounds to the ones that are farther (in the picture's background), as it happens in nature and in certain real-life experiences. When this harmonic coexistence, this cognitive perspective, is violated, it creates anxiety, curiosity, and disturbance. Hearing gunshots or someone screaming scares and disturbs us. This is also true in television picture composition. When visual and aural harmony (due to the perceptual and cognitive factors of perspective) is violated, tension is created, accompanied by uneasiness and discomfort. Unless the audio director and the production director wish to create anxiety and disturbance, the common practice should be to maintain the audiovisual perspective combination for better television composition results and for an improved overall, audiovisual communication.

The last audiovisual composition factor, stemming from the perceptual and cognitive principles of psychological closure, is the gestalt. This means simply that when we combine pictures with sounds we must consider the power exerted by the innate ability and intuitive tendency to fill in missing information and with minimum visual and auditory elements to create new configurations or gestalts. For example, we continue to see an event, even when it is over; we extend the melody we have heard or we continue to hear it although it is over. In fact, the entire process of television production and the basis on which we construct pictures and sounds in the audiovisual media derives from the principal of psychological closure and gestalt. The television picture is only a representation—a configuration—of the event; it is not the event itself; the visual field (the television picture) is the configuration, the gestalt, of the visual world. Among the various forms of psychological closure and the strongest resulting gestalt is continuity. Sounds provide a sense of continuous action and succession of events in pictures due to the principal of psychological closure.

In short, all these factors (figure–ground, visual and aural perspective, and gestalt), assist in the harmonious combination of the structuring of television pictures.

Compositional Bases in Correlating Pictures With Sounds. In addition to the perceptual and the cognitive factors in structuring visual images and in combining their audio portion with the aural, there are several other factors that we call compositional bases for correlating the pictures with their appropriate sounds in television programs. These bases are drawn from the fundamental compositional principles of the visual communication media arts, discussed earlier, and are also known as matching criteria for pictures and sounds (Zettl, 1990).

Visual balance, direction, proportion, shape and form, level of sophistication, light and color, time and motion, tension, expression, and point of view, which all television images have in varying degrees, must be combined and enriched with appropriate sounds to maintain their artistic potentials. This task is complicated and demands careful consideration not only of these visual communication media compositional factors, but the additional consideration of the diverse messages, moods, and physical structure of the pictures. Zettl (1990) grouped them into "historical-geographical, thematic, tonal, and structural" (p. 378). A brief review of these compositional bases with their corresponding examples is provided here.

Correlating pictures with sounds historically or chronologically means using the sounds of the period connoted by the visuals of the picture. For example, the picture of the Parthenon in Athens, Greece, or the Colosseum in Rome, Italy, can be matched with the ancient sounds of the flute in the first case and marching band sounds in the second case. The historical periods illustrated in the pictures are matched by the music (the sounds) of the same period.

The correlation of pictures with sounds environmentally or geographically is easily achieved with the use of sounds (music) that match the location or geography illustrated in the picture. For example, the sound of flamenco music matches the picture of Spain and the music of the Indian flute matches the picture of India, and so on.

The subject matter or thematic structural combination of pictures and sounds is achieved when we add the appropriate music to match the theme of a picture. For example, when a picture shows the interior of a church, organ music seems most appropriate. The church-related experience brings out the music we have heard and experienced in the past.

Tonal or atmospheric combination of pictures and sounds means to matching the tone, mood, or feeling provided by the picture with its corresponding music and sound. For example, tonally we correlate a funeral scene with melancholy sounds. Conversely, a happy scene is usually enhanced with joyful music, in a picture of a happy couple dancing to the tune of joyful music.

Finally, we correlate pictures with sounds structurally or morphologically, which means that we match the inner structure of the picture (the visual elements) with the corresponding internal structure of the sounds. For example, a picture of a football field is correlated with the sounds of band music, a picture of an orthodox church with the Byzantine chant or psalm, and a picture of a Catholic church with the Gregorian chant.

It is emphasized that the correlation of pictures and sounds on the basis of the historical, geographical, thematic, tonal, and structural elements of both visual and auditory elements cannot alone provide the desired results. The support of the various other components and compositional factors, mentioned earlier, is needed if they are to be effective. Also these compositional bases are only the starting point for the development of the skills needed, and the knowledge required, for the effective correlation of pictures with sounds by the individual sound director and television production director.

Video and Audio Editing

The next section discusses television editing principles and techniques. This section, however, focuses primarily on the application of sound in television editing.

When we examine the principles on which the techniques of television audio are based, we must also consider the role played by the pictorial editing to determine the audio techniques. Because the television picture incorporates the sights (visuals) with sounds (audio) and with motion editing, the proper arrangements of both the visual and the aural elements come to focus. The techniques used to edit the television pictures to tell a story cannot be effective unless the visuals and the other elements are perfectly combined and properly correlated. Therefore, when I refer (in the next section) to television editing techniques, the reader must understand that the audio portion of the picture follows the same principle and is always present. Herein are some examples of picture–sound correlations in television editing.

In the diagnostic or analytical editing technique of continuous action, the narration, the sound effects, and the theme music follow a continuous flow to match the sequence shown by the edited pictures. Usually a soundtrack is added to keep the pace and maintain the flow of events as one picture succeeds the other. In the second diagnostic editing technique of segmented action, all sounds are also segmented, matching the events, environment, and circumstances shown in the pictures with their appropriate sounds. This is more difficult to achieve than with the previously mentioned editing technique of diagnostic continuous action. However, in postproduction editing, segmented sounds can easily be added to the segmented picture editing with sounds matching the circumstances correspondingly.

In the thematic or idea associative editing technique of resemblance, the sounds correlating with the theme of one picture must also correlate with the theme of another picture that resembles the first only in terms of its theme. In this type of editing, the task of the pictorial sequencing is to compare two seemingly different pictures (e.g., a picture of a sick person and a picture of a sick animal, or a picture of crowded people with a picture of crowded animals) with the theme they resemble (sickness in the first case and crowding in the second). The edited sounds must match the edited pictures accordingly, not so much during the live video recording as in postproduction editing.

Lastly, in the thematic confrontation editing technique, the sounds correlating with the theme of one picture must also correlate with the theme of another that resembles the first only in terms of its conflicting theme. In this type of editing, the task of the pictorial sequencing is to confront or collide two different events of the same theme (e.g., an image of a healthy man with an image of a healthy child or an image of a happy couple with an image of an unhappy one). The sounds, like the pictures, must indicate the confrontation or the collision between health and sickness and between happiness and sorrow. Again, this thematic editing technique can easily be applied in postproduction editing rather than during the live television production recording.

In summary, the established television picture editing techniques of diagnostic continuous and diagnostic segmented actions and thematic resemblance and thematic confrontation actions require appropriately correlated sounds to match the pictures. Special consideration must be given to the selection and the use of the sounds so they can be equally compatible to their corresponding edited visuals.

TELEVISION EDITING:
PRINCIPLES AND APPLICATIONS

The last stage in the preparation and the recording of a television program is to review the shots as they are described in the storyboard, or to determine what shots will be selected at what particular point in the program. This decision is made by the director and the selection of the shots is executed by the switcher operator or technical director. This process, in fact, is the second form of television editing, the so-called production editing. As previously stated, however, editing occurs in three stages. It starts as the preproduction editing process, during which the television script is visualized and pictured (the mental images are made into pictures) and the program's storyboard is created. It continues during the production with the selection of the shots to narrate the program's story known as production editing. Finally, after the program is recorded, postproduction editing is often applied, during which the sequencing of the shots, the selection of the images, the timing of the program, the audio, and the sounds of the program are arranged and edited.

The enormous power of editing as an aesthetic component in television production (mostly due to its flexibility in allowing extensive manipulation of the sequential arrangement of the production's audiovisual materials) has been recognized from the very beginning of television. Unlike the sound component, television editing has been studied, experimented with, and researched considerably by many theorists, practitioners, and researchers during the last 60 years of its existence (Metallinos, 1985b). These three activities (study, experimentation, and research) center on three respected factors that generate, support, and identify television editing. These factors are *time* (and timing), *motion* (and pace), and *sequencing* (or editing). These three factors constitute the basis on which the principles of television editing are built. In fact, time, motion, and sequencing are interrelated, interdependent, and work together to create television editing as an aesthetic agent, a key compositional factor, in television production.

It is, therefore, necessary to examine first the nature, characteristics, and use of these factors in television production recording before the established principles of television editing and their application to television programs are discussed and exemplified. The presence of time, motion, and sequencing is evident in all three stages of television production in varying degrees. Consequently, these three factors are considered uniformly applicable to the entire process of television production development and completion. This section specifically examines the nature, characteristics, and functions of time and timing in television; analyzes the various forms of television motion; discusses the basic principles on which sequencing of pictures, or editing, is achieved; and reviews, underlines, and provides examples of existing television editing techniques.

Time and Timing in Television

The essence of time and the role of timing in television are the most significant factors to be considered in the study of television's compositional principles. This section defines time and underlines its importance in contemporary society and in mass media, examines the three types of time (clock, felt, and biological), and relates the past, present, and future phenomenon to the television medium.

Nature Characteristics and Functions of Time.   Perhaps the most interesting philosophical inquiry from the beginning of Western civilization has centered on the question of what time is. Throughout the centuries, philosophers, mathematicians, religious scholars, and physicists have attempted to find an answer to the question of time (its essence, its meaning, where it starts, where it ends). As one would have expected, they have provided their own points of view, definitions, and explanations about the nature of time and their statements make an interesting study that goes beyond the scope of this discussion.

There are, however, certain aspects of time that refer to its nature and reveal its characteristics. First, time relates to change. It can only be defined as the continuous process of actions, events, or conditions. For Aristotle, time was considered the measurement of the before to the after, which is also an aspect of change related to time's essence. Plato also related the nature of time with the essence of change and he believed that time is conceived as the state of being to the state of becoming, which also indicates change. This change can be progressive or regressive for the better or worse. A second aspect of time is its relation to space. In our attempt to measure time we involve space. The distance from Point A to Point B could very well be 2 hours. However, we automatically locate in space the Points A and B and we have to travel the distance by some means that we measure in spatial units (miles, meters, feet, etc.). In short, time and space are interrelated. A third characteristic of time is its duration or the period during which an action or event occurs. This duration is related to the previously mentioned change and space, and it adds a new aspect, a new characteristic of time and length that is a quantity dimension of time measured by various techniques. The duration of each time period is a very important characteristic of time relating to television that is discussed later. Another aspect of time that is also important to television is motion. Its aspect of change that occurs in space and has a certain duration involves motion and relocation of action, regardless of the speed by which motion occurs. Time involves motion; it is understood as movement of actions and occurring events in space. Motion, as is discussed later, is measured by time; they are interrelated and interdependent. Finally, an aspect of time that concerns this discussion (and is revealed by the review of literature regarding the nature and key characteristics of time) is time's relationship and involvement with everything else in the universe and in our lives. This is known as the relativity theory of time developed by Albert Einstein (1875–1955), who identified the relationship between energy (E), mass (M), and the velocity of light [(time) C] and concluded that $E = MC^2$ where energy is equal to mass, multiplied by the velocity of light in the square power (Gondsmit & Clairborne, 1961).

On the basis of these important aspects of time, which characterize and explain time in terms of its relationships with change, space, duration, motion, and relativity, several theories of time have been developed that discuss the functions of time on numerous levels and in varying degrees.

Three of these theories relate to the media of film and television, help to distinguish film and television, and underline the three most significant functions of time in television composition. They are Zeno's theory of motionless time, Bergson's theory of duration of time and motion, and Einstein's theory of relativity.

Zeno of Elea (490–430 B.C.) was a Greek philosopher who was born in the town of Elea in what is southeastern Italy today. He studied and taught at the Eleatic School (under the direction of the philosopher Parmenides) and later became the teacher of Pericles and Calias in Athens. Considered by Aristotle as the inventor of dialectical reasoning, Zeno created a series of argumentative paradoxes. One such argument is related to time, space, and motion and states, in effect, that in a spatial distance an infinite number of bisections exist, which one has to travel infinitely to arrive from one section to the next. Consequently, one cannot travel any distance in finite time, no matter how short the distance is or how fast the traveling speed is. Logically, therefore, motion is impossible, and if motion does not exist, time does not exist or, at least, both motion and time are frozen bisections, or moments. This seems to be related to the medium of film in that still pictures constitute frozen moments of time, or individual units (bisections), standing still unless they are mechanically projected and run successively with speed (24 frames per second), and create the illusion of motion (Zettl, 1990). This is further discussed in the next section, which relates motion to editing.

Bergson's basic belief (regarding time, motion, and change) was time's continuous duration, dynamic process, and continuous flow. Contrary to Zeno's theory of the existence of frozen, static, and fragmented moments of time, Bergson saw in everything an organic growth, a continuous duration of action and events uninterrupted and always evolving. This seems to be related to the medium of television in that the scanning beam that creates the television picture works continuously, organically; its motion never stops; it moves constantly to create the lines that make up the television picture. This point is also discussed in the editing section.

The relativity theory of Einstein relates the function of time in our lives and the media. According to this theory, everything relates to everything else. Therefore, time functions as a coordinator, a commodity that translates into money: Time is money. It is time we give to be rewarded. Commercial media, particularly television, survive because they sell time to advertisers to generate revenues required for the creation of television programs. Time is central to our modern lives and relates to all our activities, including the media.

In short, the review of the nature, characteristics, and key functions of time underline time's importance as a factor analyzing the structure of television composition, and time's interconnection with motion.

Time Categories and Their Relationship to Television. The visual communication media of film and television are time dependent. Their products are the results of the skillful manipulation of time and timing. The final aesthetic consideration of a film or television program is its length. It is, therefore, important that the three main categories of time as they relate to television programs, namely the biological time, the clock time, and the felt time, are distinguished.

Biological time refers to each person's biological clock that tells the person that it is time to eat, sleep, wake up, and so on. The human body arranges, in time periods, its various activities and informs the individual that it is time to change, react, repeat actions and circumstances, always in coordination with the different organs of the body. For example, we know, biologically, that it is time to go to sleep because we are tired and our eyes are closing.

It could be that our internal clock, our biological time, is the result of our own creation of habits. We decide the exact times we want to eat, sleep, work, and so on. In that respect we differ from other individuals. However, the environmental time, seasonal changes, and society's established norms are all standardized. We follow them year in and year out. This is important to the development of our biological time. The working hours (9:00 a.m.–5:00 p.m.), dinnertime (6:00–7:00 p.m.), entertainment times (usually 7:00–11:00 p.m.), and television's prime time (7:00–11:00 p.m.) are standard practice in North American societies. It would be interesting to study the degree to which television's prime-time programming affects the biological clock of the people of these societies.

Clock time refers to the physical time read on the clock. It is measured in time units (i.e., hours, minutes, seconds) and it indicates change from the before to the after.

As one of the most fundamental quantities of the physical world, time is measured objectively by time methods, namely (a) the *solar* time (which measures the motion of the sun and divides the day into 24 hours), (b) the *sidereal* time (which measures the motion of the stars and divides the year into four seasons, 12 months, etc.), and (c) the *ephimeris* time (which measures the revolution of the earth around the sun and is used by astronomers to accurately measure the various positions of planets and stars (Funk & Wagnalls New Encyclopedia, 1972). Our institutions, and in fact, our lives are run by clock time, which acts as the catalyst that unifies our daily, weekly, and yearly activities, and determines our status (wealth, involvement, etc.) in society. What we do with time and how we use it become central issues determined by the physical time that unifies our activities within the society we live in.

Felt time refers to the psychological time that we experience internally with our emotional, psychological, totally subjective involvement with an event, an action, or a situation. Felt time is measured in terms of our personal involvement and to what degree our emotional or psychological connection with the event makes us ignore clock time or attend to it. For example, if we are totally involved in reading a good book or watching an interesting film or television program we are not concerned with what time it is and we totally ignore clock time. Conversely, if we are reading an uninteresting book or watching a boring television program, clock time comes into focus; we are constantly watching the clock, anxiously awaiting its ending.

It is noteworthy that the duration of our emotional (subjective) involvement determines the degree to which we ignore clock time. As a result, we often regret having been involved for too long in various activities. Visual communication media products such as theater, film, and television have considered the need to balance the felt, or emotional, time with that of the clock, or physical time, both of which are balanced with the biological or physiological time of the individual.

In television, this uniformity of time and the needed balance of clock, felt, and biological times is often achieved with the establishment and proper manipulation of other types of times falling under the script or physical time, experienced or emotional duration time, and technologically adjusted television medium time.

The television script contains three forms of clock time. The first one is the overall clock time needed to complete the program from the opening to the closing. This is also known as *running time* of the program and its overall physical duration is determined by the type of program; for example, situation comedies usually run for 30 minutes and drama series usually run for 60 minutes. Generally, commercial television's running time is shorter than that of film or theater due to the nature of the medium and the factor of fatigue affecting the viewers.

The second type of physical script time is the total amount of clock time needed to cover the events of the *story* from the beginning to the end. This time is unpredictable; it could be covered in years or only a few hours. The occurring events are also uneven in the script's story time. For example, a historical documentary's periods are uneven; some historical periods are longer than others. However, the duration of all periods covered make up the physical time of the story of the script. Obviously, the story time must be condensed to meet the requirements imposed by the running time so that a documentary on World War II can be told in one program with a running time of no more than 60 minutes.

The last physical time of the television script is the *scene time* that measures how long the individual scenes of a script are. As theatrical plays divide into acts and each act into scenes, so do the average television programs; they divide not into acts, but into scenes or episodes. The lengths of the scenes vary in both the running time and story time. However, the sum total of the scene times makes up the program's running and story times.

In terms of the felt time, the television program is characterized by the types of such subjective or psychological times as pace, tempo, and speed.

Pace refers to the overall feeling of the show, whether it runs fast or not. Usually fast changes of shots and rapid rhythmic music create a faster overall pace and we have the feeling that everything in the visual field develops and moves faster. *Tempo* (as in music) refers to a program's individual segments' rhythm. Some segments are characterized by a faster rhythm or tempo and others by a slower one. Like pace, tempo is felt time generated psychologically by structural sounds combined with structural changes of images. *Speed* refers to the individual performers within each segment. Subjectively, we often perceive some actions within a scene as moving faster or slower than others. One example is an argument between two people: As the argument intensifies, the speed of the segment seems to increase as well and we feel the developed tension created between the people.

Technically, the medium can adjust the speed to either accelerated time or to slow-motion time, or to replay (playback) past events (often in slow motion). In all three cases the time is felt (psychological) and its application can be helpful or detrimental to the production's outcome if it is not used sensibly and justifiably. However, this refers to television's motion factors and their aesthetic consideration, which are examined in the motion section.

In summary, the three categories of television time are the biological, the felt, and the clock times and their derivatives are the running time, story time, and scene time; the pace, tempo, and speed; and the accelerated, slow-motion, and playback times. This last one brings us to the discussion of the past, present, and future phenomena in television.

Past, Present, and Future Phenomena in Television. The instant replay of a recorded event in television brings to mind past, present, and future phenomena, the aesthetic value of each, and their interdependence. In their quest to define time and time's connection with the past, present, and future phenomena, a Christian philosopher, a poet, and a contemporary scientist have given us some interesting thoughts worth reexamining.

As far back as the early days of Christianity, Saint Augustine (354–430), a Latin priest who became one of the most eminent spokespersons of the Western Church, having studied rhetoric, philosophy, and Christian dogma, came to the conclusion that the present can only be conceived of as a link or a connection of the past and the future. He suggested that when we talk about time and its connection with the past and the future, we can only talk about and underline the presence of things past, the presence of things present, and the presence of things future.

The presence of things past helps us to remember, supports our efforts to comprehend the presence of things present, and provides clues to what the future might be. This is what instant replay does in television. It gives us a better understanding of what has occurred. The presence of things future can only be comprehended as long as they are derived from experiences of the past, right now.

The American-born English poet T. S. Eliot (1888–1965), in his poem *Burnt Norton* (Eliot, 1963), wrote:

Time present and time past
Are both perhaps present in time future
And time future contained in time past.
If all time is eternally present
All time is unredeemable.

What might have been is an abstraction
Remaining a perceptual possibility
Only in a world of speculation.
What might have been and what has been
Point to one end, which is always present. (p. 189)

Although past phenomena are only an abstraction and the future phenomena are only a speculation, the fact remains that they are both interrelated with the present. The abstracted memory of television's playback pictures provides the clue for what will be coming up in the next picture, thus connecting all three to the moment of the present.

Lastly, the Nobel prize winner and professor of physical chemistry and thermodynamics Ilya Prigogine (1980), in his book *From Being to Becoming*, suggested that the connection of time's past with time's present and time's future can only be understood as a sociocultural evolutionary change. In physics these three aspects of time are not related. Prigogine (1980) concluded:

> Therefore, in a sense, anyone interested in cultural and social motion must consider, in one way or another, the problem of time and the laws of change; perhaps inversely anyone interested in the problem of time cannot avoid taking an interest in the cultural and social changes of our time.
>
> Both in classical and in quantum mechanics, it seemed that, if the state of a system at a given time were "known" with sufficient accuracy, the future (as well as the past) could at least be predicted in principle. Of course this is a purely conceptual problem; in fact we know that we cannot even predict whether it will rain in, say, one month from now.
>
> Yet this theoretical framework seems to indicate that in some sense the present already "contains" the past and the future. (p. xvii)

It is interesting that Prigogine (1980), a scientist, recognized the connection of time with change that is evident in the present of things past (cultural changes) and that they can be seen in the presence of things future (evolutionary and inescapable).

In short, the past, present, and future phenomena of time are constantly present in television production, during which visual and auditory elements move from the past to the future, presenting them both in the present (see Fig. 9.37).

Television Motions

The nature, characteristics, and functions of motion in general, and in visual communication media in particular, were discussed in Part I (Perception) and in the section referring to the fundamental compositional principles of the visual communication media arts in Part III. This section discusses the various forms of motion in television as they relate to the development of television's editing principles. Specifically, this section underlines the Bergsonean duration

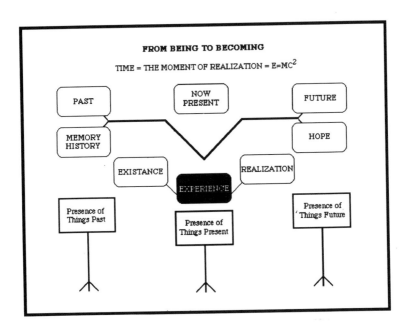

FIG. 9.37. A concept of time perception. The past, present, and future are present *now*, at the moment we realize and experience our existence.

in television motion, examines the various television motion paradoxes and pragmatics, and reviews the three key motions (primary, secondary, and tertiary) of television.

The Continuous Flow of Television Images: The Bergsonean Duré.   The key difference between film and television, in regards to the structure of their images, lies in the distinct ways by which the two media generate their pictures. Film pictures' motion is actually an illusion, a paradox, because the film pictures are still pictures that exist as testimony of past events. They have already been filmed, they have gone through the scrutiny of editing, and they are frozen moments awaiting mechanical projection and activation. Zeno's concept of a finite motion and moveless time applies to film as long as the film pictures are not projected at a speed of 24 frames per second, in which case they create the illusion of motion because of the speed at which they are projected.

Television's images, on the other hand, are the results of a continuous, ever unfolding motion of the electron beam that activates the phosphorous dots and creates the scanning lines that generate the picture frames. This continuous process creates a constant change that is a unique aesthetic factor of television, as stated previously. The Bergsonean idea of a continuous flow of time and motion applies to the television medium. Television is Bergsonean in nature, whereas film seems to be based on Zeno's finite motion idea (Zettl, 1990).

To the average film and television viewer, motions of pictures are perceived the same. A film cut looks the same as a television cut and a film zoom-in is perceived the same as a television zoom-in. The perception of motion is stable in both media, as it is also evident when we watch movies on television. So why do we insist on referring to film as Zenoen and television as Bergsonean? We do this because in framing or directing for film we must consider the static state of the film picture, which is being completed now, to the state of being. This is not the case in framing for television, which generates and changes the pictures in the state of becoming as an unfinished unit. Viewers' perception of the motion of images of the two media might be the same, but the image conceptions of the film and television media are different and the directors must be aware of it.

The continuous flow of television pictures calls for a different approach in the construction of images that is based on the real-life recording of actions and events, and therefore, for continuous recording with minimum interruptions and rerecordings of scenes. This should be a factor of paramount concern to television directors and students of television composition and aesthetics.

Unconventional Television Motions. Along with the three conventional television motions (primary, secondary, and tertiary) discussed earlier, we have such uncommon motions as motion while in motion, figure–ground reversal motion, slow motion, accelerated motion, and reversal motion.

Motion while in motion occurs when we are in a car or on an airplane, both of which are in motion, and we move forward or backward within the environment. According to Zettl (1990), this motion constitutes a paradox because television's flow from here to there has a reference point of change (a background) that changes itself. It is obvious how important the background (motion's reference point) becomes when we record an event in which there is motion within a moving background.

Figure–ground reversal motion refers to a falsely perceived motion in which we feel as though we are moving backward when we actually are motionless. This happens, for example, when we stand on a bridge watching the water moving forward and we gradually turn toward the bridge. For a moment we have the feeling that we move, with the bridge, backward while the waters remain still. This phenomenon is caused, of course, by the reversal of the figure and the background. The running waters traverse their original role as figures and assume the place of the bridge. If we record this event in television, we will have a motion paradox that would be annoying if it were not within the context of the program.

Slow motion is a common practice in contemporary commercial television used effectively in live television productions such as sports telecasts. Its purpose is to intensify the event, allowing the viewer to observe more details and follow the action more intensely. Slow motion is used mostly for playback of an event that is repeated for purposes of clarification and even to dramatize the event and to intensify the spectacle. Although the external rhythms of the pictures have slowed down, our internal rhythm of the event often increases rather than slows down. It is a paradox motion of television that can be used to increase viewers' emotional involvement with the program when used properly and within the context of the program.

Accelerated motion of television pictures is also an unconventional motion used in television productions to economize time, increase viewer interest, and break the normal pace and rhythm of the program. Events that take a long time to develop, such as the gathering of the clouds before the rain, the blooming of a flower, and the changes of the seasons, can be shown in a faster than normal motion that intensifies viewer interest and participation. This motion, also, is paradoxical and should be rarely applied and only when it is absolutely necessary.

Reversal motion is another uncommon motion available in television production, used only in rare cases and in special television programs such as instructional programs or documentaries on subjects requiring the use of reversal to demonstrate speed, acceleration, and motivation. Physics, biology, mathematics, and generally all natural sciences, instructional, and/or educational television programs often use the reversal motion to intensify and to clarify certain points and issues. Because it is uncommon, however, it should be used only when it is absolutely necessary; it is better to avoid using it altogether.

Conventional Television Motions.   An aspect of television that identifies it as a unique medium, different from all other visual communication media (except film), is that the television image is generated by the manipulation, coexistence, and collaboration of the three types of motions already discussed in Parts I and II of this book. Here, their applications are briefly examined.

Primary motion varies in degrees of speed and direction of objects and subjects moving toward or away from the camera. A horizontal (left to right and right to left) primary motion should preferably be recorded on a long shot so that the event remains within the frame. Vertical motion of objects and subjects in relation to the camera is preferable in television recording with the z-axis vectors moving toward or away from the camera to maximize space and to allow the acceleration (inward) or slowing down (outward) of motion of objects and events.

Secondary motion refers to the motions of the camera itself that vary in degrees of speed and directions, such as dollying in and out, panning right or left, tilting up and down, pedestaling up or down, trucking right or left, arcing in either direction, and booming, or placing the camera on the crane, allowing multidirectional movements of the booming camera. Evidently each of these movements is used in special circumstances as dictated by the production needs. The available choices provide greater flexibility of motions that are unique assets to the medium of television.

The third motion, which Zettl (1990) called *"tertiary motion,"* is created when we juxtapose or sequence television images to compose an event, tell a story, communicate an idea, and so on. The sequencing of visual images that create tertiary motion varies in shape and form in regard to their frequency and speed. They are controlled by the television's on-air editing device, allowing cuts, dissolves, fades, wipes, and superimpositions. Both the various transitions from one picture to the next and the placement of pictures one after the other create the tertiary motion—the actual television editing.

Principles of Television Sequencing and Editing

It was stated earlier that sequencing is a form of motion created by the juxtaposition of visuals and sounds to unfold an action. On what basis, however, do we make the selection of the audiovisual elements, the pictures that will unfold the action and will tell the story? On what principles does picture sequencing operate? Are there general guidelines that we must follow when preparing the editing of a television program? These are some of the questions confronting television directors in preparation of the program's recording.

To underline the principles of television sequencing and editing, this section discusses the process of visualization and sequencing in preproduction; examines the compositional values and aesthetic results of television's traditional devices such as the cuts, dissolves, fades, wipes, and special effects; and reviews the theory of montage and editing in film and television.

The Process of Visualization/Picturization in Television. During the preproduction stages of a television program, the television script is storyboarded. This means that the script's text is visualized by the director and transformed into mental images, which, in turn, are drawn into actual pictures, illustrations, or sketches. This is the first stage of television editing known as preproduction editing; it constitutes the basis on which the other two forms of editing (production or instantaneous editing and postproduction or final editing) are performed.

The process of visualization/picturization (or sequencing) is a deductive process during which the directors first create an overall mental image of the program stemming from the key message of the script. They then divide the program into three segments, the segments into smaller units, and so on. The segmented mental images are drawn in and are storyboarded. Finally, the production's remaining requirements such as camera placement, floor plan, lighting, and audio, are visualized and plotted with all possible details preplanted.

This process of visualization/picturization is a complex undertaking that demands special attention and careful consideration. Television production directors must closely study and must thoroughly analyze the script before they choose the sequencing of the images and the sounds accompanying the images. Obviously, the successful sequencing process will result in a better overall television production. This can be achieved by the director's own imagination, supported by close attention, thorough analysis of the script, and contextual analysis of all production requirements.

The Compositional Value of Television's Transitional Devices.   In the quest for the principles of television sequencing, we must consider the compositional or aesthetic value of each of the main transitional devices performed by the switcher.

As stated earlier, the sequencings of pictures create another type of motion generated by various forms of picture transition performed by the television switcher. In general, all transitional devices already mentioned perform a threefold function. They indicate the motion of visuals, illustrate the direction of the visuals, and assist the sequencing of the images, also known as "instantaneous editing" (Zettl, 1992, p. 526).

The compositional function of television's transitional device known as a cut is to provide an uprooted, sudden, and instant change from one picture to another. Although the change is sudden, it still illustrates transition from one event or action to the next. The specific aspects and the very nature of television production determines the use of cuts. However, as a general and overall practice, a cut should be used to connect the sequence of action moving from one shot to the next without noticeable interruption of the flow of action. In addition to the established rhythmic structure, narration, and logical evolution of the action, cutting from one shot to the next is used to sequence the unfolding event.

Within the context of sequencing and instantaneous editing, cuts should be used to provide different points of view of the event, to break the monotony of the visuals, to intensify a point in the script, or to establish the direction shot. Another compositional function of the cut is to increase or decrease the production's pace and viewers' involvement with the event. For example, the use of fast cuts in a scene involving an intense argument between two people will alter the production's rhythm and will increase spectators' involvement with the action of the scene. A final application of the cuts is to provide more details of an event. Cutting from a long shot to a closer one reveals the specific elements of the event as long as the cuts are transitionally smooth and compositionally acceptable.

Television's traditional device known as a dissolve gradually transforms the picture (or shot) to another, temporarily overlapping the first picture over the other. The dissolve is used primarily to connote the passage of time and varies in speed or duration of execution. In general, the faster the speed of the dissolve, the shorter the passage of time from one picture to the next. In addition to the three functions performed by all transitional devices, the television dissolve is effective when it is used to connect the themes of two different events. For example, the dissolve is applied in dream sequences, in traveling, and/or in visualizing the thoughts of a person.

The fade, a transitional device with special compositional values, is used, for the most part, as a motion, direction, and sequencing indicator of events that appear from black or disappear to black. A slow fade up brings the action in the visual field to life, whereas a fade out (or fade to black) connotes the end of an action or program. Often, the fade is used as an indicator of the duration (length) of an episode. Like the chapters in a book, the fades in television indicate the beginning and the end of an event. As with the dissolve, the speed of the fade is a very important factor to be considered. For example, a gradual fade up is more effective than an abrupt one and a slow fade out is more appropriate, depending, of course, on the program's particular needs.

The wipe, as a transitional device in television's instantaneous editing, indicates a gradual push (or wipe out) of one picture by another. There are soft-edge as well as regular or hard-edge wipes, and they vary in their transitional direction (e.g., left to right, top to bottom, diagonal). The main compositional value of the wipe is its ability to gradually replace one shot by another, at varying speeds and directions. Its specific use should be determined by the particular needs of the production.

Television's special effects, whether electronically generated by the switcher or digitally by the computer, are all transitional devices that are used in television recording (instantaneous editing) to fulfill the compositional needs of a production.

As stated earlier (in the discussion of television lighting techniques), the great number of these effects and their availability often hinder their real value as aesthetic agents in television composition. In television sequencing, all special effects function as motion, direction, and transition indicators. However, the individual compositional value of each of these effects cannot be pinpointed and predetermined. This is left to the discretion of the production directors, who should be driven by professional judgment and artistic sensitivity in their use of special effects in their productions.

In summary, the principles of television sequencing are based on the specific compositional values of each of the transitional devices of the medium available today in television production centers.

Theory of Montage: Philosophical Bases. In the discussion of the principles of television sequencing, the examination of the theory of montage is warranted because montage, with the visualization/picturization and the compositional value of the television transitional devices, provides the necessary background for the exploration of television's editing techniques.

Montage means to cluster together two or more events, pictures, or thoughts with different contents to produce a new event (picture or thought) stemming from the juxtaposition. The roots of montage go as far back as the ancient Greeks, and particularly Plato, who recorded the dialogues of Socrates with his pupils. During these dialogues, an idea was stated regarding an issue and it constituted the thesis of the person who stated it (usually it was Socrates who provided the thesis). The pupils were asked to state their opinions on the statement, or thesis, and their arguments constituted the antistatement, or antithesis. Combining these two opposite opinions, Socrates usually combined the two ideas into a third one that became the thesis for the continuation of the argument. Through the process of thesis and antithesis, synthesis (a new statement) was argued and resolved. This perfected dialectic to an art form and created the art of oratory.

The persuasive power of dialectic and its ability to explore and develop new thoughts and establish new theories attracted the German philosophers Hegel (1770–1831) and Marx (1818–1883). Both philosophers used dialectic to develop their theories on idealism and communism, respectively. The Hegelian theory of idealism argues that all aspects of life fluctuate between the states of being (thesis) and not being (antithesis) and they all resolve themselves into a third state known as becoming (synthesis; see Fig. 9.38).

Marx's theory of communism stems from the Hegelian dialectic theory of idealism and argues, in effect, that the capitalistic class of people (the bourgeoisie) constitute the thesis. This class must be opposed by the working

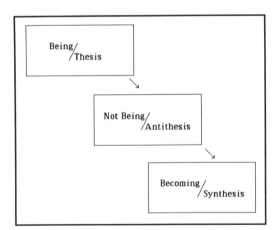

FIG. 9.38. The Hegelian dialectic. Through dialectic argumentation (thesis, antithesis, synthesis), we evolve in the state of being and arrive at the state of becoming.

class of people (the proletariat) that constitute the antithesis. The new class of people brought by the synthesis of the previous two are the communists (see Fig. 9.39).

Influenced by both German philosophers, and primarily by the Hegelian dialectic, the Russian stage and motion picture director Eisenstein (1888–1948) developed the film theory of montage suggesting that conflict and argumentation create progress. Various social, economic, and political conflicts, when argued and explored dialectically, often result in progress. Eisenstein's beliefs, argued dialectically, created a system of editing in film known as Eisenstein's theory of film montage, consisting of five basic methods of picture juxtaposition. These are the metric montage method, rhythmic montage method, tonal montage method, overtonal montage method, and intellectual montage method. They are discussed and exemplified thoroughly in two well-known books, *Film Sense* and *Film Form* (Eisenstein, 1942, 1949), which contain his numerous papers on film montage, translated and edited by Jay Leyada.

Eisenstein's film montage theory, which generated the metric, rhythmic, tonal, overtonal, and intellectual methods of sequencing pictures, has a profound similarity and resemblance to the perceptual principle of gestalt. In fact, the principle of gestalt, in which we create configurations or whole entities from interdependent elements, is what the resulted synthesis becomes after two or more pictures are placed next to each other. The concept of gestalt is closely related to both dialectic and montage, and all three constitute

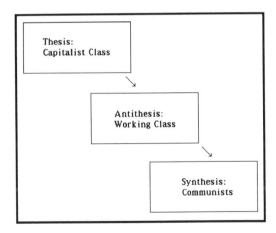

FIG. 9.39. Marx's dialectic. The Hegelian dialectic was used by Marx, who argued that the capitalistic society is the thesis, the working classes are the opponents of the capitalists, and the struggle between the two results in the communist ideal.

the basis for the exploration and understanding of television editing discussed next.

Television Editing: Strategies and Techniques

From the previous discussions on television time, motion, sequencing, and montage and from the review of such key literary sources on television editing as Millerson (1972), Robinson (1975), Wurtzel (1983), and Zettl (1990, 1992), television editing techniques fall under two major categories: continuity editing and complexity editing. This section provides an overall review of each category and examines the subsequent editing strategies and techniques in each category.

Continuity Editing Strategies. Continuity editing covers a number of strategies used to maintain the unbroken chain of events of a television program. In television, all forms of editing should provide a continuous flow of the individual events that make up the total program. However, unlike complexity editing, continuity editing is mostly concerned with the arrangement, manipulation, and control of all visual (and aural) elements that provide direction, continuity, and orientation—logical successions leading one picture to the next.

In addition to the audio, which provides continuity in the evolution of the events of a program, the video portion contains a number of graphic elements within the picture field that must be manipulated and controlled to maintain continuity in television production. The processes of arranging, controlling, and manipulating the graphic elements for the purpose of maintaining the sequencing of events are named continuity strategies in television editing.

Among all forces that operate within the visual field of the television picture, vectors constitute the ones that determine the direction and flow of visual elements. Along with the remaining forces of orientation, magnetism of the frame, attraction of mass, asymmetry of the screen, figure–ground relationships, and psychological closure (Metallinos, 1979), vectors also determine the synthesis of television pictures. As stated earlier, vectors, which are defined as directional lines that lead the viewer's eyes from one point to another, are characterized, also, by their strength, forcefulness, or magnitude and are considered "indispensable to the structure of visual images" (Metallinos, 1979, p. 212). Insofar as their direction is concerned, Zettl (1990) divided vectors into graphic, index, and motion vectors that could occur as continuous vectors or as converging ones, depending on their role within the visual field. In regard to their magnitude and forcefulness, graphic vectors are weaker than index vectors, which, in turn are weaker than motion vectors.

The first continuity strategy in television editing is the arrangement, manipulation, and control of the picture's graphic vectors, defined as stationary visual elements arranged so that they lead the eyes to a particular direction (e.g., buildings, telephone poles, street lights, long straight roads viewed from far away). To maintain direction continuity, the editing strategy calls for a logical succession of the graphic vectors. For example, from a long shot of the continuing graphic vector created by the long street, we can cut to a medium shot of the same street or any other object, as long as the graphic vectors' homogeneous direction within the picture field is maintained. In fact, this editing strategy is necessary in sequencing long shots of streets, buildings, horizons, railroad tracks, and so on, in which the graphic vectors are matched with the horizon's line to maintain the visual continuity of an event.

The second continuity strategy in television editing is the arrangement, manipulation, and control of the picture's index vectors defined as directional forces created by a stationary object that points, unquestionably, to a particular direction, forcing the eyes to follow the specific direction (i.e., a motionless pointed figure—an arrow, nose, sign, etc.). When this strategy is applied, more attention is required for the logical sequencing of events due to the greater strength of the index vector that determines, without a doubt, the direction of the action. Let us take, for example, a long shot of a spectator's profile, looking at hockey players in a rink from left to right (as we look at the screen). The spectator's body, head, nose, hands, and posture create strong continuity index vectors that lead the eyes, unquestionably, to the events in the hockey rink. The next shot of the spectator, regardless if it is a medium or close-up shot, must maintain the same index vector direction for continuity purposes. This editing strategy is necessary in sequencing extreme long shots with extreme close ups and very close shots. Any change of the index vectors' continuity strategy of television editing will result in disorientation, change of visual direction, and general confusion of action.

A third, even stronger, and more effective continuity editing strategy in television is the manipulation of the motion vectors created by objects and subjects moving within the visual field of the television picture (e.g., people walking, cars moving, or machines in motion). The strength and magnitude of the motion vectors increases, of course, with the speed of the moving object, providing an even stronger indication of both the direction of the visual elements within the picture field and continuity. If this continuity is not maintained in editing, the picture's orientation and composition become incohesive. In this editing strategy the direction of the motion of the objects or people in one picture must be maintained in the next, and so forth, until the event is completed. For example, if a car is shown moving outward, from the screen's center toward the viewer on a regular medium long shot, the logical continuation of the motion dictates that the next shot must show the car moving inward, away from the viewer, toward the picture's vanishing point. A simple example can be to match the long shot of the car moving from left to right with another shot (medium or close-up) maintaining the same screen direction. This editing strategy is effective in sequencing all types of events with intense motion as long as the logical direction of motion and the progressive evolution of visual images is maintained in the edited pictures.

In summary, the suggested main continuity editing strategies in television are based on the arrangement, manipulation, and control of the graphic, index, and motion vectors. It is important to note, however, that the greatest challenge in the application of these three strategies of continuity editing in television is the fact that these vectors are found in each television picture in various degrees. The decision as to which editing strategy must be followed should be dictated by three factors: the visual presence of the strongest vectors, the strength of the auditory elements accompanying the pictures, and the context of the event, in each of the particular scenes.

Complexity Editing Strategies.   Both terms, *continuity* and *complexity* editing were used by Millerson (1972) and Zettl (1990), who seemed to consider the former as an objective, logical, almost necessary mechanical undertaking, and the latter as a subjective, complex, and creative endeavor. The application of the techniques of complexity editing, therefore, is left to the discretion of the directors who use this technique to interpret the program in their own way, providing new insights and revealing different points of view for the viewers. The two main divisions of complexity editing techniques are the diagnostic and the thematic.

In *diagnostic editing*, the concern is to provide a continuous or sequential analysis of the action. A diagnostic continuous editing technique is applied when we provide a series of pictures that diagnose a cause–effect phenomenon. In case we want to diagnose, for example, the cause of death of a person in a continuous editing technique, the sequencing of pictures must be to first show the healthy person, then to provide a picture of the person very ill, and finally to end-up with a picture of the person dead, in a funeral scene. Here, the action is cause–effect oriented; hence, it is diagnostic in nature and continuous in its evolution.

On the other hand, when we wish to diagnose and/or to analyze an event by employing the segmented or sectional editing technique, we sequence the various segments (or sections) to make up the whole event. If, for example, the event that is to be edited segmentally is a concert, we sequence the pictures by starting with an overall view of the orchestra; we provide a close-up of the conductor, who constitutes a part of the orchestra; then we go back to the overall view of the orchestra to close up the segment. We employ a segmented editing technique to sequence the action of the concert. In short, in diagnostic editing we use either a continuous editing technique or a segmented one to analyze the action of the event.

In the *thematic editing* technique, the sequencing of the theme (or the dominant idea of the segment to be edited) is based on either the resemblance of the picture's theme or its confrontation. The resemblance editing technique compares two seemingly unrelated themes and projects one of them. For example, if the theme is war, we can resemble (compare) the picture of soldiers fighting, with animals fighting. The confrontation editing technique confronts, or collides two thematically similar events in opposite circumstances. If, for example, the theme is human conditions, a picture of a healthy person is correlated with a picture of a sick person. In confrontation editing it is important to maintain the theme in its opposite situation.

In short, in the thematic editing technique the sequencing is based on the resemblance or confrontation editing techniques to relate the action or the event.

In summary, the compositional basis for the study of television aesthetics is drawn from the examination and analyses of the arts (as explained in chap. 7), criticism (as analyzed in chap. 8), and the applied rules of composition of television programs (as examined in this chapter).

References

Adler, R., & Cater, D. (Eds.). (1975a). *Television as a social force: New approaches to television criticism.* New York: Praeger.

Adler, R., & Cater, D. (Eds.). (1975b). *Television as a cultural force.* New York: Praeger.

Allan, R. (1987). *Channels of discourse: Television and contemporary criticism.* Chapel Hill: University of North Carolina Press.

Allen, R. C. (1987). The guiding light: The soap opera as economic product and cultural document. In H. Newcomb (Ed.), *Television criticism: The critical view* (4th ed., pp. 141–163). New York: Oxford University Press.

Alten, S. R., (1994). *Audio in media* (4th ed.). Belmont, CA: Wadsworth.

Arnheim, R. (1966). *Towards a psychology of art: Collected essays.* Berkeley: University of California Press.

Arnheim, R. (1969a). *Art and visual perception: A psychology of the creative eye.* Berkeley: University of California Press.

Arnheim, R. (1969b). *Visual thinking.* Berkeley: University of California Press.

Aronoff, J. (1967). *Psychological needs and cultural systems: A case study.* Toronto: Van Nostrand.

Baggaley, J., Ferguson, F. M., & Brooks, P. (1980). *Psychology of the television images.* New York: Praeger.

Banks, J. (1991). Listening to Dr. Ruth: The new sexual prime. In L. R. Vande Berg & L. A. Wenner (Eds.), *Television criticism: Approaches and applications* (pp. 425–441). New York: Longman.

Barash, M. (1985). *Theories of art: From Plato to Winckelman.* New York: New York University Press.

Beardsley, M. C. (1958). *Aesthetics: Problems in the philosophy of criticism.* New York: Harcourt, Brace, & World.

Benedic, R. (1935). *Patterns of culture.* London, England: Penguin.

Berger, A. A. (1982). *Media analysis techniques.* Beverly Hills, CA: Sage.

Bluem, A. W. (1965). *Documentary in American television: Form, function, method.* New York: Hastings House.

Bordwell, D., & Thompson, K. (1985). Fundamental aesthetics of sound in the cinema. In E. Weis & J. Belton (Eds.), *Film sound: Theory and practice* (pp. 197–199). New York: Columbia University Press.

Brand, S. (1987). *Media lab: Inventing the future at M.I.T.* New York: Viking Penguin.

Brion, M. (1960). *Romantic art.* New York: Thames & Hudson.

Brown, J. A. C. (1963). *Techniques of persuasion: From propaganda to brainwashing.* Baltimore, MD: Penguin.

Burke, K. (1950). *A rhetoric of motives.* New York: Prentice-Hall.

Burns, G., & Thompson, R. J. (Eds.). (1989). *Television studies: Textual analysis.* New York: Praeger.

Buxton, R. A. (1991). The late-night talk show: Humor in fringe television. In L. R. Vande Berg & L. A. Wenner (Eds.), *Television criticism: Approaches and applications* (pp. 411–424). New York: Longman.

Bywater, T., & Sobchack, T. (1989). *An introduction to film criticism: Major critical approaches to narrative film.* New York: Longman.

Campbell, R. (1991). Securing the middle ground: Reporter formulas in "60 Minutes." In L. R. Vande Berg & L. A. Wenner (Eds.), *Television criticism: Approaches and applications* (pp. 331–364). New York: Longman.

Chatman, S. (1978). *Story and discourse, narrative structure in fiction and film.* Ithaca, NY: Cornell University Press.

Chesebro, J. W. (1987). Communication, values, and popular television series: A four year assessment. In H. Newcomb (Ed.), *Television: The critical view* (4th ed., pp. 17–51). New York: Oxford University Press.

Chiari, J. (1977). *Art and knowledge.* New York: Gordian.

Crombeck, B. E. (1991). Mythic portraiture in the 1988 Iowa presidential caucus bio-ads. In L. R. Vande Berg & L. A. Wenner (Eds.), *Television criticism: Approaches and applications* (pp. 254–269). New York: Longman.

D'Agostino, P. (1985). *Transmission: Theory and practice for a new television aesthetic.* New York: Tanam Press.

Davies, R. A., Farrell, J. M., & Mathews, S. S. (1982). The dream world of film: A Jungian perspective of cinematic communication. *Western Journal of Speech Communication, 46,* 326–343.

Davis, D. (1960). *The grammar of television.* London, England: Barrie & Jenkins.

Debes, J. L., & Williams, C. M. (1970). *Proceedings of the first national conference on visual literacy.* New York: Pittman.

Debes, J. L., & Williams, C. M. (1978). *Provocative papers #1: Visual literacy, languaging, and learning.* Rochester, NY: The International Visual Literacy Association.

Deming, C. J. (1985). Hill Street Blues as a narrative. *Critical Studies in Mass Communication, 2,* 1–22.

Deming, C. J., & Jenkins, M. M. (1991). Bar talk: Gender discourse in "Cheers." In L. R. Vande Berg & L. A. Wenner (Eds.), *Television criticism: Approaches and applications* (pp. 44–57). New York: Longman.

Detels, C. (1993). History and the philosophies of the arts. *Journal of Aesthetics and Art Criticism, 51,* 364–375.

Dickie, G. (1971). *Aesthetics: An introduction.* Indianapolis, IN: Bobbs-Merrill.

Dondis, D. (1973). *A primer of visual literacy.* Cambridge, MA: MIT Press.

Downey, J. (1976). Travelogues of video trans Americas. In I. Schneider & B. Korot (Eds.), *Video art: An anthology* (pp. 38–39). New York: Harcourt, Brace, Jovanovich.

Dudek, L. (1990). The idea of art. *Canadian Literare, 126,* 50–64.

Duncan, M. C., & Brummett, B. (1991). The mediation of spectator sport. In L. R. Vande Berg & L. A. Wenner (Eds.), *Television criticism: Approaches and applications* (pp. 367–387). New York: Longman.

Eagleton, T. (1984). *The function of criticism: From the spectator to post-structuralism.* London: Verso.

Eco, U. (1976). *A theory of semiotics.* Bloomington: Indiana University Press.

Edman, I. (1939). *Arts and the man.* New York: Norton.

Eisenstein, S. M. (1942). *Film sense.* (J. Leyda, Trans.). New York: Harcourt Brace Jovanovich.

Eisenstein, S. M. (1949). *Film form.* (J. Leyda, Trans.). New York: Harcourt Brace Jovanovich.

Eliot, T. S. (1963). *Collected poems: 1909–1962.* London: Faber & Faber.

Farrell, T. B. (1989). Media rhetoric as social drama: The winter Olympics of 1984. *Critical Studies in Mass Communication, 6,* 158–182.

Ferguson, F. (1961). *Aristotle's Poetics.* New York: Hill & Wang.

Ferner, J. (1991). Melodrama, serial form, and television today. In L. R. Vande Berg & L. A. Wenner (Eds.), *Television criticism: Approaches and applications* (pp. 163–177). New York: Longman.

Fisher, W. R. (1987). *Human communication narration: Toward a philosophy of reason, value, and action.* Columbia: University of South Carolina Press.

Fiske, J. (1987). *Television culture.* London: Routledge.

Fiske, J. (1991). The discourses of TV quiz shows, or school + luck = success + sex. In L. R. Vande Berg & L. A. Wenner (Eds.), *Television criticism: Approaches and applications* (pp. 445–462). New York: Longman.

Fletcher, J. E. (1979, May). *Right and left asymmetry: Assessment by magnitude estimation.* Paper presented at the annual conference of the International Communication Association, Acapulco, Mexico.

Foss, K. (1989). *Rhetorical criticism: Exploration and practice.* Prospect Heights, IL: Waveland Press.

Freud, S. (1949). *An outline of psychoanalysis.* New York: Norton.

Funk & Wagnalls New Encyclopedia, Vol. 1. (1972). New York: Funk & Wagnalls, Inc.

Gibson, J. J. (1950). *The perception of the visual world.* Boston, MA: Houghton Mifflin.

Goble, F. G. (1971). *The third force: The psychology of Abraham Maslow.* New York: Pocket Books.

Greenberg, D. (1977). *Television: Its critics and criticism.* Ann Arbor: University of Michigan Press.

Hadas, M. (1962). Climates of criticism. In R. L. Shayon (Ed.), *The eighth art* (pp. 15–23). New York: Holt, Rinehart, & Winston.

Hayakawa, S. (1964). *Language in thought and action* (2nd ed.). New York: Harcourt, Brace, & World.

Head, S. W., & Sterling, C. H. (1990). *Broadcasting in America: A survey of electronic media* (6th ed.). Boston, MA: Houghton-Mifflin.

Herbener, G. F., Van Tubergen, G. N., & Whitlow, S. S. (1979). Dynamics of the frame in visual composition. *Educational Communication and Technology Journal, 27,* 83–88.

Himmelstein, H. (1981). *On the small screen: New approaches in television and video criticism.* New York: Praeger.

Hoffer, T. W., & Nelson, R. A. (1980). Evolution of docudrama on American television network. A content analysis. *Southern Speech Communication Journal, 45,* 149–163.

Horowitz, S. (1987). Sitcom domesticus: A species endangered by social challenge. In H. Newcomb (Ed.), *Television criticism: The critical view* (4th ed., pp. 107–125). New York: Oxford University Press.

Huyghe, R. (1962). *Art and the spirit of man.* London: Thames & Hudson.

Hyde, S. (1970). *The history and the analysis of the public arts.* Unpublished course syllabus, Department of Broadcast Communication Arts, San Francisco State University, San Francisco, CA.

Isenberg, A. (1973). *Aesthetics and the theory of criticism.* Chicago: University of Chicago Press.

Kaminsky, S. M., & Mahan, J. H. (1985). *American television genres.* Chicago: Nelson Hall.

Kepes, G. (1969). *Language in vision.* Chicago: Paul Theobald.

Kepplinger, H. M., & Donshach, W. (1982). The influence of camera angles and political consistency on the perception of a party speaker. In J. Baggaley & P. Janega (Eds.), *Experimental research in TV instruction, 5,* 135–152.

Kervin, D. (1991). Gender ideology in television commercials. In L. R. Vande Berg & L. A. Wenner (Eds.), *Television criticism: Approaches and applications* (pp. 235–253). New York: Longman.

Kostelanetz, R. (1985). *Esthetics contemporary.* Buffalo, NY: Prometheus.

Lewis, C. (1968). *The TV director/interpreter.* New York: Hastings House.

Lewis, W. F. (1987). Telling America's story: Narrative form and the Reagan presidency. *Quarterly Journal of Speech, 73,* 280–302.

Littlejohn, D. (1975). Thoughts on television criticism. In R. Adler & D. Cater (Eds.), *Television as a cultural force* (pp. 147–173). New York: Praeger.

Marc, D. (1984). *Demographic vistas: Television in American culture.* Philadelphia: University of Pennsylvania Press.

Martin, W. (1986). *Recent theories of narrative.* Ithaca, NY: Cornell University Press.

Maslow, A. H. (1954). *Motivation and personality.* New York: Harper & Brothers.

Mathias, H., & Patterson, R. (1985). *Electronic cinematography.* Belmont, CA: Wadsworth.

McCain, T. A., Chilberg, J., & Wakshlag, J. (1977). The effect of camera angle on source credibility and attraction. *Journal of Broadcasting, 21,* 35–46.

McCain, T. A., & White, S. (1980, November). *Channel effects and non-verbal properties of media messages: A state of the art review.* Paper presented at the annual conference of the Speech Communication Association, New York.

McKim, R. (1980). *Experiences in visual thinking* (2nd ed.). Belmont, CA: Wadsworth.

McLuhan, M. (1964). *Understanding media: The extension of man.* New York: Signet Books.

McQuail, D. (1969). *Towards a sociology of mass communication.* London: Collier-Macmillan.

Medhurst, M. J., & Benson, T. W. (Eds.). (1984). *Rhetorical dimensions in media: A critical case book.* Dubuque, IA: Kendall-Hunt.

Metallinos, N. (1973). Criteria for evaluating the performing arts. *Interchange, 3,* 11–17.

Metallinos, N. (1979). Composition of the television picture: Some hypotheses to test the forces operating within the television screen. *Educational Communication and Technology Journal, 27,* 205–214.

Metallinos, N. (1985a). The idiosyncrasies of television: An overall view. *Journal of Visual Verbal Languaging, 5,* 43–51.

Metallinos, N. (1985b). Empirical studies of television composition. In J. R. Dominick & J. E. Fletcher (Eds.), *Broadcasting research methods* (pp. 297–311). Boston, MA: Allyn & Bacon.

Metallinos, N. (1988). Computerized television: Technology overshadows aesthetics. In R. A. Braden, D. G. Beauchamp, & L. Miller (Eds.), *Visual literacy in life and learning: Readings from the 19th annual conference of the International Visual Literacy Association* (pp. 143–155). Blacksburg, VA: International Visual Literacy Association.

Metallinos, N. (1989). Figure-ground anomalies in commercial television: A diagnostic study. In R. A. Braden, D. G. Beauchamp, L. W. Miller, & D. M. Moore (Eds.), *About visuals: Research, teaching, and applications. Readings from the 20th annual conference of the International Visual Literacy Association* (pp. 291–303). Blacksburg, VA: International Visual Literacy Association.

Metallinos, N. (1991a). Jolts: The television wasteland and the Canadian oasis. *Canadian Journal of Communication, 16,* 316–318.

Metallinos, N. (1991b). High definition television: New perceptual cognitive and aesthetic challenges. *Canadian Journal of Educational Communication, 20,* 121–129.

Metallinos, N., & Tiemens, R. K. (1977). Asymmetry of the screen: The effect of left versus right placement of television images. *Journal of Broadcasting, 21,* 21–33.

Millerson, G. (1972). *The technique of television production* (9th ed.). New York: Hastings House.

Millerson, G. (1991). *Television production techniques.* New York: Hastings House.

Moholy-Nagy, L. (1969). *Vision in motion*. Chicago: Paul Theobald & Co.

Morse, M. (1991). Post synchronizing rock music and television. In L. R. Vande Berg & L. A. Wenner (Eds.), *Television criticism: Approaches and applications* (pp. 289–310). New York: Longman.

Mumby, D. K., & Spitzak, C. (1991). Ideology and television news: A metamorphic analysis of political stories. In L. R. Vande Berg & L. A. Wenner (Eds.), *Television criticism: Approaches and applications* (pp. 313–330). New York: Longman.

Newcomb, H. (1974). *Television: The most popular art*. Garden City, NY: Doubleday/Anchor.

Newcomb, H. (1987a). *Television: The critical view* (4th ed.). New York: Oxford University Press.

Newcomb, H. (1987b). Towards a television aesthetic. In H. Newcomb (Ed.), *Television: The critical view* (4th ed., pp. 613–627). New York: Oxford University Press.

Newcomb, H., & Alley, R. S. (1983). *The producer's medium: Conversations with creators of American television*. New York: Oxford University Press.

Novitz, D. (1990). Art, life, and reality. *British Journal of Aesthetics, 30*(4), 301–310.

O'Keefe, D. J. (1990). *Persuasion: Theory and research*. Newbury Park, CA: Sage.

Ornstein, R. (1972). *The psychology of consciousness*. San Francisco, CA: Freeman.

Paik, N. J. (1976). Input time and output time. In I. Schneider & B. Korot (Eds.), *Video art: An anthology* (pp. 98–103). New York: Harcourt, Brace, Jovanovich.

Price, J. (1972). *Video-vision: A medium discovers itself*. New York: New American Library.

Prigogine, I. (1980). *From being to becoming: Time and complexity in physical science*. New York: Freeman.

Read, H. (1966). *Art and society*. New York: Schocken Books.

Reich, S. (1976). Video tape and a composer. In I. Schneider & B. Korot (Eds.), *Video art: An anthology* (pp. 104–106). New York: Harcourt, Brace, Jovanovich.

Risoner, F. (1977). An introduction to mass media and popular arts. In F. Risoner & D. C. Birch (Eds.), *Mass media and the popular arts* (2nd ed., pp. 3–13). New York: McGraw-Hill.

Robinson, J. F. (1975). *Video tape recording: Theory and practice*. New York: Hastings House.

Rybacki, K., & Rybacki, K. (1991). *Communication criticism: Approaches and genres*. Belmont, CA: Wadsworth.

Schneider, I., & Korot, B. (Eds.). (1976). *Video art: An anthology*. New York: Harcourt, Brace, Jovanovich.

Schrang, R. L. (1991). Sugar and spice and everything nice versus snakes and snails and puppy dog's tails. Selling social stereotypes on Saturday morning television. In L. R. Vande Berg & L. A. Wenner (Eds.), *Television criticism: Approaches and applications* (pp. 220–232). New York: Longman.

Scodari, C., & Thorpe, J. M. (1992). *Media criticism: Journeys in interpretation*. Dubuque, IA: Kendal–Hunt.

Seldes, G. (1956). *The public arts*. New York: Simon & Schuster.

Seldes, G. (1957). The public arts. In B. Rosenberg & D. M. White (Eds.), *Mass culture: The popular arts in America* (pp. 557–561). New York: The Free Press.

Seldes, G. (1961). *The great audience*. New York: Viking.

Shanks, R. (1976). *The cool five: How to make it in television*. New York: Vintage Books.

Shayon, R. L. (Ed.). (1962). *The eighth art*. New York: Holt, Rinehart, & Winston.

Shayon, R. L. (1971). *Open to criticism*. Boston, MA: Beacon Press.

Shoemaker, D. E. (1964). *An analysis of the effects of three vertical camera angles and a three lighting ration*. Unpublished doctoral dissertation, Indiana University, Bloomington.

Sklar, R. (1980). The Fonz, Laverne & Shirley, and the great American class struggle. In *Primetime-America: Life on and behind the television screen* (pp. 15–28). New York: Oxford University Press.

Smith, L. D. (1988). Narrative styles in network coverage of the 1984 nominating convention. *Western Journal of Speech Communication, 52*, 63–74.

Smith, R. R. (1980). *Beyond the wasteland: The criticism of broadcasting* (Rev. ed.). Urbana, IL: ERIC Clearinghouse on Reading and Communication and the Speech Communication Association.

Steinberg, C. S. (Ed.). (1974). *Broadcasting: The critical challenges.* New York: Hastings House.

Stewart, C. J., Smith, C. A., & Denton, R. E. (1984). *Persuasion and social movements.* Prospect Heights, IL: Waveland Press.

Stone, L. A., & Collius, L. G. (1965). The golden section revisited: A perimetric explanation. *American Journal of Psychology, 78,* 503–506.

Summers, R. E., & Summers, H. B. (1966). *Broadcasting and the public.* Belmont, CA: Wadsworth.

Tarroni, E. (1979). The aesthetics of television. In H. Newcomb (Ed.), *Television: The critical view* (2nd ed., pp. 437–461). New York: Oxford University Press.

Tatti, B. (1976). Video art. In I. Schneider & B. Korot (Eds.), *Video art: An anthology* (pp. 130–131). New York: Harcourt, Brace, Jovanovich.

Taylor, J. F. A. (1964). *Design and expression in the visual arts.* New York: Dover.

Thompson, R. J. (1991). Stephen J. Cannell: An auteur analysis of the adventure/action genre. In L. R. Vande Berg & L. A. Wenner (Eds.), *Television criticism: Approaches and applications* (pp. 112–126). New York: Longman.

Tiemens, R. K. (1965). Some relationships of camera angle to communication credibility. *Journal of Broadcasting, 14,* 483–490.

Timberg, B. (1987). The rhetoric of the camera in television soap opera. In H. Newcomb (Ed.), *Television criticism: The critical view* (4th ed., pp. 164–178). New York: Oxford University Press.

Toogood, A. (1978). A framework for the exploration of video as a unique art form. *Journal of the University Film Association, 30,* 15–19.

Turner, K. J., & Sprague, R. (1991). Musical and visual invention in "Miami Vice": Old genre, new form. In L. R. Vande Berg & L. A. Wenner (Eds.), *Television criticism: Approaches and applications* (pp. 273–288). New York: Longman.

Vande Berg, L. R., & Wenner, L. A. (Eds.). (1991). *Television criticism: Approaches and applications.* New York: Longman.

Walhout, D. (1986). The nature and function of art. *British Journal of Aesthetics, 26,* 16–25.

Walker, J. R. (1987, Summer). Persuasive impact of production techniques: Previous research and future directions. *Feedback,* pp. 11–16.

Webster's Ninth New Collegiate Dictionary. (1989). Springfield, MA: G. & C. Merriam.

Wenner, L. A. (1991). One part alcohol, one part sport, one part dirt, stir gently: Beer commercials and television sports. In L. R. Vande Berg & L. A. Wenner (Eds.), *Television criticism: Approaches and applications* (pp. 388–407). New York: Longman.

Williams, S. (1991). Bugs Bunny meets He-Man: A historical comparison of values in American cartoons. In L. R. Vande Berg & L. A. Wenner (Eds.), *Television criticism: Approaches and applications* (pp. 201–219). New York: Longman.

Wilson, B. P. (1980). *The design, application, and evaluation of stereophonic television: A production model.* Unpublished master's thesis, San Francisco State University, San Francisco.

Wolfe, M. (1985). *Jolts: The television wasteland and the Canadian oasis.* Toronto: James Lorimer & Co.

Write, W. (1975). *Six guns and society. A structural study of the westerns.* Berkeley: University of California Press.

Wurtzel, A. (1983). *Television production* (2nd. ed.). New York: McGraw-Hill.

Zettl, H. (1973). *Sight, sound, motion: Applied media aesthetics.* Belmont, CA: Wadsworth.

Zettl, H. (1978). The rare case of television aesthetics. *Journal of the University Film Association, 30,* 3–8.

Zettl, H. (1990). *Sight, sound motion: Applied media aesthetics* (2nd ed.). Belmont, CA: Wadsworth.

Zettl, H. (1992). *Television production handbook* (5th ed.). Belmont, CA: Wadsworth.

Conclusion and Future Research Directions

It is disheartening to see how little has been done in visual communication media aesthetics research. Even so, a variety of avenues have been taken in establishing an overabundance of personalized techniques, practical guidelines, and untested hypotheses, particularly in the area of television aesthetics. Observers, practitioners, and theoreticians of television have recognized the importance of aesthetics in the medium's development. However, only recently has empirical work begun to support television's link to aesthetics. The field of television aesthetics needs to continue its pioneering efforts to built new models for the study of television aesthetics, to develop the constructs of the three axes of television aesthetics (perception, cognition, and composition), to refine the theories and research paradigms, and to generate appropriate research questions that produce scientifically tested answers.

We must persuade our students and our colleagues in the field to be more adventurous and more courageous in engaging in vigorous empirical research studies of television's perceptual, cognitive, and compositional properties. The future of the field of television aesthetics seems to move in this direction, as it is shaped by parallel empirical research in related academic fields. We must persuade our colleagues that it is both a pleasure and a privilege to be a part of this creative evolution of the field of television aesthetics.

Author Index

Subject Index

DATE DUE

GAYLORD		PRINTED IN U.S.A.